Marxist Left Review

Number 25 – Autumn 2023

Editor
Omar Hassan

Editorial committee
Mick Armstrong
Sandra Bloodworth
Omar Hassan
Louise O'Shea

Reviews editor
Alexis Vassiley

© Social Research Institute

Published by Socialist Alternative
Melbourne, March 2023

PO Box 4354
Melbourne University, VIC 3052

www.marxistleftreview.org

marxistleftreview@gmail.com

Contributions to *Marxist Left Review* are peer-reviewed

ISSN 1838-2932
rrp. $17

Subediting and proofreading
Tess Lee Ack
Diane Fieldes

Layout and production
Oscar Sterner

Cover
Oscar Sterner

Printed by IngramSpark

Marxist Left Review is a theoretical journal published twice-yearly by Socialist Alternative, a revolutionary organisation based in Australia.

We aim to engage with theoretical and political debates on the Australian and international left, making a rigorous yet accessible case for Marxist politics. We also seek to provide analysis of the social, political and economic dynamics shaping Australian capitalism.

Unless indicated otherwise all articles published reflect the views of the individual author(s).

We rely on our readers' support to continue publication.
You can help by subscribing at *marxistleftreview.org*

Marxist Left Review

Number 25 – Autumn 2023

FEATURES

1   OMAR HASSAN
    Editorial: Toil and trouble

13 JORDAN HUMPHREYS
    "Beware of the Black Bourgeoisie": The growing role
    of Indigenous elites in Australian capitalism

53 NICK EVERETT
    "Closing the gap"? Labor's dismal
    record on Indigenous rights

81 LUCA TAVAN
    Workerism and autonomism in Italy's "Hot Autumn"

125 MICK ARMSTRONG
    The sixties radicalisation and the emergence
    of Trotskyism on the Australian left

153 TESS LEE ACK
    East Germany 1953:
    Workers' forgotten rebellion against Stalinism

REVIEWS

195 SAM PIETSCH
    Analysing Australian imperialism

203 DUNCAN HART
    An insight into inequality in Australia today

continued on next page →

SAGE JUPE
Socialism in the United States

OMAR HASSAN

Editorial: Toil and trouble

Omar Hassan is the editor of *Marxist Left Review*. He has been active in anti-fascist and Palestine solidarity work, and has written extensively on the Middle East.

TWENTY TWENTY-TWO was the year of the central bankers. As inflation has continued to dominate discussions of world politics, these unelected mandarins have moved to centre stage. Their monthly proclamations on interest rates are observed by all, from the most desperate mortgagees to the captains of industry. Every word and phrase is obsessively analysed by those hoping to find meaning (and profits) in their sermons.

The reason for this almost comic obsession is that 2022 was a terrible year for investors. In a recent piece summing up the year, the *Financial Times* explained the scale of the catastrophe, sometimes described as a "richcession":

> Long-term US government bonds staged the biggest drop since 1788. Investors' classic blend of bonds and equities has put in the worst performance since 1932. At its lowest point this year, the S&P 500 index had shed $11tn in market capitalisation... that is similar to the entire annual economic output of Germany, Japan and Canada combined.[1]

---

1. Martin and Agnew 2022.

The high priests of capitalism have clearly decided that it is worth sacrificing these unimaginable sums to stop inflation. Why do they care so much? Partly, as Ben Hillier outlined in a piece for *Red Flag*,[2] inflation hurts lenders – especially the big banks – by reducing the value of the debt owed. Bankers aren't the types to suffer in silence, so they're engineering a global recession to protect their profit margins. This argument assumes that the banking sector has an overwhelmingly dominant sway over the fundamental settings of the world economy, but the aftermath of the 2008 crisis proved that this is not the case.

The ruling class has more fundamental problems with consistently high levels of inflation. For one thing, it is hard for institutions to make sensible investment decisions when assumptions about future prices, costs and returns are so unreliable. If currency exchanges, commodity prices and debt markets all rely on the value of money being relatively stable, so too do decisions made about expanding the productive capacity of the real economy. While some bosses will find ways to make profits in any scenario, the overall health of the system is inevitably compromised by a sustained period of inflation.

Higher inflation also has social and political ramifications. A sharp rise in the cost of living discredits the ruling class generally, and the ruling political party in particular, by exposing their inability to shield workers and the poor from the vicissitudes of the market. At the same time, the scrutiny that central banks are subjected to in these times peels back some of the mystery that surrounds economic policy and the choices that are made to shape it in particular ways. This can be partially ameliorated by the propaganda defending the need to reduce workers' wages and spending, but there are always plenty who will reject such an argument, if only out of righteous self-interest. The most important consequence of rising inflation is the possibility of a more bitter round of class struggle. When the currency is relatively stable workers' living standards can improve steadily, even as wages stagnate amid soaring profits. But inflation means social struggle becomes necessary just to hold ground, let alone go forward.

---

2. Hillier 2022.

If investors were initially the biggest victims of the new era of higher inflation and interest rates, then that would be just fine. Nobody at the *Marxist Left Review* is shedding any tears for these parasites. But there is another side to the crisis. Workers across the world are seeing their real incomes squeezed as wages fall relative to the price of goods and services. In November the International Labor Organization released a report[3] on workers' wages that estimated that global monthly wages fell by 0.9 percent in the first half of 2022 alone: the first time this century that real global wage growth has been negative. The situation is worse in the US, where real weekly earnings for 106 million production and non-supervisory employees – the closest statistical proxy for the working class that exists there – is down by 2 percent since last December, which in turn was down by 2 percent from the December before that.[4] In the EU and Eastern Europe, real wages fell by 2.4 and 3.2 percent in the first half of 2022. In Australia, real wages were down by 3.5 percent in the year to June, bringing wages down to levels last seen in 2011. This is class war of the most raw kind.

Rising prices are causing disproportionate pain for low-income workers, who spend more of their income on essentials. The situation is particularly acute for workers and the poor in the global south. There the UN estimates that the combination of COVID and inflation will have increased the number of people living in extreme poverty by 75 million compared to pre-pandemic forecasts.[5] While workers in the global south suffered more during the first year of the pandemic than in the last two years, wage growth there remains weak, and in many cases is falling. But even in the advanced capitalist world there are widespread reports of supermarket shoppers cutting spending on unnecessary goods and shifting to cheaper options.

Of course, the situation remains highly fluid. It is possible that inflation will now fall steadily. Central bankers are currently planning to continue increasing rates for some time, and then to hold them higher for longer. If they stick to that approach, the pressure on the financial system will continue to grow, especially on leveraged investors, zombie

---

3. ILO 2022.
4. U.S. Bureau of Labor Statistics 2022.
5. United Nations n.d.

companies and indebted nations in the global south. Profit rates will fall, unemployment will grow and a subsequent recession could be quite deep. Others are betting that central banks will begin easing interest rates sooner rather than later. The main rationale for this argument is that debt levels are at historic heights across the economy, and that the financial elite will forsake the cleansing destruction of a crisis in favour of another round of stimulus and kicking the can down the road. Time will tell which road the ruling class chooses to take, with each presenting its own dangers.

The economic data published so far in 2023 point to some kind of global recession, but it would be premature to make predictions. There is a huge number of variables, including the development of the war in Ukraine, whether China's economy can grow, shifts in monetary policy, further geopolitical instability, and more. But regardless of how the immediate situation develops, the war on workers will continue.

Working-class politics

Despite the harsh attacks on workers' living standards, there is still no sign of a generalised response, either industrial or political. How to explain the lag? Decades of class war from above have devastated trade unions and essentially pulverised the radical left, leaving most workplaces bereft of agitators and organisers, let alone democratic institutions of coordination and struggle. Another factor is that living standards, in the advanced capitalist world at least, are yet to fall as drastically as headline inflation figures would suggest. Partly this is because many workers accumulated substantial savings during the pandemic, which are yet to be fully exhausted. As well, unemployment remains at historic lows, which provides a double buffer. Firstly, it means there are opportunities for extra overtime, internal promotions and second jobs. Secondly, it means that the pain is distributed relatively evenly: there is not yet a section of the core working class that is being acutely impoverished by job losses or industry restructuring. So while fears and insecurities about the future abound, the mass of people are yet to feel the crushing burden of unemployment and economic ruin. The final and most intangible factor is the impact of the pandemic. Lockdowns were disorienting and politically pacifying, but so too has been the reopening, with most prepared to wear the heightened risks of sickness, long COVID and death in order to take advantage of the freedom to consume and travel.

For all of that, there continues to be an audience for the radical left. The *Financial Times* recently published a report which noted that millennials are bucking the trend of shifting to the right as they age.[6] This fits with anecdotal evidence of a generation that is hyper-aware of its downward mobility, imbued with a hatred of the rich, indifferent to conservative social values and angry about the destruction of the planet. This common sense has been shaped by the US wars in the Middle East, the Global Financial Crisis, the left populism of the Occupy Wall Street movement and recurring climate disasters. It manifests in enormous mobilisations around Black Lives Matter and other issues, and also in the popularity of neo-reformism when it appears genuine and disruptive, as with Corbyn, Syriza, and so on. Thus even if the working class and social movements are relatively passive in most places, there is an instinctive anti-capitalism in broad sections of society, especially concentrated among younger workers and students.

The UK and France are the countries in the advanced capitalist world where this potential is being mobilised to the greatest extent. In the UK, industrial action has seen a relatively sustained and substantial uptick in recent months. In part this is a product of that country's uniquely dysfunctional political institutions and economic performance. Wages in the UK are less than they were in 2008. Among the G20 only Mexico and Italy have been worse over that time frame. Brexit has been a big problem for the British ruling class, not only severely undermining their economic prospects but entrenching in the majority of young people a hostility to racism, nationalism and other elements of conservative politics. The situation there also shows that reformism springs eternal, with left-wing workers projecting much the same hopes onto Mick Lynch (Secretary-General of the National Union of Rail, Maritime and Transport Workers) as they did on Corbyn. Though the union officials, Lynch included, are doing their best to stifle and contain industrial action, the intransigence of the Tory

---

6. Burn-Murdoch 2022.

government and the energy of the rank and file means there is no sign it will abate any time soon. The situation is characterised by a plethora of local struggles over wages and conditions, punctuated by highly publicised and disruptive national strikes in public services.

The French struggle looks quite different. It is an explicitly political movement against Macron's attempt to increase the retirement age to 64. Where left-wing British workers have been unsuccessful in winning the argument for general strikes, the French movement has so far been defined by multiple days of coordinated national strike action, with more planned as we go to print. This has obvious advantages in terms of the size and scope of the movement, with more than 2 million striking and marching on multiple occasions already. The scale of such a movement means it is very much in the hands of the officials, who have been typically hesitant to call for the indefinite strike action needed to decisively defeat the proposal. Yet the 7 March strikes and demonstrations were the largest yet, with a number of important unions shifting gears into renewable indefinite strikes.

In the global south, it is Iran and Peru where class and social struggles have been most sustained, and where the ruling classes have been besieged by ongoing mass mobilisations. The perseverance and courage of the Iranian movement continues to impress, with months of joint protests by Kurds, women, students and conscious workers now renewed following the poisoning of young girl activists. Regardless of the outcome, the rebellion will surely leave a significant legacy for organisers to build on. In Peru, the coup against the mildly reformist Castillo has backfired badly, with workers and peasants taking to the streets in enormous numbers. Attempts to wind up the struggle by granting concessions and by firing on unarmed protesters have both failed. The congress has refused to call new elections, a demand supported by the vast majority of the public, 70 percent of whom also agree with the left's proposal to rewrite the authoritarian constitution.[7] As this journal went to print, the situation remained deeply unstable. Given that Peru is one of Latin America's largest economies and is traditionally on the right wing of regional politics, this level of crisis

---

7. Dutra 2023.

and resistance can be important for the development of politics across the whole region. Much more so than the victory of a chastened Lula in Brazil, who has aligned himself with sections of the far-right establishment, or yet another moderately reforming pink tide leader.

Imperialism

The tectonic plates of world imperialism are moving at multiple speeds in all sorts of directions. This is producing immediate eruptions, such as Putin's war on Ukraine, and a long-term build-up of pressures that threaten even greater catastrophe, as with the new cold war between the US and China.

The situation in Ukraine continues to grind on. After almost half a year of stasis on the Eastern front, Russia seems to be on the cusp of gaining a victory in Bakhmut, though at enormous cost. Ukraine's success in retaking Kherson in November last year stimulated a new round of military aid from the West, but the prospects for further advances seem less clear. For now, reports that NATO stockpiles of essential weapons are starting to run low are motivating a new round of investment into the means of producing death, also known as the military-industrial complex. But it's possible that there could be an abrupt about-face in the Western attitude to the war. Some US commentators in particular are indicating that the recent decision to send American and German tanks, artillery and anti-aircraft weaponry could be one of the last shipments of heavy weapons that Ukraine receives. A lot depends on the results on the battlefield: Ukrainian victories will make it harder for the West to blackmail them into surrendering.

The war has been highly controversial on the left. A minority have tended to apologise for Putin's invasion, blaming the West for encroaching on Russia's sphere of influence. Others clearly condemn Putin's decision to invade, but emphasise the need to oppose Western aid as a reckless escalation of the conflict. For the latter group, opposing the escalation of inter-imperial tensions generated by the war overrides their support for Ukrainian national rights. Another tendency sees the war as a straightforward attack by Russia on Ukraine, with little attention given to the broader imperial dynamics. For some in this group, support for Ukraine has at times slid into apologism or indifference to Western imperialism. This is deeply problematic, given that the war has been used to re-legitimise and relaunch Western imperialism for a new era of global conflict.

For our part, Socialist Alternative believes it is impossible to separate the dynamics of the war and the inter-imperial jostling that surrounds it. We therefore support the Ukrainian resistance, but neither call for nor oppose arms shipments to Ukraine. While the national resistance has the right to call for weapons to fight, we cannot lend our support to the growing militarisation of NATO and its allies, including Australia.

Putting aside these nuances, it is clear that the Ukraine war has had a deeply reactionary impact on politics in the West. In Europe, the US and the UK the conflict has been aggressively used to buttress right-wing governments, and the public's legitimate concern for Ukraine's rights has been used to ram through a massive expansion of the arms industry. Germany, previously known for the strong pacifist traditions on the left and in broader society, allocated €100 billion in new funds to the *Wehrmacht* last year. Some in the SPD cabinet, including the defence minister, are now calling for mandatory conscription to be reintroduced and for the military fund to be increased to €300 billion. This comes on top of a broad explosion in arms expenditure prior to the war, with Canada and the EU having already increased their military budgets by $130 billion from 2016 to 2020.

In the US, military spending has continued to grow under Biden, as has the aggression directed against China. The recent shooting down of spy balloons, alongside a handful of unidentified flying objects,[8] has taken tensions between the countries to a new level. This escalation is occurring despite China very openly signalling that it wants to cool the diplomatic and economic conflicts between the two nations. But the Democratic administration has shown little interest in any sort of detente, instead instigating multiple rounds of crippling sanctions and working increasingly closely with Taiwan's political and military institutions. The constraints being put on China's capacity to import

---

8. We hope that our alien comrades understand that conscious proletarians are opposed to interstellar warfare.

and produce microchips are designed to hold back China's technology and artificial intelligence industry for years, if not decades, and is part of a concerted strategy to entrench US hegemony in a field that will likely determine the future of warfare and industry.[9] US corporate behemoths such as Apple are quietly resisting this shift to a cold war footing, fearful of losing access to China's enormous domestic market. Yet it seems inevitable that they will be forced into line.

If open conflict between the US and China seems unlikely in the short term, the long-term prospects look increasingly dire. China is a rising power that is expanding in all sorts of important ways, including its military capacity, domestic consumption, productive capacity, share of international trade, and more. It has a big advantage in a handful of key sectors, including renewables and rare earth minerals. Yet recent events have shown that the US empire should not be underestimated. It has unrivalled power to reshape the parameters of the world economy and geopolitical landscape, using a range of strategies including fiscal and monetary policy, sanctions and deeply embedded international institutions, all backed by the unprecedented military power of NATO. The US-led network of military and political alliances is stronger than ever, and includes the entire advanced capitalist world as well as most of the regional powers in the global south.

How these dynamics play out, and the speed with which the contradictions develop, is an open question. It's possible the internal contradictions of Chinese state capitalism will prevent it from becoming the systemic challenger to the US that many assumed was inevitable a few years back. Alternatively, Chinese elites may seek to deflect domestic weakness by engaging in a more aggressive imperial policy. Either way, the overall risk of global conflict and nuclear war is higher than it has been since the Cuban missile crisis of 1962. The tensions will also lead to long-term economic shifts, most notably the unwinding of some elements of globalisation that have weakened the US and allowed China to grow, including just-in-time production and lengthy supply chains. Instead we are likely to see the growing division of the world into competing economic blocs, as countries seek

---

9. Hassan 2023.

to reshore or "friendshore" key industrial sectors. Together with the growing costs involved in responding to climate change and dealing with ageing populations in China and the West, there are many reasons to think that baseline inflation rates will be higher than they have been for some time.

Australia

After decades of relative prosperity, Australia is at something of an inflection point. As of October last year inflation had wiped out every cent of the (pitiful) wage rises workers had gained since 2011. Meanwhile, rapidly rising interest rates are squeezing working families, who suffer from one of the world's highest debt to disposable income ratios: 50 percent greater than the UK and double that of the US.[10] Those without a mortgage are not being spared, with rental prices shooting up in the major cities as landlords pass on increased costs and take advantage of a shortage in supply (which does not include the many investment properties deliberately left empty for tax purposes). While living standards are far from collapsing, this is the first real decline in living standards for decades.

Into this maelstrom steps the Labor Party, which has taken power for the first time in almost a decade. But far from taking a stand in defence of workers' living standards, the Albanese government has happily accepted that cuts to living standards are necessary to restore economic stability. Treasurer Jim Chalmers has been emphasising the need to balance the budget: refusing to increase Australia's derisory welfare payments, and making the "tough" decision to raise taxes on low- and middle-income families. All of this to avoid undercutting the Reserve Bank's explicit goal of slashing demand – ie, workers' living standards.

Labor's stance on China has been equally hawkish, despite the facade of friendlier relations between the two nations. Foreign Minister Penny Wong has been involved in an endless and aggressive round of regional diplomacy to shore up allies in the Pacific. Labor's austerian approach to government spending clearly doesn't apply when it comes

---

10. OECD n.d.

to investing in killing machines, with the military budget set to grow from 1.96 percent of GDP in 2022–23 to 2.23 percent by 2030. And that's before the cost of the AUKUS nuclear-powered attack submarines is taken into account, estimated at an eye-watering $368 billion.

If the ALP has essentially maintained the capitalist status quo, their strategy has been to promote a series of symbolic gestures as transformational policies. This is the case on climate, on women's pay, on robodebt and most importantly, the Indigenous Voice to parliament. Peter Dutton has taken a strong oppositional stance to basically every Labor policy, hoping to repeat the successes of the hard-right Tony Abbott Opposition of a decade earlier. So far there is no sign of this having an impact, but it is yet to be seen how long a right-wing Labor government can hold on to its support in a context of falling living standards. One thing is for sure: Albanese lacks the principles or the savvy to stand up to serious political pressure.

Unions and the broad left have shown no interest in challenging the many attacks on workers and the poor. Instead, they've been signing deals with bosses that will allow them to trade wages for conditions, signing off on public service contracts that offer less than 2 percent wage rises, and championing the Labor Party's symbolic proposal for an Indigenous Voice to parliament. Amid the news of falling wages and housing unaffordability, the unions are currently campaigning in support of the Labor Party's $3 million cap on superannuation. Aside from the fact that this pathetic proposal continues to offer substantial tax breaks to the rich, it will raise a pittance and does nothing to address the profit and power of the super-rich, whose share of national income continues to grow.

Overall then, we face a world system riven with tensions and contradictions, though not, importantly, in permanent crisis. Given the instabilities described here, it is inevitable that there will be flashpoints of struggle and resistance. The rebuilding of an international revolutionary left is as urgent as ever.

References

Burn-Murdoch, John 2022, "Millennials are shattering the oldest rule in politics", *Financial Times*, 30 December. https://www.ft.com/content/c361e372-769e-45cd-a063-f5c0a7767cf4

Dutra, Israel 2023, "Why should we support the popular rebellion in Peru?", *International Viewpoint*, 27 January. https://internationalviewpoint.org/spip.php?article7967

Hassan, Omar 2023, "The new frontier for global imperialism: Review of 'Chip War' by Chris Miller", *Red Flag*, 13 February. https://redflag.org.au/article/new-frontier-global-imperialism-review-chip-war-chris-miller

Hillier, Ben 2022, "Crunch time", *Red Flag*, 3 October. https://redflag.org.au/article/crunch-time

ILO 2022, "Global Wage Report 2022–23". https://www.ilo.org/wcmsp5/groups/public/---ed_protect/---protrav/---travail/documents/publication/wcms_862569.pdf

Martin, Katie, and Harriet Agnew, "A year of pain: investors struggle in a new era of higher rates", *Financial Times*, 30 November. https://www.ft.com/content/c93f3660-821f-458b-ae0f-23ac05b8f03f

OECD n.d., "Household debt". https://data.oecd.org/hha/household-debt.htm

United Nations n.d., "End poverty in all its forms everywhere". https://unstats.un.org/sdgs/report/2022/goal-01/

U.S. Bureau of Labor Statistics 2022, Real Earnings News Release, 12 January. https://www.bls.gov/news.release/archives/realer_01122022.htm

JORDAN HUMPHREYS

"Beware of the Black Bourgeoisie": The growing role of Indigenous elites in Australian capitalism

Jordan Humphreys is a socialist activist in Sydney and has written extensively on Indigenous oppression and working-class history. His book *Indigenous Liberation and Socialism* is forthcoming from Red Flag Books.

> I would argue that today the Black middle class are as great a problem as anything else that the Aboriginal community confronts. In the same way as the Black middle class in the African American situation has been the buffer between the ruling-class establishment and the shitkickers.
>
> – Gary Foley, 2021[1]

OVER THE OCTOBER Labour Day long weekend in 1977, 200 Aboriginal activists and their supporters met at the Black Theatre in Redfern to discuss the launching of a new campaign for land rights. It was out of this meeting that the NSW Aboriginal Land Council was born. Its first convenor was Kevin Cook, a left-wing trade unionist and radical Aboriginal activist, and the committee was filled with activists who had been forged out of the struggles of the 1960s and '70s. The conference also established the Trade Union Committee on Aboriginal Rights (TUCAR) to link the land rights campaign with working-class organisations.

---

1. From the *Melbourne Calling* video interview "Gary Foley the Godfather of Aboriginal activism speaking the truth" on YouTube. https://www.youtube.com/watch?v=VH_W_G4uBz4

Forty-five years later, a very different meeting involving the Land Council took place in Redfern. On 2 August 2022 an emergency community meeting was held at the National Centre of Indigenous Excellence to protest against the closure of the centre and the summary dismissal of 50, mostly Indigenous, staff members. The sacked workers had been offered a humiliating $700 if they would sign non-disclosure agreements with the owners of the centre, who just happened to be the NSW Aboriginal Land Council.[2]

Co-founder and CEO of Redfern Youth Connect Margaret Haumono told the meeting that she and others had spoken to the Land Council and had been told that the closure was "not our [the Land Council's] problem". The meeting responded with cries of "gutless dogs" and "shame". Wiradjuri, Yuin and Gadigal woman Nadeena Dixon, granddaughter of the Aboriginal trade union activist Chicka Dixon, said that "too many of our community leaders have become dictators", while fired staff expressed disgust at being thrown out the door with little communication.

As if to confirm Dixon's words, two representatives from the Land Council then pushed their way to the front of the meeting and demanded the right to reply to their critics. One of the representatives berated the crowd, explaining that "we can't run this place on a loss" and that the only alternative to closing down the centre was to sell off the whole site to developers.

The other representative argued that there wasn't any money to be made out of swimming pools and gyms, and revealed that the Land Council was considering handing over the whole operation to the PCYC (Police and Community Youth Club). This was met with outrage from the crowd, most of whom were all too familiar with the history and culture of the police in Redfern. It certainly didn't help that Land Council representatives had been given a police escort to the meeting.

The Land Council had gone from an organisation run by a bunch of radicals, unionists and socialists to an organisation dominated by a group of Indigenous bureaucrats dedicated to

---

2. The following description of the NCIE protest meeting is based on personal observation by the author, reported in Humphreys 2022a.

fostering private enterprise and respectability. Its incorporation into the capitalist system is emblematic of a broader shift in many Indigenous organisations.

Originally, the NSW Land Council had been a voluntary grassroots activist group without any government funding. It relied on the resources of Tranby College, which had been established by the unions, for its land rights campaigning. In the wake of the passage of the Aboriginal Land Rights Act (NSW) in 1983 the Land Council was formally constituted as a statutory corporation. At first, continuity seemed to outweigh change: Cook was made chairperson and the Council still had a number of prominent left-wing figures.[3]

However, by the 1990s the Land Council had undergone a significant transformation. From 1983 to 1998 it accumulated $281 million from land tax payments made in compensation for the loss of land. This money – far less than Indigenous people deserve in reparations – allowed the Council to become a self-funding independent body. At the same time, it served as the basis for the strengthening and expansion of an increasingly conservative and capitalist-minded Indigenous bureaucracy. A key moment in this process took place in 1990, when a series of amendments were passed to the Land Rights Act that gave the NSW Land Council and its subsidiaries the ability to sell, mortgage or exchange the land they had gained through land rights claims. The same amendments also made the NSW Land Council elected councillor positions full-time salaried ones.

In 2012 the impact of these amendments became clear when the NSW Land Council applied for a coal seam gas permit covering 321,300 square kilometres, with a non-disclosed business partner. This application came after the Land Council had made three petroleum exploration licence applications earlier in the same year. While pushed by the full-time leaders of the Land Council, the application was met with widespread opposition from Indigenous people and the local land councils, particularly in the Northern Rivers and Illawarra regions where the coal seam gas projects were being proposed.[4] Fed up with the Land Council's schemes, a number of left-wing Indigenous activists

---

3. See Norman 2015 for the history of the NSWALC.
4. Howden 2012.

set up the NSW Aboriginal Land Rights Association Inc in 2021. It was designed to be "a grassroots Aboriginal Community Controlled Organisation with a mandate centred around upholding the purpose of the NSW Aboriginal Land Rights Act 1983".[5]

The development of the NSW Aboriginal Land Council was not an anomaly. The Aboriginal Housing Company (AHC) was similarly established out of the struggles in Redfern during the 1970s to maintain Indigenous control over the area known as the Block. In the 2000s, the AHC helped initiate the Pemulwuy Project, which was supposed to regenerate the local Aboriginal community area. However when designs became public in 2014, it became clear that the AHC was primarily interested in realising the untapped commercial value of the land, with space overwhelmingly allocated to retail, office space and expensive student housing. This led local Aboriginal activists to establish the Redfern Aboriginal Tent Embassy, which resisted the development for over a year. Eventually, federal Aboriginal Affairs minister Nigel Scullion brokered a deal in which 62 homes would be built for Indigenous families at the same time as any commercial development of the Block.

Similarly, the Condobolin Local Aboriginal Land Council has come under sustained criticism for years from Aboriginal residents who say their housing has fallen into disrepair, with black mould, termites, electrical faults and broken sewerage pipes. "We've got our elders who are in their 70s and 80s that are living in houses with black mould, where the roofs are peeling off, the walls have deteriorated", Kira-Lea Dargin, a Wiradjuri woman and advocate for several of the residents, told ABC News. In July 2021, the Land Council signed 18 eviction notices after residents refused to pay rent. Writing for ABC News, Ella Archibald-Binge summed up the situation well, noting that this "crisis has become a microcosm of a broader issue across NSW, as relationships break down between Aboriginal communities and the local bodies set up to represent them".[6]

---

5. NSW Aboriginal Land Rights Association Inc n.d.
6. Archibald-Binge 2021.

The emergence of a new Indigenous middle class

Underpinning the conflicts with these organisations is the emergence of an Indigenous middle class in Australia. There have of course always been political differences among Indigenous people in Australia. In particular, there has long been a minority of Indigenous people who have found a place within the capitalist establishment. But until the later decades of the twentieth century, this was confined to a tiny number of individuals who were easy to dismiss as sell-outs. The emergence of a broader Indigenous middle class, and the development of a small but growing Indigenous capitalist class, adds new dimensions to the differentiation within the Indigenous population.

Probably the most public manifestations of the growing influence of this Indigenous middle class are the proposals for an Indigenous Voice to parliament, the various state-based treaty processes currently underway, and the prospect for more in the future – including on a federal level. There have also been shifts with regard to government and corporate policies, from Indigenous employment opportunities to economic partnerships to cultural recognition and a range of other issues, as well as broader cultural shifts in how Indigenous culture and history are understood and discussed in the media, the education system and so forth.

These shifts are related to broader changes in the dynamics of race relations and multiculturalism in modern Australian capitalism. Throughout the twentieth century, the struggles of Indigenous people and non-Indigenous activists overturned discriminatory laws and racist practices, challenged public attitudes, exploitative bosses and government bureaucracies, and legitimised the struggle for Indigenous rights. While racism towards Aboriginal people continued despite these wins, the collective impact of these reforms was significant.

Alongside developments in the sphere of Indigenous politics, the liberal idea of multiculturalism broadly came to replace assimilation as the main strategy for race relations. Multiculturalism involved seeing Australia as made up of a series of different, but internally homogeneous ethnic groups, each with their own legitimate cultural heritage. Rather than asking these communities to abandon their culture in order to integrate, the new policy aimed, at least on paper, to create a pluralistic society that celebrated the diversity of cultures contained within Australia. Within this framework, Indigenous people are widely seen as the first and most legitimate minority culture.

This has now been further tweaked with the development of modern identity politics. People are more than ever encouraged to embrace whatever identities they are connected with. For a significant section of academics, public servants and journalists, modern Australia is – or should be – a cosmopolitan society based on a multitude of ever-increasing numbers of intersecting racial, cultural, sexual, political and social identities. The more identities, the better. This is strongly, if often unconsciously, related to a hyper-individualistic capitalist world view in which we are all defined as individual consumers made up of an amalgamation of different intersecting personal attributes.

In the process, a curious transformation has taken place. In the not-so-distant past, a left-wing commentator on Indigenous issues could say:

> Neoliberal politics, in part, rejects a politics of recognition. Addressing historical and cultural injustice through recognition and Indigenous rights is seen as irrelevant and, at its most extreme, as a hindrance to Indigenous advancement.[7]

Today however the mainstream of neoliberalism openly embraces the politics of recognition. Governments and corporations promote and profit from oppressed identities as part of public relations campaigns and necessary checklists in the rollout of new brands or programs. This newfound institutional "wokeness" has absolutely nothing to do with any struggle for rights or liberation. The promotion of respectable spokespeople from minority groups and proposals for constitutional recognition are attempts to whitewash a system that relies on the ongoing subjugation of all sorts of oppressed groups. A conservative

---

7. Morris 2014, p.10.

critique of the politics of recognition and identity is now the purview of the hard right of society.

Nowhere is this gulf between the image and reality clearer than with regard to Indigenous people in Australia. The ABC can play footage of smiling Indigenous kids singing the classic hit "I am Australian" in their Indigenous languages at the same time that it is reported that 100 percent of the children in detention in the Northern Territory are Indigenous. Albanese's government can be hailed for beginning a process of decolonisation with its support for an Indigenous Voice to parliament, while leaving in place the key pillars of the inherently racist Northern Territory Intervention. The bosses of the mining industry, the Business Council of Australia and the Murdoch media can shake their heads at the failure to close the income, health and education gaps between Indigenous and non-Indigenous people, while overseeing the system of exploitation, privatisation and corporate greed that makes this inevitable.

Indeed there is almost an inverse relationship between the frequency with which we hear passionless acknowledgements of past wrongs and the making of real progress towards liberation.

These shifts are sometimes dismissed as mere tokenism. It's true that they will not radically transform the oppressive conditions most Indigenous people live under. But it is mistaken to think that these shifts will have no impact at all. They will lead – and indeed already have led – to substantial benefits for a subsection of Indigenous society – what historian and activist Gary Foley calls the "Blak Bourgeoisie".[8]

Italian Marxist Antonio Gramsci describes this process well in his *Prison Notebooks*, when he explains how ruling classes gradually absorb a layer of people from antagonistic oppressed or exploited groups, in order to give greater legitimacy to their rule and widen the social base of those who have a material interest in its continuation. This is particularly marked in oppressed groups that contain within themselves class divisions, such as women, migrants and LGBTI people.

---

8. Hall 2023.

The emergence of a new Indigenous elite is the result of a number of processes coming together. First of all, there is the creation of what academic Tim Rowse has called the "Indigenous Estate":

> In the last third of the 20th century, nearly one-fifth of the Australian land mass was transferred to Indigenous Australians' ownership. By 2013, Indigenous interests had been recognised over more than half of Australia – a combination of land rights, native title, and Indigenous Land Use Agreements enabled by the assertion of native title. To this estate, hectares will be added every year through purchases by the Indigenous Land Corporation (ILC), a statutory authority set up by the Keating government in June 1995. As long as the ILC's endowment yields an annual purchase fund, there is no limit to the acreage that can be, to some degree, Indigenous land.[9]

There are very stringent limits to this "Indigenous Estate": mainly that it cannot infringe on commercial interests such as mining, tourism and farming. Nevertheless, in combination with myriad urban-based Indigenous businesses, consultancy firms, NGOs and community organisations, this estate has created "thousands of organisations making up the 'Indigenous sector', the joint product of Indigenous political mobilisation and state funding and legislation".[10] As well there has been an expansion in the employment of Indigenous people in traditional middle-class academic, legal, media, governmental and cultural roles within institutions such as universities, law firms, media companies, state bureaucracies and cultural projects.

Of course, any progress for Indigenous people entails some degree of bureaucratisation. If Indigenous people win greater control over their own affairs, then organisations will be set up to facilitate this, and in the context of capitalist society, such organisations will inevitably develop some degree of institutional conservatism. This isn't unique to Indigenous people; any oppressed or exploited group that manages

---

9. Rowse 2017, p.287.
10. Rowse 2017, p.380.

to win some degree of acceptance in society develops similar problems. In the wake of the civil rights movement in the United States, there was a flowering of Black bureaucracies in government departments and private businesses. Even the workers' movement has developed bureaucratised organisations within the trade union movement in response to its partial victories.

The problem arises when the dangers and challenges posed by these developments are ignored or downplayed.

Another factor in the development of an Indigenous elite has been the conscious intervention of the state and sections of private capital. This has been necessary because prior to the 1970s there was little class differentiation among the Indigenous population. Unlike Indigenous groups in New Zealand or North America, pre-invasion Aboriginal societies did not have class hierarchies, and after colonisation Indigenous groups were unable to develop any kind of independent economic base. Thus government and private capital have played a key role in creating opportunities for Indigenous businesses and bureaucracies to grow.

This new approach reflects a major shift in ruling-class thinking on Indigenous issues. An early sign was the Howard government's 1998 amendment to the Native Title Act, which both weakened and entrenched the legislation. Native title has now gone from being one of the most controversial political issues in Australia to one on which there is now a large degree of consensus, as David Ritter has explained:

> On and off between 1992 and 1998, native title was staggeringly divisive and controversial; the subject of immense political storm and legal battles giving rise to numerous banner headlines, blockbuster parliamentary debates and marathon litigation in front of the High Court. At times, wilder opinion forecast the break-up of Australia, the collapse of the economy and outbreaks of violence... Students born in the last twenty years often look up from their desks in some puzzlement when one tries to evoke the hysteria and volume of debate that once existed over the recognition of native title... Native title is now

just part of the furniture; or maybe, so dim is the collective awareness of the legal doctrine once dubbed a "revolution", that it can be thought of as no more than a design on the national wallpaper.[11]

This is largely because the leaders of the mining, pastoral and tourism industries have come to see that they can get most of what they desire through the framework of native title. Whatever constraints or conflicts it might occasionally give rise to are offset by the ease with which their plans can be approved under the cover of "consultation". Clear victories for Indigenous communities are rare and hard fought for, and the spirit of "consensus" between Indigenous community leaders and mining bosses has largely benefited the latter.

In general terms Australia is going down a path similar to that forged by Canada and New Zealand decades ago. As in those places, the new policies will not end or even significantly ameliorate Indigenous oppression. However it will increase the scale and significance of the Indigenous upper and middle classes in Australian society, and irreversibly change the contours of Indigenous politics.

Black capitalists

From the political establishment, there seems to have been a clear push towards "partnerships" with Indigenous leaders in the wake of Tony Abbott's campaign to close 150 Indigenous communities in Western Australia during 2015. While there was general agreement within government policy circles that "rationalising" the number of Indigenous communities was a worthy goal, Abbott's gung-ho attitude had generated more opposition than they were comfortable with, particularly as there was also growing public consciousness around issues such as racist policing and Australia Day. What these policy advisors proposed was greater engagement and partnerships with Indigenous leaders to try to avoid such opposition emerging in the future. The fruits of this can be seen on a number of fronts.

---

11. Ritter 2009, p.xii.

The Morrison government made a concerted effort to develop an Indigenous capitalist and middle class. From September 2020 to September 2021 the federal government's Indigenous Procurement Policy saw 10,920 government contracts, valued at $1.09 billion, awarded to 943 Indigenous businesses. This is set to increase in coming years, with Albanese maintaining the goal that 3 percent of the value of Commonwealth contracts be awarded to Indigenous businesses from 2022. It is notable that it is often government departments traditionally associated with the hard right of politics that have had some of the biggest contracts with Indigenous businesses. The largest number of contracts is with the Department of Defence, which signed 6,476 contracts (valued at $610 million) in 2020–21. State and territory governments have their own Indigenous procurement policies as well, similarly running into the hundreds of millions of dollars.[12]

To take just one example, the Department of Defence signed a $452 million contract with Indigenous-owned construction company Pacific Services Group Holdings (PSG) to work on redeveloping Garden Island dockyards. The director of PSG is Indigenous man Troy Rugless, a former rugby league player, who has been involved in the construction industry for years as a director of several companies. Through the government's procurement policy PSG has gone from a small cleaning service in a rundown warehouse to a multi-division construction company aiming towards listing on the Australian stock exchange.[13]

The Indigenous Procurement Policy has helped to facilitate the rapid growth in Indigenous business owners, albeit from a very low base. Many start on more lucrative government jobs before competing in the private sector. Between 2006 and 2018, the number of Indigenous businesses jumped by almost 74 percent. The gross income for these businesses increased by 115 percent and in 2018 was $4.88 billion. This probably underestimates the numbers as it only includes businesses that are both at least 50 percent Indigenous-owned and are officially registered as Indigenous businesses. Other

---

12. National Indigenous Australians Agency 2021.
13. Australian Defence Force Magazine 2019.

estimates put the number of Indigenous owner-managers at around 17,900 in 2016 (an increase of 30 percent compared to 2011), a figure that would be even higher today.[14]

While Indigenous businesses are still a very small section of capital, they are growing disproportionately. The percentage of non-Indigenous people who are business owners is of course far higher than among Indigenous people, but the gap is narrowing. Interestingly, registered Indigenous companies are larger than non-Indigenous counterparts, with a report published in 2018 finding they had an average gross income of $1.6 million and 14 employees, compared to $400,000 and two employees for the wider community.[15] A report by Supply Nation, an organisation that connects Indigenous and non-Indigenous businesses, found that despite the impact of COVID-19 in the years from 2019 to 2021, "there was an increase in Indigenous businesses across all types of business ownership with the most growth observed in the number of registered sole traders and partnerships".[16]

Private capital has also played a role in promoting the formation of Indigenous businesses. In 2011 Fortescue Metals Group (FMG) awarded just $20 million in contracts to two Indigenous-owned companies. By 2021 that had risen to $3 billion. One of these was with the Indigenous-owned mining maintenance contractor Warrikal Engineering, which recently signed a contract worth $350 million. Warrikal was only founded in 2017 and has already had major contracts with Rio Tinto and Pilbara Minerals. The company's workforce is around 20 percent Indigenous and Warrikal's chief executive is Amanda Healy, a Wonnarua Koori woman, who has run several different businesses and was recently appointed Adjunct Professor at Curtin University's business school.[17]

In 2019 the Business Council of Australia (BCA) launched the "Raise the Bar" initiative which pledged businesses to collectively spend $3 billion on contracts with Indigenous businesses over the

---

14. Evans et al. 2021 and Shirodkar et al. 2018.
15. Evans et al. 2021.
16. Supply Nation 2022, p.8.
17. Smit 2021a and Smit 2021b.

next five years. The businesses that signed up include Qantas, the Commonwealth Bank, Lendlease, BHP, BP, Rio Tinto, BAE systems and Westpac. Reconciliation Action Plans have also become widespread in the business world, particularly in some of the largest companies in Australia, including BHP, LendLease and 44 companies on the ASX200.[18]

Mining companies, in particular, have been keen to reset their relationships with the Indigenous community. This is particularly the case in the wake of Rio Tinto's deliberate destruction of 46,000-year-old artifacts in Juukan Gorge, and further revelations that they dumped heritage material from the Marandoo mine into a Darwin rubbish dump in the 1990s. The Wintawari Guruma Aboriginal Corporation, whose land the Marandoo mine is on, has cut ties with Rio Tinto and a moratorium has been placed on mining in the Juukan Gorge. This has caused a reduction of about 2 million tonnes in Rio Tinto's production. In the aftermath of this disaster, their rivals BHP have taken the opportunity for some Black-washing, by pushing for the South Australian and Western Australian governments to introduce strict penalties for companies that damage heritage sites as well as giving Indigenous communities a greater ability to appeal heritage decisions. This cynical campaign is being launched with the full knowledge that they will be less affected by such legislation than their rivals in Rio Tinto.[19]

The goal of these mining groups is to neutralise the morally powerful opposition to their projects posed by Aboriginal activism. The new agreement that BHP signed in 2021 with the Barada Barna Aboriginal Corporation is a case in point. It is chock full of cheap symbolism, like giving a local airport an Indigenous name and painting Indigenous cultural murals at the airport and the mining site. At the same time, it prioritises building up Indigenous corporations and consciously seeks to enmesh them in the mining industry in order to undermine potential criticisms. This includes a historic level of investment, training and contracts for local Indigenous businesses that will last for multiple generations. Both BHP and the

18. BCA 2019.
19. Knowles 2021.

Barada Barna Aboriginal Corporation frame this project as one of "self-determination", which shows how much this term has become detached from any radical let alone anti-capitalist association. Barada Barna Aboriginal Corporation chairperson Luarna Walsh celebrated the agreement as one that

> sets Barada Barna on a path of self-determination. It will ensure BBAC is sustainable into the future and help our next generation of descendants achieve their goals through schooling and university, and employment and training. This Agreement also provides BBAC with the ability to diversify our income streams, by creating Traditional Owner business that can tender for a variety of contracts on Country.[20]

Black bureaucrats

The promotion of a layer of Indigenous people with a material interest in Australian capitalism isn't confined to a few thousand business owners. Alongside this has developed a broader layer of middle-class Indigenous people, involving tens of thousands of managers, bureaucrats and professionals.

In the ten years from 2011 to 2021, the number of Indigenous managers grew from 9,406 to 21,218. This is an increase of 125.5 percent, the largest increase in any Indigenous occupation outside of sales assistants. There has also been a modest increase in the percentage of Indigenous people who are managers compared to other occupations. In 2006 only 3.8 percent of employed Indigenous people were managers, in 2021 it was around 8.2 percent.[21]

Similar changes can be seen in in the number of Indigenous professionals. From 2011 to 2021 this layer almost doubled, from 19,358 to 36,013. ABS data is too imprecise to draw a clear line between middle-class and working-class people in that group, but presumably some thousands more middle-class people have been created in the process of this growth. These figures do not include the significant

---

20. BHP and BBAC 2021.
21. The following statistics are all from ABS 2022.

number of Indigenous writers, artists, musicians and political commentators who play an increasingly prominent part in shaping political discussion and popular culture, far beyond their numbers. While income levels aren't an exact guide to class differences, the widening levels of economic inequality within the Indigenous population are also a sign of growing class differentiation, as Ross Gittins has explained:

> While the gap between the two groups [Indigenous and non-Indigenous] has been narrowing, the gap within the Indigenous group has been widening. If you take the weekly disposable personal incomes of all Indigenous people aged 15 or older, adjust them for inflation, rank them from lowest to highest, then divide them all into 10 groups of 10 percent each, you discover some disturbing things.
>
> Between 2011 and 2016, the average income of those in the top decile rose by $75 a week, compared with $32 a week for those in the middle decile. Individuals in the bottom decile had no income (possibly because they were students or at home minding kids), while those in the second and third lowest deciles saw their incomes fall.[22]

Similarly, the 2021 census records that while 52.2 percent of Indigenous households had an average median weekly income of less than $1,000, only 36.7 percent of households earned above this threshold.[23]

The Voice: representation or cooption?

The emergence of an Indigenous elite and shifting attitudes in the Australian ruling class have combined to produce calls for new institutions to better manage Indigenous affairs. A range of options have been canvassed, the most notable of which is the Voice to parliament.

The origins of the Voice lie in debates around the issue of constitutional recognition for Indigenous people which coalesced in

---

22. Gittins 2018.
23. ABS 2022.

2012 with the launching of the Recognise campaign. This multimillion-dollar advertising project was overseen by the NGO Reconciliation Australia and received widespread support from major businesses such as BHP and Qantas, and right-wing politicians like former Liberal prime ministers John Howard and Tony Abbott. While a minority of conservative Indigenous figures supported the Recognise campaign, it fell apart in the face of strident grassroots opposition by many Indigenous people who saw it for the face-saving sham it was, and was finally disbanded in 2017.

The inadequate symbolism of constitutional recognition fuelled interest in an alternative proposal for a constitutionally enshrined Indigenous Voice to parliament created through a national referendum. This would be a political body that would serve in an advisory capacity for government Indigenous policies. A constitutionally recognised Indigenous Voice to parliament was one of the main proposals in the Uluru Statement of the Heart endorsed at the Referendum Council's Regional Dialogues and the National Constitutional Convention, held at the Ayers Rock Resort near Uluru in May 2017.

Advocates of the Uluru Statement present the Indigenous Voice to parliament as the first step in a process that will deal with the structural dimensions of Indigenous oppression, end the powerlessness that plagues Indigenous communities and, along with a Makarrata Commission of truth-telling and agreement-making, lead to genuine Indigenous self-determination for the first time since colonisation.

In reality, while the Voice goes beyond merely recognising the existence of Indigenous people in the constitution, it too is an almost entirely symbolic gesture. The proposed model of the Voice will be an advisory body only, with no actual power over government policy. Parliament will have to listen to its views – which it can then freely ignore.

While the Voice was developed by a layer of Indigenous academics and lawyers it has gained broad support in ruling-class circles and within the Albanese government. It was strongly endorsed by 86 percent of the public submissions to the Joint Select Committee on Constitutional Recognition relating to Aboriginal and Torres Strait

Islander Peoples. These included public submissions by most of the key sections of the Australian capitalist class. The submission by the Business Council of Australia for instance stated:

> The Business Council and its members are committed to the empowerment of Aboriginal and Torres Strait Islander peoples (in this report referred to as Indigenous Australians) and the creation of opportunities for full participation in the Australian economy and accordingly supports meaningful constitutional recognition of a Voice to the Parliament for Indigenous Australians. Without recognition of Australia's First Peoples, the Australian Constitution cannot be complete...
>
> ...The Business Council believes this issue is too important to be kicked into the weeds as we approach an election year. Equally, we do not support the politicisation of constitutional recognition and would not want to see a question put alongside next year's federal election. The Business Council believes the question should be agreed, formulated and put to the Australian people via referendum within 12 months of the next federal election.[24]

For the Labor government the Voice is seen as a part of Albanese's broader strategy of presenting a progressive gloss to the public while pursuing a right-wing alliance with big business, the mainstream media and wealthy but socially liberal Australians. The Labor Party hope to strengthen their hold over governmental power by isolating the Liberals and the Nationals – presenting them as incompetent dinosaurs out of touch with both urban middle-class voters and corporate Australia, both of whom have shifted to embrace cultural recognition for Indigenous people over the last couple of decades. In the process they also hope to be able to neutralise the healthy and progressive anti-racist sentiment in society by folding it into a tame-cat institution unlikely to upset the status quo. This approach is hardly

---

24. BCA 2018.

unique to Indigenous issues: on everything from climate change to union rights, foreign policy and LGBTI issues, hollow progressive symbolism dominates current government practice.

On the other side of politics a significant section of conservative politicians are trying to cohere a right-wing campaign against the Voice. This is centred around the federal National Party and Pauline Hanson's One Nation; however Liberal leader Peter Dutton has also attacked the Voice, although in more veiled terms. These right-wingers are trying to galvanise the existing racist sentiment in Australian society against Indigenous people into what they hope will be a humiliating defeat for the Labor Party in the referendum – a hope made possible by the weaknesses of the proposed reform itself.

There are however some fractures within the right, with prominent moderates from the Liberal Party backing the Voice proposal. The NSW Liberal Party in particular is dominated by pro-Voice Liberals such as NSW MP Julian Leeser, Senator Andrew Bragg and the moderate Liberal Party power broker Matt Kean. In February the NSW Liberal Premier Dominic Perrott pledged to run a joint Yes to the Voice campaign with the Albanese government if the Liberals were re-elected in the NSW state election.

Support for the Voice from mining bosses and Liberal moderates reflects the fact that the proposal can hardly be described as a reform. It will be an advisory body with no real control over funding, legislation or communities. It will not make any difference to the lives of the vast majority of Indigenous people, but will further the social and political capital of a small section of the Indigenous middle class. Most importantly, a victory will give progressive legitimacy to an insipid Albanese government that refuses to address either the specific issues facing Indigenous communities or the wages crisis facing the working class more broadly.

The Voice essentially represents a balancing act by the dominant parts of the Australian ruling class, concerned with the need to appear modern and anti-racist on one hand, but without giving Indigenous people any real power.

Opposition to the Voice has been dominated by right-wingers but there is a minority of figures critical of the Voice from a progressive direction. This was on display at the Invasion Day rallies this year, which in most cities stridently attacked the Voice, and when the former Greens senator Lidia Thorpe resigned from her party over the issue. Concern over the Voice goes back in fact to the 2017 Constitutional Convention, which saw a breakaway group of seven delegates and their supporters from Victoria, Canberra and New South Wales, including Lidia Thorpe and long-standing Indigenous activists Jenny Munro and Lyall Munro Jr, walk out in protest of what they saw as a charade that had been stitched up by conservative Indigenous leaders such as Noel Pearson. A statement by Les Coe, Nioka Coe and Ruth Gilbert condemned the Constitutional Convention as a "scandalous, deceitful process" dominated by the "Conservative Black Political elite" in which any genuine discussion about sovereignty and self-determination was marginalised in favour of surface-level changes.[25]

There is then at least some awareness of the growing role of Indigenous elites, although the debates around the Voice also reveal the difficulties in developing concrete alternatives. For instance, treaties are often presented as a more left-wing alternative to moderate proposals like the Voice. But while there has been relatively more reluctance about the granting of treaties by the Australian establishment, there have been shifts on this front too.

The Victorian state government for example is involved in an already quite developed treaty process. This has led to the establishment of a First Peoples' Assembly of Victoria, which in conjunction with the state government, has created a Treaty Authority that is supposed to be an independent body overseeing treaty negotiations, a Treaty Negotiation Framework that sets the parameters of these negotiations, as well as a Self-Determination Fund that is supposed to provide financial resources to Indigenous people in Victoria so they can participate in these negotiations on a more equal footing with the state government.

Socialists should be sceptical about the ultimate outcome of treaty processes such as that being pursued in Victoria. After all, governments

---

25. See the Walkout Statement: Aboriginal Embassy Statement from the Sacred Fire at https://nationalunitygovernment.org/content/walkout-statement-aboriginal-embassy-statement-sacred-fire

in New Zealand and Canada have not allowed Indigenous political bodies, truth and reconciliation commissions, or even treaties to stop them from violating land rights in the pursuit of profit. In 2020, the Canadian government persevered with a multibillion-dollar gas pipeline project, despite fervent opposition from the Wet'suwet'en First Nation representatives. In New Zealand, successive governments have repeatedly rejected the Waitangi Tribunal's recommendation that the Māori be given foreshore and seabed rights.

Whether it is an Indigenous voice to parliament or a treaty, or some combination of both, there is significant and growing support for some kind of Indigenous political representative body. Of course, the left cannot be against such a body in principle. But for it to have a real impact it needs to be a step towards self-determination and justice, involving real funding and control. The alternative is just another committee like the many we've seen before, which enriches and empowers the minority who are lucky enough to be part of it, while doing nothing for Indigenous people more broadly.

One example of such a body is the Coalition of Peaks. This is a grouping of over 50 Indigenous organisations formed in 2019. Within a few months it had established an agreement with the Council of Australian Governments (COAG). In 2020 a National Agreement on Closing the Gap was signed between the Coalition of Peaks, the prime minister, premiers, chief ministers and the president of the Australian Local Government Association. The National Agreement was ostensibly motivated by the lack of Indigenous input into Closing the Gap programs. While this is a valid critique, the inclusion of the Coalition of Peaks doesn't appear to have made much of a difference. The problem is not to be found in the colour of the skin of the bureaucrats implementing the program, but in its fundamentally neoliberal nature. As the National Agreement states:

> This Agreement builds on, and replaces, the NIRA. It continues the successful elements of the NIRA, strengthens others and addresses foundational areas previously excluded from consideration. The most significant of those was that NIRA was only an Agreement between Australian governments whereas in

this Agreement, for the first time, representatives of Aboriginal and Torres Strait Islander people are also parties.[26]

Despite this supposedly landmark agreement, the 2022 Closing the Gap report stated that the targets for adults in prison, deaths by suicide, children in out-of-home care, children being school-ready and income inequality were either "not on track" or worsening.[27]

Indigenous elites in Canada and New Zealand

We can look at other countries where the class divisions within the Indigenous population are more developed to see where this all leads. Across Canada there are now more than 250 First Nations, Metis and Inuit development corporations, with collectively several billion dollars in assets. Strong ties have been built between the Indigenous capitalist class in Canada and the resource-extractive industry in particular, which is now the largest private employer of Indigenous people in Canada.

The Haisla Nation for instance has established strong links with the liquified gas industry (LNG) and its Working Group boasts that Suncor Energy spent more than $4 million with Haisla-owned businesses in 2013, and that there are now 19 Petro-Canada stations owned and operated by First Nations companies. In 2016 the Haisla Nation-owned Cedar LNG obtained a 25-year LNG export licence from the Canadian government. The most controversial decision of the Indigenous capitalists who run the Haisla Nation though has been its participation in the $40 billion LNG Coastal GasLink pipeline project. The project has been endorsed by elected chiefs and councils from 20 Indigenous nations but has been rejected by some of the Wet'suwet'en people, including a number of hereditary chiefs. In 2020 this clash led to a substantial movement across Canada by both Indigenous and non-Indigenous protesters who drew attention to the environmentally destructive and profit-driven nature of the Coastal GasLink pipeline.[28] Another expression of the convergence of interests that has arisen

---

26. Closing the Gap 2020.
27. Closing the Gap 2022.
28. Nowlin 2020.

between First Nations elites and fossil fuel capitalists is the alliance of West Australian mining billionaire Gina Rinehart with the leaders of the Piikani Nation in the Rocky Mountains of Canada. They are seeking to overturn a court-ruled environmental ban on a proposed coal mine.[29]

Canada also has an extensive network of Indigenous political structures such as the Assembly of First Nations (AFN), which represents First Nations peoples living on reserves, and the Congress of Aboriginal Peoples, which represents those living in other rural or urban areas. Both bodies have substantial government funding and access to private capital (including a First Nations bank), and they play a key role in overseeing the implementation of treaty processes and negotiations. The existence of these bodies has not ended, or even demonstrably lessened, the structural racism oppressing Indigenous communities. Despite these bodies existing for decades, the proportion of the prison population that is Indigenous skyrocketed from 17 percent in 1999 to over 30 percent in 2020.[30]

Instead, bodies like the Assembly of First Nations have played a key role in cohering an Indigenous elite that has become disconnected from the interests of the vast majority of First Nations people.

In 2007, AFN National Chief Phil Fontaine publicly criticised the National Aboriginal Day of Action protests for encouraging illegal road blockades and confrontations with the police. An article in the *Star* newspaper revealed that Fontaine secretly met with the Canadian Police in a coordinated attempt to suppress the protests. This was followed by the resignation in 2012 of AFN National Chief Shawn Atleo, who came under pressure because of his open hostility towards the Idle No More movement. During the 2020 Wet'suwet'en protests, the AFN, led by National Chief Perry Bellegarde, unanimously supported the pipeline and pressured First Nations activists to back down. They even deployed identity politics to try and wedge the movement, attempting to paint it as a group of outsider white "professional" protesters.

---

29. de Kruijff 2021.
30. Report of Dr Ivan Zinger, Correctional Investigator of Canada, quoted in Public Safety 2020.

These political divides should not be surprising. All communities are divided, most importantly by politics and by class. Bellegarde is close to Justin Trudeau – the undisputed champion of fake symbolism – and last year invited him to be the first Canadian prime minister to attend a national meeting of the AFN. As Yellowknives Dene First Nation activist and writer Glen Coulthard has explained in his book *Red Skin, White Masks: Rejecting the Colonial Politics of Recognition*, the AFN's vision of "self-determination" is based on a consensus between the AFN and the Canadian government, in which the AFN accepts neoliberal capitalism in return for a bigger seat at the table.

New Zealand is different again. There has always been a section of Māori elites willing to play an intermediate role with capitalism, expressed in the system of tribal councils and reserved Māori parliamentary seats during the nineteenth and twentieth centuries. But the adoption of a policy of "biculturalism" by the Labour government during the 1980s ushered in a new era, allowing for the greater development of both a conservative Māori bureaucracy in the state sector and a Māori capitalist class.

The Labour government did this in two ways. First, they devolved – ie, semi-privatised – programs and services formerly delivered by the NZ central government to local tribal authorities. Secondly, they expanded the role of the Waitangi Council that had been first established in 1975 in response to the Māori protest movements of that time. The plan then was to coopt Māori activists from these movements by giving them state jobs to oversee programs for the Māori community. This strategy of co-opting Māori activists was significantly expanded during the 1980s and 1990s, and by the late '90s "Māori units, divisions or secretariats had been established in Ministries of Education, Environment, Health, Inland Revenue, Justice, Labour, Social Welfare and Women's Affairs".[31]

These state jobs were complemented by the creation of another section of the Māori state bureaucracy to staff the specialist Māori advisory and liaison bodies set up to oversee the new consultative

---

31. Poata-Smith 2001, p.261.

arrangements and treaty discussions between the NZ government and local and pan-tribal Māori bodies from the late 1970s onwards.

At the same time there was an explosion in the Māori private capitalist class. This was centred on Māori-owned consultancy companies which were contracted to

> help government to incorporate Māori values and perspectives into the operating procedures and management styles of mainstream government departments and to identify and remove discriminatory and culturally prejudicial practice.[32]

The Marxist Māori writer ES Te Ahu Poata-Smith has explored how the career paths of two prominent Māori activists from the 1970s and early 1980s, Donna Awatere and Ripeka Evans, highlights the role of these consultancy companies:

> Awatere established Ihi Communications Consultancy in 1985, which developed into a million-dollar annual enterprise providing expert Māori advice to government agencies and the private sector organisations delivering programmes and services to the public. Meanwhile, Ripeka Evans became the "Cultural and Planning Assistant" to the chief executive of State owned Television New Zealand, which under the influence of biculturalism, increased its Māori staff by seventy percent over three years by 1989.[33]

The Labour government helped create a Māori "tribal capitalist" class by concentrating control over Māori community assets in the hands of a small number of "tribal executives".[34] A key role was played, as in other countries, by the new bodies set up to administer compensation funds that were granted in response to the land struggles of the 1960s and '70s. At first these Trust Boards simply administered these funds but during the late by the 1980s

---

32. Poata-Smith 2001, p.261.
33. Poata-Smith 2001, pp.261–62.
34. Poata-Smith 2001, p.261.

their role had expanded into overseeing the economic development of Māori communities, pursuing commercial ventures and settling land disputes.

The Labour government's move to substantially expand a Māori ruling class was made easier by the development of Māori politics during the 1980s, as Poata-Smith explains:

> Unfortunately, the fourth Labour Government's attempt to appease Māori discontent was made easier by a qualitative change in the direction of the Māori protest movement itself with the proliferation of "identity politics". In the absence of mass struggles against oppression with the decline of the working class movement internationally and the rise of the New Right, many of the assumptions of identity politics were reflected in the New Zealand context with an emphasis on cultural identity as the determining factor in Māori oppression. The inherent traits of Pakeha were seen as the basic causes of an oppressive and unequal society, while the traditional and egalitarian virtues of the Māori community were critical for their resolution. Such a "cultural" explanation for Māori inequality was easily accommodated by the state because unlike the demands of the earlier movement, cultural nationalism did not represent a fundamental threat to the underlying social relations of capitalism. In fact, the partial adoption of bicultural rhetoric by the state and the co-optation of elites into state institutions gave the illusion of a "partnership" as espoused under the Treaty of Waitangi, while marginalising the more radical demands.[35]

During the 1990s there was a revival of Māori protest movements. An important factor shaping this revival of protest was that the "commercial interests of Māori tribal executives, Māori corporate enterprises, and the Māori bureaucracy" were "increasingly at odds with the interests of the vast majority of working-class Māori families".[36]

---

35. Poata-Smith 2001, p.276.
36. Poata-Smith 2001, p.276.

These divergent class interests were highlighted as the NZ government and the capitalist class pushed for greater neoliberal reforms, and tried to limit the fiscal impact of unresolved treaty claims. In order to achieve this the National government started secret negotiations with a select group of Māori capitalists who agreed with the free market economic model being promoted by the NZ government and capital. When the content of these deals became public, they led to widespread anger among the Māori population. This was notable in the negotiations between the National government and commercial Māori fishing interests and tribal executives over the purchase of Sealords, at the time the largest single fishing company in New Zealand. The National government agreed to provide $150 million so Māori fishing interests could buy half of Sealords shares. In return, this deal was to be a full and final settlement of all Māori claims over sea, coastal and inland fisheries. This was the first step in the National government's plan to resolve all treaty claims through a $1 billion fiscal cap. While the Sealords deal generated substantial Māori opposition, activists were unable to stop it from being signed and then endorsed in the courts. In the aftermath of the deal there was a further push to cement free market ideas as the economic model for Māori development and a growing corporate "militancy of Māori commercial interests both at the tribal and individual level". During the 1990s,

> there was a consistent advertising expose on the success of certain Māori businesses and the emphasis on Māori commercial development in both individual and tribal forms as the key to successful Māori economic and social development. The Māori-owned press, radio and television repeatedly saturated the Māori community with the idea that Māori business was the way forward for Māori and the "corporate warrior" philosophy emerged as the catch-cry for Māori development in the 1990s. It was convenient for a government faced with the fiscal pressures of a recession, that advocates of Māori capitalist development argued, like the New Right ideologues in treasury and the Business Roundtable, that the welfare system had held Māori back and that real

self-determination and liberation for Māori can only be achieved under unrestrained, free market capitalism.[37]

The National government's broader aim of a final settlement for all treaty claims however faced sustained opposition. Hundreds of protesters dramatically disrupted the official Waitangi Day celebration in 1995, booing conservative Māori leaders and scuffling with the police. Then Whanganui Māori occupied Moutoa Gardens on 28 February 1995, initiating the largest act of collective civil disobedience for decades. The protest sparked a wave of occupations involving thousands of protesters throughout 1995.

While these protests revealed the gulf that had opened up between the majority of working-class Māori and the Māori elite, the activists who led the protests had a limited awareness of political implications of the class divisions among the Māori. The vast majority of activists were still strongly influenced by cultural nationalist politics and its fundamental idea "that all Māori, despite class or gender differences, are bound to each other by their overriding common interests as Māori".[38] The conservative Māori leaders and business interests were seen as breaking with Māori culture, selling out their people and adopting a white European mindset, rather than expressing the class interests of the social layer within the Māori population. This cultural nationalist outlook continues to shape Māori politics in New Zealand to the present day. Poata-Smith argues:

> [I]t has become increasingly difficult to sustain the notion that all Māori share the same sets of experiences of inequality, and that Māori, irrespective of their place in production relations, are united as a community of resistance. While it is certainly the case that successive governments have been responsible for establishing a settlement framework that locks Māori self-determination into a free-market, capitalist economic framework, it is also **a notorious fact** that the political ideologies and practices that have dominated Māori protest politics since the

---

37. Poata-Smith 2001, p.293.
38. Poata-Smith 2001, p.6.

early 1980s have left the majority of Māori ill-equipped to resist the repressive and anti-working class policies that successive governments have introduced to restore the economic conditions for profitable capital accumulation. In particular, the insistence that Māori are a culture united in their resistance against Pakeha has failed dramatically as a strategy for the majority of working class Māori whanau.[39]

Class analysis and Indigenous politics

Indigenous people are often understood, even by people on the socialist left, in a sympathetic, but ultimately romantic, ahistorical and stereotyped fashion. A noble desire to reject the long-standing racist assumptions about Indigenous people, propagated for decades by many of the key institutions of capitalist societies, can easily lead anti-racists to portray Indigenous peoples as homogenous, exotic and incapable of change. Preconceived and moralistic notions of Indigenous people then get in the way of trying to unpack the actual class relations within Indigenous groups, and the contradictory and often complex economic and political developments within them.

It is notable that writers on the socialist left have been far more hesitant to discuss questions of class in Indigenous groups than they have among other oppressed peoples under capitalism. This is in large part because of the dominance of identity politics within academic and left-wing political circles. As Samuel W Rose has explained in the context of debates in North American anthropology:

> The Marxist turn in the 1970s saw the proliferation of anthropological work about Native North America, including the expansion of the historical critique of indigenous articulations with capitalism as well as the beginning of the critique of contemporary Native American political economy… An indigenist critique emerged in the 1980s, which was in reaction to this proliferation of Marxist thought. The critique,

---

39. Poata-Smith 2001, p.11.

while having unique characteristics, should be viewed as part of the postmodern turn in theorizing in academia and within the political Left itself. In this postmodern vein, it is part of the larger turn where class politics give way to identity politics as the central organizing concept. The indigenist critique focuses on Marxism's Western and modernist origins and theoretical connections, using this foreignness as a means to discredit Marxism. As such, they denounce Marxism as another face of the colonial project.[40]

Even when writers on the left have acknowledged the emergence of Indigenous elites they have often understood them not in class terms but rather through what is still an essentially cultural identity framework. So the activist-academic Nandita Sharma can reveal the limitations of confining Indigenous liberation to a nationalist, and ultimately pro-capitalist, framework but she does not link this to the emergence of class divisions within Indigenous societies.[41] Partly this reflects the elasticity of class relations inside Indigenous communities for whole periods of history. It can appear that other differences between Indigenous people, such as the divides between "assimilated" and traditional, so-called "half-caste" and "full blooded", reservation and urbanised, militants and moderates, or between different Indigenous nations, are more decisive than those between different social classes within Indigenous groups. Certainly, in some periods of history they actually were more important.

However as Indigenous people have been drawn into capitalist development a sharper differentiation of social classes within Indigenous groups, replicating those within capitalist societies as a whole, is inevitable. The exact way in which this differentiation occurs is shaped both by the previous history of socio-economic development within the Indigenous group in question, as well as the particular interests and concerns of non-Indigenous capital and the state. The development of class divisions within Indigenous groups to the point at which an Indigenous elite emerges from within them

---

40. Rose 2015.
41. See Humphreys 2022b.

doesn't inherently lead to a generalised advance for the majority of Indigenous people in that group. Instead, such a development tends to lead to the entrenchment of inequalities within Indigenous groups as the elite gain greater material advantages, political influence and cultural legitimacy.

Indigenous elites are often criticised because they have in some way "sold out" to non-Indigenous interests, and contemporary Indigenous bodies such as the proposed Voice to parliament are condemned because they are apparently non-Indigenous settler political projects. This ignores the fact that Indigenous capitalists have a shared material interest, along with their non-Indigenous counterparts, in exploiting all workers in the production process – whether Indigenous or not.

Indigenous bosses and bureaucrats are thus not hapless victims of non-Indigenous capital and states. They are eager collaborators with them, always pursuing their own class interests, which are increasingly distinct from and antagonistic to the interests of the Indigenous working class and poor. This doesn't mean that the interests of Indigenous elites and non-Indigenous capital and states are totally harmonious. The interests of the Indigenous elites can clash to a greater or lesser extent with the priorities of non-Indigenous capital and governments. After all, the primary concern of non-Indigenous capitalists and states is the accumulation of profits and the continuation of the exploitative class relations that make those profits possible, not the creation of Indigenous elites. But often these goals are compatible and mutually reinforcing, as is the case in the mining industry.

The emergence of an Indigenous elite then becomes a barrier for the future advance of the interests of the majority of working-class Indigenous people, due to the differing class interests between the two, and the way in which those conflicting interests are often obscured by a shared Indigenous heritage. This necessitates a more serious *political* engagement with Indigenous struggles, in which the socialist left should be sensitive to the differing interests and arguments of the various actors. The rejection of any serious discussion about the relationship between class, capitalism and Indigenous people by most contemporary progressive writers on Indigenous issues only obscures the vital issues involved, and makes it harder to set on the path for true liberation.[42]

The Indigenous working class and capitalism

The flipside to the emergence of Indigenous elites is of course the growth of an Indigenous working class. The Indigenous population in Australia is becoming increasingly proletarianised and urbanised. During the nineteenth and most of the twentieth centuries, the vast majority of the Indigenous population was confined to the fringes of capitalist society, whether on the missions, in urban slums or in remote communities. Today the majority of the Indigenous population is a part of the working class, and a significant section has been integrated into the urbanised blue- and white-collar working class. Fewer than 100,000 Indigenous people now live in the remote and very remote communities in the Northern Territory and Western Australia. The vast majority of the other 700,000 Indigenous people counted in the census live in coastal cities and large rural towns, particularly in New South Wales and Queensland. The 2021 census revealed that 37.1 percent (or over 300,000) of Aboriginal and Torres Strait Islander people lived in capital cities, and that the fast growing Indigenous populations were found in the more urbanised eastern states of NSW, Queensland and Victoria, while Western Australia and the Northern Territory, which have larger Indigenous populations living in remote areas, have recorded very little population growth.[43]

Greater Western Sydney is emblematic of this trend. The Indigenous population doubled between 2006 and 2021: from 26,467 to 55,128 people. This population is overwhelmingly working-class: only 7.1 percent in the region are managers and 10.7 percent are professionals, with most working in manual labour, manufacturing, transport and social and community services.[44] This compares to the 11.1 percent

---

42. For a more substantial elaboration of this argument see *Indigenous Liberation and Socialism*, forthcoming from Red Flag Books.
43. Statistics from 2021 are from ABS 2022.
44. Lawton 2016.

of non-Indigenous people who are managers and 23.9 percent who are professionals.

The same pattern can be found in Queensland, the state with the second largest Indigenous population. More than one-third of Indigenous people live in what statisticians call the Brisbane Indigenous Region (which includes Brisbane, the Sunshine Coast and the Gold Coast). The Indigenous population in this area now includes over 100,000 people: roughly one-eighth of the entire Indigenous population.[45] As in western Sydney, Indigenous people living in the Brisbane Indigenous Region are overwhelmingly working-class. Out of the 80 percent in either full- or part-time work, 35.7 percent are employed as labourers, tradespeople and transport workers, a further 38.1 percent as retail, social and office workers and only 22.1 percent are either professionals or managers.[46]

Importantly, this proletarianisation of Indigenous people has not led to assimilation, with all the negative connotations that has, but to a progressive cultural fusion. Positive references to Indigenous culture and politics are increasingly part of public life in the major cities, particularly in working-class institutions like trade unions. As well, the number of people identifying as Indigenous is growing, as more discover and celebrate their previously repressed heritage. These social changes partly explain why support for Indigenous rights is so hegemonic among younger generations.

These shifts have important implications for the future of Indigenous struggle. Issues such as land rights will remain an important part of Indigenous politics – even for those Indigenous people who live in urban environments – due to their historic significance. But the central site of exploitation for the vast majority of Indigenous people is in the heart of the capitalist economy itself. The greater integration of Indigenous people into the working class significantly strengthens both their potential power to advance their interests and the greater likelihood, although it is not guaranteed, that such action could win support from non-Indigenous workers. At the same time the continued racism that Indigenous workers face gives lie to the idea that racism

---

45. ABS 2022.
46. ABS 2022.

against them will be overcome merely through greater integration into the mainstream of capitalist society.

These facts are often downplayed by commentators on the left internationally. So Glen Coulthard, a Yellowknives Dene writer, while acknowledging that most Indigenous people in Canada today are wage earners living in urban areas, still insists that "dispossession, not proletarianization, has been the dominant background structure shaping the character of the historical relationship between Indigenous peoples and the Canadian state". From this he draws the necessary conclusion that Indigenous anti-capitalist resistance "is best understood as a struggle primarily inspired by and oriented around the question of land".[47]

Similarly the Vancouver-based socialist Indigenous activist Mike Krebs argues that it is wrong for the socialist left "to frame the Indigenous struggle in Canada as one of an oppressed minority without taking up the question of land and the question of Indigenous people as nations". Krebs argues that this "approach unscientifically separates the discrimination that Indigenous people face from its material base".[48] However, as Roxanne Dunbar-Ortiz has argued, "all capitalism starts with expropriation of land from the producers, and not just in the Americas but as the prerequisite for the development of capitalism in Europe". The dispossession of the European peasantry of control over land, often achieved via state force, was necessary to create an industrial proletariat during the industrial revolution.[49]

Socialists of course support the demand for land rights and reparations. But this insistence that land dispossession remains the central element of Indigenous oppression today is totally unscientific.

This framework has serious political implications. For example, Tom Keefer's work on Indigenous reserves in Canada wildly exaggerates their anti-capitalist potential:

> As counterintuitive as it may seem in an advanced capitalist country like Canada, the transition to capitalism remains

---
47. Coulthard 2014.
48. Krebs 2008, pp.3–4.
49. Dunbar-Ortiz 2016.

incomplete on Indigenous reserves, and the Indian Act – designed as a means to control and disenfranchise Indigenous populations destined for extinction – now acts as the primary blockage to the full penetration of capitalist social relations into these reserves.[50]

This argument is not merely counter-intuitive, it is utter rubbish. The reserves themselves are a product of capitalism, and were incorporated into the broader Canadian economy long ago. Societies do not need to look like Toronto or Melbourne to be capitalist.

More importantly, this analysis fails to see that the primary faultline in capitalist societies – including those with Indigenous populations – is the class cleavage between a multiracial working class that has the potential to unite within itself all the oppressed and exploited, and those social classes that have a stake in the continuation of capitalism, including those of Black and Brown heritage.

As Poata-Smith has argued, the key weakness of Māori cultural nationalist politics in New Zealand is that it ignores

> the significance of the location of the majority of Māori in the working class within New Zealand's class structure and therefore in their objective interest, along with other members of the working class, in collectively transforming and ultimately transcending the exploitative and oppressive foundations of capitalist society.[51]

This same weakness plagues Indigenous identity politics, and the left more broadly, in Australia today.

Conclusion

The emergence of an Indigenous middle class is an expression of the fact that Indigenous people have been able to win greater acceptance for themselves from Australian society in recent years. The natural consequence of this is that sections of the Indigenous population have been able to integrate themselves into the broader

---

50. Keefer 2010.
51. Poata-Smith 2001, p.319.

Australian middle class, even while most Indigenous people struggle at the bottom of our class-divided society.

Recognising the development of this elite Indigenous layer is vital for understanding some of the dynamics of modern Indigenous politics. The political horizons of the Indigenous elite are narrowly focused on the classic middle-class themes of political and cultural representation, integration into institutions of power and the accumulation of private wealth as key to personal fulfilment.

The narrow self-interest of this elite is obscured, and worse, promoted, by the language of identity politics. The establishment of more Indigenous-owned businesses is thus presented as a step towards self-determination, the creation of yet another Indigenous advisory body is hailed as the dawn of true reconciliation, the upward mobility of an influential Indigenous figure is interpreted as an advance for all Indigenous people.

Invocation of identity politics also suits the Indigenous elite because of their particular position within capitalist society. While their growth has been significant, they remain a small social layer that is highly dependent upon the capitalist state and to a lesser degree private capital for social advancement. This layer lacks an independent economic base, unlike Māori in New Zealand or Indigenous groups in Canada, and so campaigns aggressively for its own advancement. This is however presented as being in the interests of Indigenous people as a whole, mirroring the trajectory of middle-class women, migrants and African Americans.

Rather than accepting the agenda of the Indigenous elite, the left must advocate a strategy based on mass movements that seek to disrupt the status quo by building united action from below. Throughout the twentieth century it was precisely movements of this kind that led to the greatest advances for the largest numbers of Indigenous people, including the famous land rights and Black Power struggles of the 1960s and '70s, but also the post-war campaigns to end racial segregation that involved both Indigenous and non-Indigenous left-wing trade unionists.

Such movements will inevitably spring from specific outrages and injustices facing Indigenous people. There are many demands and issues that need to be taken up, including genuine land rights, stopping Black deaths in custody, ending structural racism, and so on. But while supporting and strengthening any such campaigns, socialists also have an obligation to make the case for the need to dismantle the capitalist system.

It is the capitalist system that is the root cause of the oppression and exploitation of Indigenous people in particular, alongside the majority of the population. It is capitalism with its racism, inequality and inexhaustible desire for greater profits that stands in the way of true liberation. The sooner this is recognised, the quicker we can begin to build a movement to challenge it.

References

ABS 2022, "2021 Census Aboriginal and/or Torres Strait Islander people QuickStats". https://www.abs.gov.au/census/find-census-data/quickstats/2021/IQSAUS

Archibald-Binge, Ella 2021, "Black mould, termites and no electricity or hot water: Inside the Aboriginal housing divide", *ABC News*, 13 October. https://www.abc.net.au/news/2021-10-13/condobolin-aboriginal-tenants-houses-mould-termite-faults/100530342

Australian Defence Force Magazine 2019, "Garden Island project drives Indigenous engagement", 31 January. https://www.australiandefence.com.au/business/garden-island-project-drives-indigenous-engagement

BCA (Business Council of Australia) 2018, *Submission to the Joint Select Committee on Constitutional Recognition Relating to Aboriginal and Torres Strait Islander Peoples*, June.

BCA 2019, *Indigenous Engagement Survey*, 1 December. https://www.bca.com.au/2019_indigenous_engagement_survey1

BHP and BBCA (Barada Barna Aboriginal Corporation) 2021, *Joint statement Historic Agreement to provide intergenerational benefits to the Barada Barna people*. https://www.bhp.com/news/media-centre/releases/2021/08/joint-statement-historic-agreement-to-provide-intergenerational-benefits-to-the-barada-barna-people

Closing the Gap 2020, *National Agreement on Closing the Gap*, July. https://www.closingthegap.gov.au/national-agreement/national-agreement-closing-the-gap

Closing the Gap 2022, Annual Report, 30 November. https://www.niaa.gov.au/resource-centre/indigenous-affairs/commonwealth-closing-gap-annual-report-2022

Coulthard, Glen 2014, *Red Skin, White Masks: Rejecting the Colonial Politics of Recognition*, University of Minnesota Press.

de Kruijff, Peter 2021, "Australian billionaires face steep challenge to mine coal in Canada's Rocky Mountains", *Sydney Morning Herald*, 27 July. https://www.smh.com.au/business/companies/australian-billionaires-face-steep-challenge-to-mine-coal-in-canada-s-rocky-mountains-20210625-p584ag.html

Dunbar-Ortiz, Roxanne 2016, Interview: "'A sense of hope and the possibility of solidarity: Colonialism, capitalism, and Native liberation", *International Socialist Review*, 103, Winter 2016–17. https://isreview.org/issue/103/sense-hope-and-possibility-solidarity/

Evans, M, C Polidano, J Moschion, M Langton, M Storey, P Jensen and S Kurland 2021, *Indigenous Businesses Sector Snapshot Study*, Insights from I-BLADE 1.0, University of Melbourne. https://fbe.unimelb.edu.au/cibl/assets/snapshot/RFQ03898-M-and-M-Snapshot-Study.pdf

Gittins, Ross 2018, "Finally, an Indigenous middle class emerges", *Sydney Morning Herald*, 9 February. https://www.smh.com.au/business/finally-an-indigenous-middle-class-emerges-20180209-h0vtrh.html

Hall, Bianca 2023, "Division over Voice as huge crowd turns out for Invasion Day rally", *Sydney Morning Herald*, 26 January. https://www.smh.com.au/national/we-are-sovereign-tens-of-thousands-take-to-streets-for-invasion-day-rally-20230126-p5cfpr.html

Howden, Saffron 2012, "Plan to explore for gas under 40% of state", *Sydney Morning Herald*, 8 December. https://www.smh.com.au/national/nsw/plan-to-explore-for-gas-under-40-percent-of-state-20121207-2b11e.html

Humphreys, Jordan 2022a, "Fury over Indigenous centre closure", *Red Flag*, 2 August. https://redflag.org.au/article/fury-over-indigenous-centre-closure

Humphreys, Jordan 2022b, "Review: Indigenous people vs 'settler' migrants?" *Marxist Left Review*, 24, Winter. https://marxistleftreview.org/articles/review-indigenous-people-vs-settler-migrants/

Keefer, Tom 2010, "Marxism, Indigenous Struggles, and the Tragedy of 'Stagism'", *Upping the Anti: a journal of theory and action*, 10, 18 May. https://uppingtheanti.org/journal/article/10-marxism-indigenous-struggles-and-the-tragedy-of-stagism

Knowles, Rachel 2021, "BHP pulls out in front as Rio Tinto flounders", *National Indigenous Times*, 22 July. https://nit.com.au/22-07-2021/2170/bhp-pulls-out-in-front-as-rio-tinto-flounders

Krebs, Mike 2008, *For the Land! Roots and Revolutionary Dynamics of Indigenous Struggles in Canada*, Socialist Voice. https://www.marxists.org/history/etol/newspape/socialist-voice-ca/pamphlets/For%20the%20Land.pdf

Morris, Barry 2014, *Protest, land rights and riots: postcolonial struggles in Australia in the 1980s*, Berghahn Books.

National Indigenous Australians Agency 2021, *Indigenous Procurement Policy*. https://www.niaa.gov.au/indigenous-affairs/economic-development/indigenous-procurement-policy-ipp

Norman, Heidi 2015, *What do we want? A political history of Aboriginal land rights in New South Wales*, Aboriginal Studies Press.

Nowlin, Christopher 2020, "Indigenous Capitalism and Resource Development in an Age of Climate Change: A Timely Dance with the Devil?", *McGill Journal of Sustainable Development Law*, 17 (1). https://www.mjsdl.com/annualreview/volume17-1

NSW Aboriginal Land Rights Association Inc n.d., https://chuffed.org/project/nsw-aboriginal-land-rights-association-inc

Poata-Smith, ES Te Ahu 2001, *The political economy of Māori protest politics, 1968-1995: a Marxist analysis of the roots of Māori oppression and the politics of resistance*, unpublished PhD thesis, University of Otago.

Public Safety Canada 2020, News release: "Indigenous People in Federal Custody Surpasses 30% Correctional Investigator Issues Statement and Challenge", 21 January. https://www.canada.ca/en/public-safety-canada/news/2020/01/indigenous-people-in-federal-custody-surpasses-30-correctional-investigator-issues-statement-and-challenge.html

Ritter, David 2009, *Contesting Native Title: From Controversy to Consensus*, Allen and Unwin.

Rose, Samuel W 2015, "Marxism and mode of production in the anthropology of native North America", *FocaalBlog*, 17 November. www.focaalblog.com/2015/11/17/samuel-w-rose-marxism-and-mode-of-production-in-the-anthropology-of-native-north-america

Rowse, Tim 2017, *Indigenous and other Australians since 1901*, UNSW Press.

Shirodkar, S, B Hunter and D Foley 2018, "Ongoing growth in the number of Indigenous Australians in Business", *Working Paper, Centre for Aboriginal Economic Policy Research*, ANU College of Arts and Social Sciences.

Smit, Sarah 2021a, "Empowerment is the key to FMG's joint ventures", *National Indigenous Times*, 16 June. https://nit.com.au/16-06-2021/2058/empowerment-is-the-key-to-fmgs-joint-ventures

Smit, Sarah 2021b, "Warrikal earns landmark deal with FMG", *National Indigenous Times*, 3 August. https://nit.com.au/03-08-2021/2187/warrikal-earns-landmark-deal-with-fmg#:~:text=Warrikal%20has%20been%20awarded%20a,for%20the%20Aboriginal%20contracting%20business.

Supply Nation 2022, *State of Indigenous Business: An analysis of procurement spending patterns with Indigenous businesses 2019–2021*. https://supplynation.org.au/research-paper/an-analysis-of-procurement-spending-patterns-with-indigenous-businesses-2019-2021/

NICK EVERETT

"Closing the gap"? Labor's dismal record on Indigenous rights

Nick Everett is a socialist activist and author of the chapter "Solidarity with the Pilbara Aboriginal Station Hands Strike" in *Radical Perth, Militant Fremantle*.

Well, I heard it on the radio
And I saw it on the television
Back in 1988
All those talking politicians
Words are easy, words are cheap
Much cheaper than our priceless land
But promises can disappear
Just like writing in the sand…

– Yothu Yindi, "Treaty", 1992[1]

IN HIS ELECTION VICTORY SPEECH, Labor Prime Minister Anthony Albanese committed his government to implement the Uluru Statement from the Heart in full, beginning with a referendum to create an Indigenous Voice to parliament in its first term. Supporters of the Uluru Statement present the Voice as the first step in a process that, along with a Makarrata Commission of truth-telling and agreement-making, will lead to genuine self-determination for Indigenous people.

1. Lyrics to "Treaty" available at http://www.schoolsreconciliationchallenge.org.au/wp-content/uploads/2018/07/TreatyYothuYindiTextBlock.pdf.

Alyawarre woman and human rights advocate Pat Anderson argues:

> Establishing the Voice will lead to immediate, important outcomes. It will set the scene for addressing the centuries of injustice. It will create an effective process to address the intergenerational disadvantage many communities suffer. It will help overcome the historical exclusion of First Nations people from public forums. And crucially, it will offer an important symbolic gesture of acknowledgement and recognition that the days of *vox nullius* ("voicelessness"), the primary intention and consequence of *terra nullius*, are at last over.[2]

Yet the proposed Indigenous Voice to parliament will not be able to compel the federal government to listen to its advice, nor will it exercise any veto power over the enactment of legislation that will be harmful to Indigenous people. Voice advocates have been at pains to insist that it will be an advisory body only, with no legislative power. Prime Minister Anthony Albanese has similarly stressed that the Voice is "not a radical proposition [but] a sensible one" and that it is in keeping with the nation's traditions of Westminster democracy.

"The architects of our Federation understood that democracy is dynamic, not static. And that change driven by the people is not a threat to the system – it is a vital and necessary part of it", he told the National Press Club on 5 February.[3]

The Voice initiative hardly represents the first time Labor governments have committed to consulting with Indigenous people to address the deep social and economic inequality they face. The establishment of the National Aboriginal Consultative Committee (NACC), by the Whitlam Labor government in 1973, and the Aboriginal and Torres Strait Islander Commission (ATSIC), by the Hawke Labor government in 1990, were similarly accompanied by much fanfare about a new beginning for the government's relations with First Nations peoples. In February 1973, Labor Prime Minister Gough Whitlam told a meeting of Aboriginal leaders that he hoped his

---

2. Anderson 2022.
3. Albanese 2023.

government would be remembered for bringing "back justice and equality to the Aboriginal people".[4]

A decade later, Labor was returned to power on a platform of implementing national land rights legislation. In 1988, during the bicentenary year, Prime Minister Bob Hawke responded to the Barunga Statement – a call by Indigenous people for land rights and self-determination – by committing his government to negotiate a treaty with First Nations people by 1990. And in 1992 Hawke's successor, Paul Keating, called for an act of recognition for First Nations people. He told a mostly Aboriginal audience in Sydney's Redfern Park:

> We took the traditional lands and smashed the traditional way of life.
>
> We brought the diseases. The alcohol.
>
> We committed the murders. We took the children from their mothers.
>
> We practised discrimination and exclusion.
>
> It was our ignorance and our prejudice.
>
> And our failure to imagine these things being done to us.[5]

Similarly, in 2008 Labor Prime Minister Kevin Rudd issued a national apology to the Stolen Generations, a decade after a government apology was recommended by the national inquiry into the Stolen Generations *Bringing Them Home* report.[6] Following the apology, the Rudd government, alongside state governments, pledged to take action to close the gap between Indigenous and non-Indigenous Australians in health, education and employment.

---

4. Quoted in Foley 2001b, p.2.
5. Keating 1992.
6. Human Rights Commission 1997.

As the Yothu Yindi song "Treaty" reminds us: "words are easy, words are cheap".

No Australian government has ever implemented national land rights legislation or a nationwide treaty with First Nations peoples. Aboriginal incarceration and deaths in custody have skyrocketed since the Royal Commission handed down its report 32 years ago. There has been no compensation to the Stolen Generations (also recommended in the *Bringing Them Home* report), and paltry compensation from state governments for stolen wages. In the 15 years since federal and state governments adopted six Closing the Gap targets to address Indigenous disadvantage, negligible improvement has been made.

In several of the Closing the Gap target areas the gap continues to widen. The 2022 report found that only a third of children commencing school were developmentally on track in 2021; overrepresentation of Indigenous children in out-of-home care and Indigenous adults in prison continues to increase, as do Indigenous suicide rates. In 2021, Indigenous children were eleven times more likely than their non-Indigenous peers to be in out-of-home care and Indigenous youth (aged between 10 and 17 years) were eighteen times more likely to be locked up.[7] It was also reported that a staggering 22,000 Indigenous children are removed from their families each year, with only around 16 per cent of those being reunited with family.[8]

This article will examine Labor's record in office since the 1967 referendum. It will review the Whitlam government's response to the land rights movement, following the establishment of the Aboriginal Tent Embassy on the lawns of federal parliament in 1972, and the Hawke government's subsequent abandonment of national land rights legislation. It will argue that Keating's adoption of native title legislation and the rhetoric of reconciliation, as well as Rudd's 2008 apology, were largely symbolic gestures that failed to meaningfully address land rights, self-determination and equality for First Nations People. Labor's embrace of the Voice follows a well-worn path: it seeks to amplify the most conservative Aboriginal voices and divert protest

---

7. Productivity Commission 2022, p.33.
8. Morse 2022.

down bureaucratic channels. But first, it is necessary to review the position long held by socialists towards the ALP.

The Labor Party

Formed in the wake of the defeats of the 1890 Maritime and 1891 Shearers' strikes, the Australian Labor Party was captured early on by small business and farming interests. At the time of federation, in 1901, its platform centred around the objectives of support for the White Australia Policy, arbitration of industrial disputes and defence of Empire. Racial exclusion was the cement that bound together Labor's first federal caucus, which was otherwise divided between opposing camps of protectionists and free-traders.[9]

While Labor began as a party articulating the demands of the early labour movement and retains links with the much-emaciated trade union movement today, it has consistently proved willing to rule in the interests of Australian capital. There have been ten periods of federal Labor government since the 1910 federal election, with Labor typically being the Australian ruling class's preferred party of government in times of crisis, including during two world wars and the Great Depression. The longest period of Labor government – 13 years – coincided with the implementation of neoliberalism and a massive transfer of wealth from wages to profits during the Hawke and Keating years, between 1983 and 1996.[10]

Up until the 1960s, Labor supported and implemented protectionist and assimilationist policies at state and federal levels. Labor governments shielded police and vigilantes from any state sanction for their role in the massacres of Aboriginal people and defended the interests of pastoralists and, later, mining companies. During the 1946 Pilbara strike, when 800 Aboriginal workers walked off pastoral stations, it was a Labor state government that jailed Aboriginal strike leaders for defying the repressive provisions of the Aborigines Act 1905 (WA).

---

9. Markey 1988, p.295.
10. See Bramble and Kuhn 2011, chapter 7.

The 1967 referendum

In 1958, state-based Aboriginal rights organisations began organising on a national basis, under the umbrella of the Federal Council for Aboriginal Advancement (renamed the Federal Council for the Advancement of Aborigines and Torres Strait Islanders, FCAATSI, in 1964). They demanded equal citizenship rights, equal pay and improved welfare for Indigenous Australians. In the early 1960s, under the influence of more conservative forces within the movement, including members of the Communist Party, the ALP and Church leaders, FCAATSI's focus turned towards lobbying federal parliamentarians for a referendum on constitutional amendments that would transfer primary responsibility for Aboriginal affairs from the states to the Commonwealth.

At the same time, a series of protests by Indigenous people and their supporters had led to a groundswell of support for Indigenous rights. The 1965 Freedom Ride, a 15-day bus journey by Sydney University students through regional New South Wales, drew national attention to the appalling living conditions and racism experienced by Aboriginal people in country towns. In 1966, a strike erupted at the Wave Hill cattle station in the Northern Territory. At first it was a strike about wages and living conditions. However, it subsequently became a determined campaign for land rights by the Gurindji people.

On 27 May 1967, the referendum for which FCAATSI had long advocated was put to voters by the Holt Liberal government. It won 90 percent support, including a majority in all states and territories. However, there was little appetite by subsequent conservative federal governments to act on this mandate to deliver any meaningful improvements for Aboriginal people. At the state level, the winding back of responsibility for Aboriginal affairs in the wake of the referendum had detrimental effects. Historian and activist Gary Foley describes how, when the New South Wales government dismantled its Aborigines Welfare Board in 1969, 20,000 Aboriginal people on 45 reserves around the state were effectively left destitute.[11] This accelerated a movement of Aboriginal youth to the cities, looking

---

11. Bennett 1985, pp.26–31.

for work. Many arrived in Redfern, forming the nucleus of the Black Power movement.

In a belated response to the Gurindji strikers' demands, the federal Arbitration Court awarded equal wages to Aboriginal pastoral workers in 1968. It proved a pyrrhic victory: with no anti-discrimination legislation to protect Aboriginal workers from dismissal, they were sacked *en masse*, resulting in great hardship for workers who had been the backbone of the Northern Territory and West Australian pastoral industries. Aboriginal communities now faced destitution on the outskirts of town centres, forced to depend on meagre welfare payments. However, the Gurindji people's walk-off, and the Yolngu people's fight against bauxite mining in Arnhem Land, began to move the issue of land rights to the centre of Aboriginal politics.

Meanwhile, Redfern activists, drawing inspiration from the Black Power movement in the United States, began to create Aboriginal community-controlled organisations such as the Redfern Aboriginal Legal Service, free health clinics, housing co-operatives and a Breakfast for Children program. Similar initiatives followed within urban Aboriginal communities centred in Fitzroy and South Brisbane. During the 1970 Vietnam moratorium campaign and the mass protests against the national tour of the all-white South African Springbok rugby team in 1971, Aboriginal activists began to make common cause with non-Indigenous radicals on a more equal footing than had been the case in the FCAATSI.[12]

The Aboriginal Tent Embassy

It was in this context that one of the most famous Aboriginal protests emerged: the Aboriginal Tent Embassy on the lawns of federal parliament. The immediate impetus was a speech by Liberal Prime Minister Billy McMahon, on 26 January (Invasion Day) 1972, in which he rejected the notion of Aboriginal land rights. McMahon had failed to offer Aboriginal communities any redress following the long-awaited outcome of the Gove land rights case in the NT Supreme Court. In April 1971, Justice Blackburn sided with mining company Nabalco,

---

12. Foley 2010, pp.10–14.

asserting that any claim Yolngu people may have had to ownership of their land had been extinguished by British colonisation.[13] In response, the Black Caucus in Redfern dispatched a group of four young men, Michael Anderson, Billy Craigie, Bert Williams and Tony Coorey, to Canberra to set up a protest on the lawns of Parliament House. Coorey told the media that McMahon's statement had effectively made Indigenous people "aliens in our own land" and therefore they should have an embassy of their own to represent them.[14]

The protest proved enduring, in part because more liberal laws in the ACT provided no pretext for the police to arrest the Embassy activists. In May 1972, the McMahon government changed the law to enable their eviction. A series of mass confrontations took place over the following months on the Parliament House lawns, drawing national and international attention.

The Whitlam-led Labor Opposition took a more pragmatic approach. Whitlam met with Embassy activists and committed a future Labor government to addressing their concerns. Whitlam became prime minister in a landslide election victory in December 1972, in a period of great social and political upheaval and high expectations. The Labor Party had promised to abolish conscription and to legislate for universal health care, free education and Aboriginal land rights. However, Whitlam's election also took place on the eve of a global recession. It soon became evident that mining company executives were in no mood to concede land rights that might impinge on their mining rights and corporate profits.

The Whitlam government

Labor, once in government, moved very cautiously. A gulf between the expectations of Aboriginal activists and what the Whitlam government was prepared to deliver resulted in rapidly strained relations between the two. Whitlam's first Aboriginal Affairs minister was Gordon Bryant, a former president of the Aboriginal Advancement League and executive member of FCAATSI. Bryant had been a part of FCAATSI's old guard, opposing an Aboriginal takeover of the Council at its 1970

---
13. Agreements, Treaties and Negotiated Settlements Project 2020.
14. Foley 2001a, pp.10–14.

conference and clashing with younger Aboriginal activists who split away to form the Tribal Council.[15] Thus, he was already alienated from the new Indigenous leadership with whom he was now expected to work.

In 1973, Bryant established the National Aboriginal Consultative Committee (NACC) as an advisory body to government. Unlike the proposed Voice to parliament, NACC's 41 representatives were directly elected by Aboriginal constituents. Under pressure from its base to secure immediate action from Labor on land rights, NACC failed to do what the Whitlam (and later Fraser and Hawke) governments wanted it to do. From the outset, there were two competing views about NACC's purpose. Aboriginal activists wanted NACC to be an autonomous and democratic body that would faithfully articulate their demands. Bryant, on the other hand, wanted a subservient body that would implement government policy.

Additionally, Bryant came into conflict with Department of Aboriginal Affairs (DAA) head Barrie Dexter. The conflict led to Whitlam's sacking of Bryant in November 1973. After just ten months in the role, Bryant was replaced by long-time union official and now senator, Jim Cavanagh, who had no background in Aboriginal affairs. Foley expresses just how incredulous activists were of Cavanagh's appointment:

> Jim Cavanagh was an old-style ALP apparatchik, promoted only because of his union influence and with attitudes toward Aboriginal issues that were paternalistic and bordering on racist. They were appalled that Prime Minister Whitlam could impose on Aboriginal Affairs such a political Neanderthal, and they came to regard this appointment as the end of their political "honeymoon" with Whitlam.[16]

Like his predecessor, Cavanagh was soon at war with the activist wing of NACC. Cavanagh also came into conflict with Charles Perkins, the most senior Aboriginal bureaucrat in Canberra, who he ordered be

---
15. Foley 1999a, p.11.
16. Foley 2001b, p.4.

suspended from the DAA. Whitlam was forced to reinstate Perkins and Cavanagh resigned soon after, in June 1975.

Perkins was no radical. He was opposed to Asian immigration and anti-union. He was also viewed with suspicion for having taken a role as a senior public servant. However, he also needed to demonstrate he was no government puppet at a time when the Black Power and the land rights movements were a force to be reckoned with. The conflict in which both Bryant and Cavanagh found themselves reflected the stark divide between the Whitlam government's rhetoric of support for Aboriginal self-determination and its practice of ignoring Aboriginal voices.

The most significant legacy of the three-year Whitlam Labor government for Aboriginal people was the Woodward Commission of Inquiry into land rights. Activist Kevin Gilbert criticised the inquiry for

> the lack of Aboriginal representation on and participation in its deliberation, that the inquiry was to be restricted to the Northern Territory, that mineral rights would continue to be reserved to the Crown, the lack of consideration of their claims for compensation...[17]

The land rights movement

The outcome of the Woodward Commission was land rights legislation implemented in the Northern Territory only, enacted by the Fraser Liberal government. While the Aboriginal Land Rights Act (NT) 1976 recognised the concept of inalienable freehold title, it enabled only claims on "unalienated Crown land" (ie, land that no one else – including mining companies and pastoralists – had any claims on). The Hawke Labor government subsequently amended the Act to introduce a sunset clause that prohibited any further claims after 1997.

The Act also established a trust account administered by the minister for Aboriginal Affairs that accumulates so-called "royalty

---

17. Quoted in Read 1990.

equivalent" income from mining on Aboriginal land. Thirty percent is paid to Aboriginal corporations. The rest – allocated to community grants and administration – is under the minister's control. Land Council representatives are given only an advisory role.[18] Nonetheless, over the following decade, this influx of funds transformed Northern Territory land councils from activist bodies dependent upon volunteer labour to state-funded bodies increasingly integrated into the business of government. In his biography of Aboriginal activist Rob Riley, historian Quentin Beresford says of the Northern Land Council:

> In the mid-1980s, the NLC had a staff of about a hundred spread over several regional offices, and a multimillion-dollar budget. It was organised along classic public service lines with separate departments.[19]

In the mid-1970s, the homelands movement was gaining momentum. Aboriginal communities such as the Arrernte, Pitjantjatjara and Warlpiri peoples in central Australia were leaving church-run missions and state reserves to re-occupy ancestral lands. The community of Noonkanbah (aka Yungngora) was established in the Kimberley in 1976 and soon after thrust into the spotlight in a bitter confrontation with the Charles Court Liberal government and over mining exploration.[20] While land rights protests at Noonkanbah failed to stop a scab (non-union) crew from undertaking drilling on Yungngora land, the protests marked a high point of collaboration between unionists and land rights activists.[21]

Legislation in South Australia – the Pitjantjatjara Land Rights Act 1981 and the Maralinga Tjarutja Land Rights Act 1984 – returned land to some Aboriginal communities. The NSW Land Rights Act 1983, introduced by the Wran Labor government, acknowledged title to some reserves, but validated the takeover of others. The Act allowed some

---

18. See Central Land Council 2023.
19. Beresford 2006, p.207.
20. See Hawke and Gallagher 1989.
21. Vassiley 2021.

limited claims on Crown land and allocated a proportion of land tax to a fund that would enable land councils to buy back some freehold land.[22] According to NSW Land Council chair Kevin Cook, "[the Act was] not what we wanted... [it] has forced a compromise on us... our traditional right to lands...have never been ceded by treaty or overturned by conquest... we maintain they still exist".[23]

In Queensland and Western Australia, governments beholden to mining and pastoral interests doubled down. In 1984, the National Party government in Queensland passed a law to block land claims in the Torres Strait by several Meriam Islanders, including Eddie Mabo. The law was subsequently disallowed by the High Court in the Mabo case as it breached the 1975 Race Discrimination Act.

In Western Australia, the Burke Labor government was elected in February 1983. Like conservative premier Charles Court before him, Brian Burke was committed to currying favour with the state's mining magnates, including Lang Hancock (Gina Reinhart's father), and other industry tycoons, such as property developers Alan Bond and Laurie Connell. The WA Inc. inquiry later revealed that Burke held a slush fund in his office to pay off anyone who got in his way.[24]

The election of the Hawke Labor government

Just three weeks after Burke's election, in March 1983, the Hawke Labor government was elected on a platform of support for national land rights legislation. Later that year, the federal parliament passed a resolution moved by Minister for Aboriginal Affairs Clyde Holding committing to comprehensive land rights legislation. The resolution recognised the principles of Aboriginal land to be held under inalienable freehold title, protection of Aboriginal sites, Aboriginal control in relation to mining on Aboriginal land, access to mining royalty equivalents, and compensation for lost land. Holding told parliament that the human rights of Aboriginal Australians must take precedence over state rights.[25]

---

22. NSW Government n.d.
23. Quoted in Wilkie 1985, p.v.
24. Beresford 2008.
25. Foley 2001b, p.9.

Holding also committed to consult with the National Aboriginal Conference (NAC), which was established as NACC's successor by the Fraser government. NAC had been effectively starved of funding during the Fraser years but was now brought back in from the cold. In September 1983, NAC and land council representatives were appointed to the newly established Aboriginal Land Rights Steering Committee (ALRSC). They faced strong headwinds from a mining industry lobby determined to sink any prospect of land rights legislation.

Mining bosses soon went on the offensive, led by Western Mining's executive director Hugh Morgan. In May 1984, at an Australian Mining Industry Council (AMIC) seminar, Morgan attacked the granting of Aboriginal land rights as "a symbolic step back to the world of paganism, superstition, fear and darkness". Traditional vengeance killings took more Indigenous lives than "any depredations by the Europeans" claimed Morgan. Charges of genocide were "nonsense", aimed "to incite resentment and animosity within the Aboriginal community", "to arouse...white middle-class guilt", and "to create expectations of compensation payments".[26] In an Australia Day speech the following January, Morgan warned: "Our national sovereignty, and the legitimacy of the settlement that began formally on 7 February 1788, is under threat".[27]

AMIC launched an advertising campaign that portrayed land rights as an attack on suburban backyards. Newspaper ads featured a "Keep Out" sign with the accompanying warning: "This land is part of Western Australia under Aboriginal claim". Television commercials ramped up this theme by depicting a pair of black hands building a brick wall across a map of Western Australia.[28]

Labor soon buckled. In October 1984, Hawke told AMIC that he would water down the proposed legislation. Newly elected NAC chair Rob Riley responded with a scathing criticism of Hawke at a National Press Club address, claiming that the ALSRC was being treated as though it were a rubber stamp for the Aboriginal Affairs minister.[29]

---

26. Quoted in Markus 2001, pp.60–62.
27. Markus 2001, p.70.
28. Beresford 2006, pp.164–65.
29. Riley 1984.

WA Premier Brian Burke, however, threatened to resign if the legislation was not shelved in its entirety. In May 1985, hundreds of Aboriginal activists mobilised in Canberra, rallying at federal parliament on 14 May and invading DAA two days later.[30] The protests, however, were to no avail. In March 1986, in what the *Canberra Times* described as a "shameful backdown",[31] Holding announced that land rights legislation would not be implemented at a national level and would now be up to the states. The only concession federal Labor was prepared to make was the symbolic handback of Uluru, in 1985.

Labor's capitulation reflected its commitment to an "economic rationalist" (ie, neoliberal) agenda that favoured the big end of town. Labor had no appetite for a public education campaign that could beat back the mining companies. And the unions, with a few notable exceptions, failed the test also. Having entered into the straitjacket of the Prices and Incomes Accord with the incoming Labor government in 1983, the Australian Council of Trade Unions was not prepared to defy federal Labor and lend the kind of support necessary for the land rights movement to prevail.

Labor's betrayal also accelerated a crisis of identity for the NAC that mirrored that of its predecessor, the NACC. While Aboriginal activists wanted a democratic organisation that represented their interests, federal governments wanted an organisation that would do their bidding. During the 1984 debate on land rights, this played out between one wing led by Riley,[32] who viewed the NAC as an instrument of grassroots-run land councils, and "Sugar" Ray Robinson,[33] who prioritised a collaborative relationship between the NAC and the

---

30. Read 2001.
31. *Canberra Times*, 6 March 1986.
32. Rob Riley, like his mother and grandmother, was a member of the Stolen Generations. In the 1970s, he joined the Perth-based Aboriginal rights organisation Black Action. He was a field officer and later executive officer for the Aboriginal Legal Service and a central activist in the Noonkanbah land rights dispute. After working as an advisor to Labor minister Gerry Hand and RCIADC commissioner Patrick Dodson, he returned to the ALS in 1990, where he campaigned around the issues of Aboriginal incarceration and recognition of the Stolen Generations. He took his own life on 1 May 1996. See Beresford 2006.
33. Robinson later served as deputy chair of ATSIC between 1996 and 2003, under the Howard government.

Labor government. NAC's leadership was now fraught with infighting and entered an interminable crisis. In June 1985, indignant at Riley's criticism of Labor's land rights betrayal, the federal government abolished the NAC.

In the lead-up to the 26 January 1988 bicentenary celebrations, Indigenous activists again began to plan national protests. The National Coalition of Aboriginal Organisations (NCAO) was formed to coordinate campaigns over sovereignty, land rights and Aboriginal deaths in custody. Under the theme of "Boycott the Bicentenary" and "Don't Celebrate '88", activists around the country travelled to La Perouse in Sydney, the site of Arthur Phillip's first landing 200 years earlier. From there they marched to Redfern and into Sydney CBD, holding a 40,000-strong demonstration.

The Hawke government was forced to offer up some concessions. The first was the announcement of a Royal Commission into Aboriginal Deaths in Custody (RCIADC). The second was the abolition of the NAC and the DAA and their replacement with the Aboriginal and Torres Straits Islander Commission (ATSIC). And the third was the creation of the Council for Aboriginal Reconciliation (CAR). All of these initiatives were intended to deflect public anger and were largely symbolic in their outcomes. A national campaign had long demanded action on Aboriginal deaths in custody, following the deaths of 21-year-old Eddie Murray in Wee Waa police station in 1981 and 16-year-old John Pat in a Roebourne lock-up in 1983. The campaign was spearheaded by the Murray and Pat families.

The RCIADC was established in 1987 and handed down its report in 1991, at a cost of $50 million. It made 339 recommendations, many of which have never been implemented. The federal government was not prepared to force state governments to implement reforms to their criminal codes and police and prison systems that could have reduced Indigenous incarceration. Instead, the WA and NT governments proceeded to introduce mandatory sentencing laws in the 1990s. In state elections, both parties engaged in bidding wars about who was most "tough on crime". The result has been the maintenance of racist policing measures and ever-increasing Aboriginal incarceration, especially among youth.

The Aboriginal and Torres Straits Islander Commission

In July 1987, the Hawke government also announced the abolition of the reviled DAA, established under the Whitlam government in 1973. The DAA was staffed by mostly non-Indigenous public servants. Some came from Aboriginal Protection Boards and other state institutions that had overseen child removal and regulated Aboriginal people's lives. Others had patrol officer experience in the Northern Territory or in the former Australian colony of Papua New Guinea. Thus, the DAA proved incapable of delivering on Whitlam's promise of self-determination and, during the Fraser years, worked to marginalise and undermine the NAC.

Hawke and his newly appointed Aboriginal Affairs Minister Gerry Hand were determined to move quickly to placate growing public protest. In January 1988, Hand and DAA Secretary Charlie Perkins embarked on a whirlwind tour of Aboriginal communities, undertaking 46 meetings and travelling over 56,000 kilometres. However, many communities regarded this as a token exercise, angered at the government's land rights betrayal two years earlier.[34] ATSIC was due to begin operation in July 1988. However, Hand and Perkins soon fell out, leading to Perkins' dismissal from his role in DAA. With Hand now having to find a new appointee to lead ATSIC, the body's creation was postponed until 1990.

ATSIC was given a broader mandate than its predecessors. Its functions were to advise governments at all levels, advocate for Australian Indigenous affairs and deliver and monitor Indigenous programs and services. The latter role was one that had been demanded by the NAC, but never conceded. Yet, as Foley observes, there were fundamental flaws in the machine.[35]

The first was that ATSIC's elected councillors lacked a popular mandate. In 1973, when the Whitlam government established the NACC, it also established an Aboriginal electoral role that included about 70 percent of Indigenous people eligible to vote.[36] According to Foley, in the 1973 NACC elections more than 80 percent of Aboriginal

---

34. See Smith 1996, p.23; Read 2001, p.314.
35. See Foley 1999c.
36. Beresford 2006, p.122.

voters participated.[37] In contrast, only Indigenous people on the mainstream Australian electoral roll were eligible to participate in ATSIC elections. Foley estimates that in ATSIC's first national election, in 1990, less than 30 percent of eligible Indigenous people voted.[38] This was due not only to the low level of Aboriginal electoral enrolment, but also because several Aboriginal activist organisations, disenchanted with the process, called for a boycott. According to Foley, among the 35,000-strong Koori community in Sydney, fewer than 1,000 voted.[39]

It was not, however, just the lack of voter participation that ensured ATSIC was not representative of Indigenous people. ATSIC was composed of a nominally representative wing, consisting of over 400 councillors representing 60 regions (reduced to 36 regions in 1993) and a board of 18 commissioners. Alongside this structure was an administrative body composed entirely of unelected public servants drawn for the most part from the old DAA bureaucracy. ATSIC staff were not accountable to ATSIC's elected councillors, but instead to the federal government and its Aboriginal Affairs minister. Presiding over the whole body was a government-appointed ATSIC chairperson, Lowitja O'Donoghue, who had been a senior Commonwealth bureaucrat since 1975.

ATSIC's structure ensured the same tensions arose that had plagued the NAC and NACC. Was ATSIC intended to be an independent and democratic decision-making body or an advisory one? What control would it exercise over funding and allocation of resources?

In a report to minister Hand prior to her appointment as ATSIC chair, O'Donoghue recommended that ATSIC's powers be limited to an advisory role only. This proposal, adopted in the Aboriginal and Torres Strait Islander Act 1989, ensured that ATSIC councillors had no effective decision-making power over development in the regions that they were elected to represent. That power was vested in an unelected bureaucracy. In 1994, HC Coombs, a former Commonwealth bureaucrat and founder of the Aboriginal Treaty

---

37. Foley 1999c, p.6.
38. Foley 1999c, p.10.
39. Foley 1999c, p.10.

Committee during the Fraser years, made the following observation of ATSIC's functioning:

> [T]he Commission is not, as yet, an Aboriginal organisation working for and accountable to Aboriginal society and importantly...is not thought of as such by many Aborigines [sic]. Rather, it continues to be seen by many as an instrument of the Commonwealth Government and of the central ATSIC bureaucracy in Canberra. It does not, therefore, adequately serve the purposes of either government or Aborigines.[40]

What Coombs alludes to here is that the federal government needed an Indigenous body that could be widely seen to be representative of Indigenous interests while, at the same time, implementing government policy. This contradiction only sharpened in the years to follow, as programs delivered by ATSIC were pared back. ATSIC councillors were now left with the job of explaining to their constituents why they were implementing cuts to health, housing and employment programs. This was entirely consistent with ATSIC's *raison d'être* from the beginning. Foley says of ATSIC's formation:

> Thus, a small, elite group of indigenous public servants, academics and ATSIC commissioners began a process of cultivating, and being cultivated by, the Government. This elite, unrepresentative group would become indispensable during the next four years of anxiety and debate about the next major indigenous issue to confront the government, that of Mabo and native title.[41]

Before addressing this vexed issue, another Hawke government initiative is worthy of mention: the Council for Aboriginal Reconciliation (CAR). As Foley and other activists have pointed out,[42] reconciliation was not an issue that had emerged spontaneously

---

40. Coombs, *Aboriginal Autonomy: Issues and Strategies*, Cambridge University Press, Melbourne, 1994. Cited in Coombs and Robinson 1996, p.10.
41. Foley 2001b, p.16.
42. Foley 1999b.

from either the Indigenous or non-Indigenous communities. Rather it proved a useful diversion from the anger Aboriginal activists felt in response to Labor's betrayals.

CAR was established in 1991 with much fanfare. It was one of the few recommendations of the Royal Commission into Aboriginal Deaths in Custody to be implemented. According to the Reconciliation website, CAR "invested ten years of research, promotion, partnership-building, consultation and educating into the reconciliation process".[43]

However, in reality, CAR achieved very little. It took six years for another royal commission to hand down the *Bringing Them Home* report on Australia's Stolen Generations, in 1997, and a further decade before the newly elected Rudd Labor government apologised to the Stolen Generations (albeit without compensation). Hundreds of thousands participated in reconciliation bridge walks, sponsored by Labor state governments, in June 2000. However, their demands were limited to calling on the conservative Howard government to apologise to the Stolen Generations. Howard was in no mood to listen. Thus, the mobilisations served only to build a platform for Labor based on a purely symbolic gesture.

Native title and land rights

The High Court's Mabo decision, handed down on 3 June 1992, was described by Aboriginal Affairs Minister Robert Tickner as "one of the most important decisions the High Court of Australia will ever deliver and elevated the process of reconciliation".[44] However, Aboriginal activists had a more sceptical view of its significance. With an immediate and sustained backlash from mining interests, reminiscent of the earlier debate on land rights legislation, the Keating Labor government came under immense pressure to implement native title legislation that would protect mining and pastoral interests. Once again, a media campaign was unleashed about the Mabo decision's supposed threat to suburban backyards.

In July 1993, a year after Mabo and weeks after the Wik people lodged a significant native title claim, the federal cabinet decided

---

43. See https://nrw.reconciliation.org.au/
44. Tickner 2001, p.86.

that "Aboriginal people would have rights to negotiate with miners and others, with unresolved disputes to be determined by the Native Title Tribunal to be created by the proposed legislation".[45] Thus, Aboriginal people would once again be deprived of any veto over mining on their land.

Indigenous leaders were divided. An elite, self-appointed group (known as the A-team), including Noel Pearson, Sol Bellear, Marcia Langton and others, was ushered into negotiations with government, arriving at what they claimed was a "compromise" agreement. A second group of Indigenous negotiators, led by Michael Mansell, dubbed themselves the B-team and met with Democrat and Green senators in an effort to force concessions from the government. They failed.

The resulting Native Title Act 1993 established a very high benchmark for recognition of title. Only Crown land could be claimed, and it was available only to Aboriginal people who could prove continuous association with that land: a very difficult thing to do after centuries of dispossession. With most Aboriginal communities having experienced forced removal or expulsion from their land, confinement and the removal of their children, such connections to country were all too often severed. Rob Riley, one of the "B Team", accused the government of "having sold out the rights of Aboriginal people to the pastoralist, mining and tourist industries".[46]

A subsequent High Court case in 1996 produced the Wik judgment, which required pastoralists and mining companies to negotiate with Aboriginal people for limited access to the land. However, even this was watered down, such that native title holders face protracted court battles to secure meagre compensation. Consequently, very few Aboriginal people are native title claimants, and those who are successful are obliged to seek redress through compensation from mining and commercial interests, instead of exercising rights of control over development on their land.

---

45. Tickner 2001, p.144.
46. Quoted in Tickner 2001, p.201.

The Northern Territory Intervention

In March 1996, the conservative Howard Liberal government was elected in a landslide, in an election where Pauline Hanson's anti-Aboriginal and anti-Asian agenda featured prominently. This set the scene for Howard to launch an attack on even the most meagre gains Aboriginal people had won in the preceding Hawke and Keating years. In 1997, Howard vehemently rejected a government apology to the Stolen Generations proposed in the *Bringing Them Home* report. Siding with right-wing commentator Keith Windschuttle in the "history wars", he castigated truth-telling about Aboriginal massacres as a "black armband" view of history.

The culmination of Howard's backlash was the Northern Territory Emergency Response (better known as the Northern Territory Intervention), launched in June 2007 on the eve of a federal election. The pretext was the *Little Children are Sacred* report of the Northern Territory Board of Inquiry into the Protection of Aboriginal Children from Sexual Abuse. However, the measures Howard implemented bore no resemblance to the nearly 100 recommendations of that report. Instead, Howard seized on an opportunity to improve his flagging electoral fortunes with a military invasion of Aboriginal communities. As commentator Guy Rundle observed at the time, Howard was seeking to replicate the "war on terror" on home soil.[47]

The NT Intervention included welfare quarantining (so-called "income management" via the Basics Card), the abolition of the Community Development Employment Projects (CDEP) and their replacement with work for the dole. The federal government compulsorily acquired 65 Aboriginal communities, granting them only five-year leases to Crown land. The permit system that had previously regulated government access in remote communities was suspended. Federal and state police, as well as the army, were mobilised to crack down on alcohol consumption and pornography, supposedly to aid the welfare of Aboriginal children. Demeaning signs were erected at the entrance to communities (most of which were already "dry") declaring them to be alcohol- and pornography-free zones.

---

47. Rundle 2007, p.37.

The NT Intervention was continued under the subsequent Rudd and Gillard Labor governments under the misnomer of "Stronger Futures". Cosmetic changes were made: the original Intervention legislation had breached the federal Anti-discrimination Act. However, Rudd and Gillard's commitment to the Intervention demonstrate the shallowness of Rudd's Stolen Generations apology.

Today, Aboriginal communities are still suffering from the dismantling of the CDEP employment program carried out during the Howard and Rudd years, and the punitive welfare measures that followed. Housing overcrowding remains a key issue. A 2021 Australian Institute of Health and Welfare report found that while one in five Indigenous people live in overcrowded housing, in remote communities the statistic is one in four and, in very remote communities, one in two.[48] The consequence is dramatically reduced health outcomes. As of January 2023, the COVID-19 mortality rate for Indigenous people was 1.5 times higher than for non-Indigenous people, but a shocking 3.5 times higher in remote and very remote communities.[49]

The Indigenous Voice to parliament

Albanese's announcement of a referendum on the Indigenous Voice to parliament continues in the tradition of previous Labor governments. It represents rhetorical commitment to Indigenous rights, while failing to address structural forms of racism that are heavily embedded in Australian capitalism. As Jordan Humphreys has observed:

> In reality, the Voice is an almost entirely symbolic gesture. The proposed model of the Voice will be an advisory body only, with no actual power over government policy. Parliament will have to listen to its views – which it can then freely ignore.[50]

The idea of an Aboriginal Voice in/to federal parliament is not a new one. From the mid-1920s, the NSW-based Australian Aboriginal

---

48. Australian Institute of Health and Welfare 2021.
49. ABS 2023.
50. Humphreys 2023.

Progressive Association advocated for an Aboriginal board to advise the Commonwealth government, and for state control over Aboriginal lives to be abolished. These demands were raised as part of a comprehensive platform that included land rights and an end to the removal of Aboriginal children by the NSW Aboriginal Protection Board.

In 1929, AAPA president Fred Maynard told a Sydney meeting of the Labour League that the AAPA advocated an Aboriginal representative "in the Federal Parliament, or failing it, to have an [A]boriginal ambassador appointed to live in Canberra to watch over his people's interests and advise the Federal authorities".[51] Four years later, Koori man Joe Anderson famously addressed a nationwide Cinesound news broadcast as the self-proclaimed "King Burraga". He declared: "All the black man wants is representation in Federal Parliament".[52]

However, the Voice will be far from representative of *all* Indigenous people's interests. The model proposed by a government-appointed advisory panel, which includes NT Intervention supporters Marcia Langton and Noel Pearson, rejects direct election of Indigenous Voice representatives by Indigenous communities at large on the basis that this would not "accommodate the vast diversity of cultures and ways in which cultural authority works in Aboriginal and Torres Strait Islander communities".[53] Harking back to ATSIC, they also cite low voter turnout as threatening the legitimacy of the Voice.

Instead, they recommend a model in which national Voice members are drawn from "Local and Regional Voices", based "on relevant arrangements in place that work well". They place emphasis on "shared decision making in partnership with governments".[54] The relevant arrangements referred to above presumably refer to land councils and bodies initiated in partnership with state governments, such as the First Peoples' Assembly in Victoria and the recently legislated First Nations Voice in South Australia.

---

51. Quoted in Maynard 2020.
52. Maynard 2020.
53. National Indigenous Australians Agency 2021, p.7.
54. National Indigenous Australians Agency 2021, p.6.

Each of these state-based models, like the national Voice to parliament, are (or will be) legislated into existence and can therefore be replaced as governments see fit. Moreover, they operate within a neoliberal framework in which governments view Indigenous self-determination as synonymous with granting government contracts to Aboriginal corporations to deliver "culturally appropriate" services. This model differs from the Hawke government's ATSIC service delivery model in so far as it provides a much greater role for the market to determine who can turn a profit in building Aboriginal housing or keeping children in out-of-home care or detention.

Today there are many more Aboriginal corporations positioned to bid for government contracts. As of 30 June 2022, there were 3,521 corporations registered under the Corporations (Aboriginal and Torres Strait Islander) Act 2006.[55] The last "Top 500" report published by the Office of the Registrar of Indigenous Corporations (ORIC), in 2016, found that the combined income of the top 500 Indigenous corporations had more than doubled in the previous decade, from $865 million in 2005–6 to $1.92 billion in 2015–16. The equity of these corporations had grown even faster, at 11.9 percent per year. Total equity of the top 500 in 2015–16 was more than $1.9 billion.[56]

Unsurprisingly, this accumulation of wealth has not "trickled down" to those most in need. In 2016, the poverty rate for Indigenous Australians was 31 percent, and was twice as high in very remote communities (54 percent) as in major cities (24 percent). Australian National University researchers Markham and Biddle observe that the income disparity between urban and remote Indigenous communities continues to grow.[57]

This entrenched wealth disparity is the consequence of decades of neoliberal policy pursued by both Labor and Coalition governments. Labor governments have felt a much greater need to appeal to liberal opinion by consulting with Indigenous "representatives" in designing and implementing "public policy, programs and service delivery" in accordance with neoliberal logic. However, the extent

---

55. National Indigenous Australians Agency 2022.
56. Office of the Registrar of Indigenous Corporations 2017.
57. Markham and Biddle 2018.

to which these "representatives" are listened to depends upon how willing and able they are to articulate the interests of the above-mentioned Indigenous corporations and a small, but growing, Aboriginal middle class.[58]

Incorporating the Indigenous Voice to parliament in the Australian constitution won't make it more representative or more democratic. Rather, it signals Labor's intention to continue down the path it has adopted since the Whitlam years, half a century ago. That is, a strategy that gives lip service to Aboriginal empowerment, while at the same time entrenching elite interests. Combatting institutional racism and inequality will require a different approach: one built from the ground up.

Addressing a Rainbow Alliance conference back in 1988, Gary Foley concluded his talk by arguing that: "The only sort of Australia that I think Aboriginal Australia can ultimately live alongside in true harmony is some form of socialist republic Australia where racism, sexism and exploitation have been eliminated".[59]

That's not just the type of society we should all aspire to, but one we need to organise to fight for, together.

References

Agreements, Treaties and Negotiated Settlements Project 2020, *Milirrpum v Nabalco (1971) 17 FLR 141*. https://database.atns.net.au/agreement.asp?EntityID=1611

Albanese, Anthony 2023, "Address to the Chifley Research Conference", National Press Club, Canberra, 5 February. https://www.pm.gov.au/media/address-chifley-research-conference

Anderson, Pat 2022, "Why a First Nations Voice should come before Treaty", *The Conversation*, 21 October. https://theconversation.com/why-a-first-nations-voice-should-come-before-treaty-192788

Australian Bureau of Statistics (ABS) 2023, "COVID-19 Mortality in Australia: Deaths registered until 31 January". https://www.abs.gov.au/articles/covid-19-mortality-australia-deaths-registered-until-31-january-2023

---

58. For a further discussion of the rise of an Aboriginal middle class see Jordan Humphreys' article in this issue of *Marxist Left Review*.
59. Foley 1988.

Australian Institute of Health and Welfare 2021, "Indigenous housing: Snapshot", 16 September. https://www.aihw.gov.au/reports/australias-welfare/indigenous-housing

Bennett, Scott 1985, "The 1967 Referendum", *Australian Aboriginal Studies*, 2, Aboriginal Studies Press, Canberra. https://search.informit.org/doi/10.3316/ielapa.860402932

Beresford, Quentin 2006, *Rob Riley: An Aboriginal Leader's Quest for Justice*, Aboriginal Studies Press.

Beresford, Quentin 2008, *The Godfather: the life of Brian Burke*, Allen & Unwin.

Bramble, Tom and Rick Kuhn 2011, *Labor's Conflict: Big Business, Workers and the Politics of Class*, Cambridge University Press.

Central Land Council 2023, "The Aboriginal Land Rights Act". https://www.clc.org.au/the-alra/

Coombs, HC and Robinson, CJ, 1996 "Remembering the Roots: Lessons for ATSIC", in Patrick Sullivan (ed.), *Shooting the Banker: Essays on ATSIC and Self-Determination*, North Australia Research Unit, Australian National University.

Foley, Gary 1988, "For Aboriginal sovereignty", *Arena* (83), republished at the *Koori History Website*. http://www.kooriweb.org/foley/essays/speech1.html

Foley, Gary 1999a, "Whiteness and Blackness in the Koori Struggle for Self-Determination", *Koori History Website*. http://www.kooriweb.org/foley/essays/pdf_essays/whiteness%20and%20blackness%20in%20the%20koori%20struggle.pdf

Foley, Gary 1999b, "Reconciliation: fact or fiction?", *Koori History Website*. http://www.kooriweb.org/foley/essays/pdf_essays/reconciliation.pdf

Foley, Gary 1999c, "ATSIC: Flaws in the machine", *Koori History Website*. http://www.kooriweb.org/foley/essays/pdf_essays/atsic.pdf

Foley, Gary 2001a, "Black Power in Redfern 1968–1972", *Koori History Website*. http://www.kooriweb.org/foley/essays/pdf_essays/black%20power%20in%20redfern%201968.pdf

Foley, Gary 2001b, "The Road to Native Title: Aboriginal Rights and the ALP 1973–1996", *Koori History Website*. http://www.kooriweb.org/foley/resources/pdfs/227.pdf

Foley, Gary 2010, "A Short History of the Australian Indigenous Resistance 1950–1990", *Koori History Website*. http://www.kooriweb.org/foley/resources/pdfs/229.pdf

Hawke, Steven and Michael Gallagher 1989, *Noonkanbah: Whose Land, Whose Law*, Fremantle Arts Centre Press.

Human Rights Commission 1997, *Bringing Them Home:* Report of the National Inquiry into the Separation of Aboriginal and Torres Strait Islander Children from Their Families. https://humanrights.gov.au/sites/default/files/content/pdf/social_justice/bringing_them_home_report.pdf

Humphreys, Jordan 2023, "A voice to parliament will do little for Indigenous justice", *Red Flag*, 224, 20 January. https://redflag.org.au/article/voice-parliament-will-do-little-indigenous-justice

Keating, Paul 1992, Speech at the Australian launch of the International Year for the World's Indigenous People, Redfern, 10 December. https://pmtranscripts.pmc.gov.au/sites/default/files/original/00008765.pdf

Markey, Raymond 1988, *The Making of the Labor Party in New South Wales 1880–1900*, New South Wales University Press.

Markham, Francis and Nicholas Biddle 2018, *Income, poverty and inequality – Census Paper 2*, ANU Centre for Aboriginal Economic Policy Research. https://openresearch-repository.anu.edu.au/bitstream/1885/145053/1/CAEPR_Census_Paper_2.pdf

Markus, Andrew 2001, *Race: John Howard and the remaking of Australia*, Allen & Unwin.

Maynard, John 2020, "The Voice to parliament isn't a new idea – Indigenous activists called for it nearly a century ago", *The Conversation*, 3 January. https://theconversation.com/the-voice-to-parliament-isnt-a-new-idea-indigenous-activists-called-for-it-nearly-a-century-ago-122272

Morse, Dana 2022, "Closing the Gap report shows four targets going backwards as experts call for efforts to 'empower communities'", *ABC News*, 30 November. https://www.abc.net.au/news/2022-11-30/closing-the-gap-report-released/101713892

National Indigenous Australians Agency 2021, *Indigenous Voice Discussion Paper*, Commonwealth of Australia. https://voice.niaa.gov.au/sites/default/files/2021-03/indigenous-voice-discussion-paper-2_0.pdf

National Indigenous Australians Agency 2022, "Appendix D – Register of Indigenous Corporations Annual Report 2021–22", *Annual Report 2021–22*. https://www.transparency.gov.au/annual-reports/national-indigenous-australians-agency/reporting-year/2021-22-36

NSW Government n.d., "The Aboriginal Land Rights Act 1983". https://www.aboriginalaffairs.nsw.gov.au/land-rights/the-aboriginal-land-rights-act-1983-alra/

Office of the Registrar of Indigenous Corporations 2017, *The Top 500 Aboriginal and Torres Strait Islander Corporations 2015–16*. https://www.oric.gov.au/sites/default/files/documents/11_2017/Top500_2015-16.pdf

Productivity Commission 2022, *Closing the Gap Annual Data Compilation Report*, July. https://www.pc.gov.au/closing-the-gap-data/annual-data-report/report/closing-the-gap-annual-data-compilation-report-july2022.pdf

Read, Peter 1990, "'Cheeky, Insolent and Anti-White': the split in the Federal Council for the Advancement of Aboriginal and Torres Strait Islanders – Easter 1970", *Australian Journal of Politics and History*, 36 (1), April, pp.73–83.

Read, Peter 2001, *Charles Perkins: A Biography*, Penguin.

Riley, Rob 1984, Address at the National Press Club on 11 October 1984 [sound recording], *Trove*. https://nla.gov.au/nla.obj-222466426/listen

Rundle, Guy 2007, "Military humanitarianism in Australia's North", in Jon Altman and Melinda Hinkson (eds), *Coercive Reconciliation: Stabilise, Normalise, Exit Aboriginal Australia*, Arena.

Smith, Diane 1996, "From Cultural Diversity to Regionalism", in Patrick Sullivan (ed.), *Shooting the Banker: Essays on ATSIC and Self-Determination*, North Australia Research Unit, ANU.

Tickner, Robert 2001, *Taking a Stand: Land Rights to Reconciliation*, Allen & Unwin.

Vassiley, Alexis 2021, "Noonkanbah 1979: when unionists stood up for Aboriginal rights", *Red Flag*, 17 February. https://redflag.org.au/node/7540

Wilkie, Meredith 1985, *Aboriginal Land Rights in NSW*, Alternative Publications Co-operative and Black Books.

LUCA TAVAN

Workerism and autonomism in Italy's "Hot Autumn"

Luca Tavan has been involved in campaigns against education cuts, for refugee rights, and in solidarity with Palestine. He has written a series of articles on the *Biennio Rosso*.

So there we were, with the three-hour union strike, and the two of us got together with five or six other comrades and contacted a few people from Lotta Continua. Then we set off; just the seven of us. And by the time we got to the head offices where all the staff hung out, there were about seven thousand of us!... The staff were all looking out of the windows, and saw us down below. They didn't know what to do. And the few guards on the doors were terrified. It was beautiful...this year we started with seven of us and ended up with seven thousand. Next time we'll start with seven thousand and end up with seventy thousand, and that'll be the end of FIAT. Goodbye, Agnelli.[1]

– Interview with a FIAT worker, 1970

ITALY'S "HOT AUTUMN" was one of the most profound moments of the global radicalisation of the late 1960s, a period of massive strikes, student revolt and social struggle. In the factories a state of permanent warfare reigned, which was so bitter and confrontational that some militants likened their position to that of Vietnamese

---

1. Georgakas 1971, pp.33–34.

guerrillas fighting the US occupation. On the streets, waves of social movements for education, housing rights and women's liberation transformed the conditions and social expectations of millions of people.

Italy's decade-long period of social contention, which historian John Foot has described as "quite easily the most radical, interesting, and, in the end, violent of all the world's '1968s'",[2] led to an explosion of revolutionary politics and organisation. In the 1970s, the revolutionary left won the loyalty of tens of thousands, and published three daily papers.[3] Socialist activists who had been marginalised during the post-war boom could now find an audience among radicalising workers, and were given an unparalleled opportunity to put their ideas and strategies to the test.

The workerists were one such grouping. In the early 1960s, they had attempted to rediscover the revolutionary heart of Marxism by turning their attention to the tensions emerging in the large factories in the country's industrial north. They focused on self-organised, militant struggle as the motor for social change, in opposition to the gradualist approach of the mainstream union leaders and the parliamentarism of the Italian Communist Party. At the peak of the struggles, their militancy allowed them to exert a serious influence on sections of the working-class vanguard that were looking to make a revolution.

But as the industrial struggle receded in the 1970s, many workerist intellectuals abandoned an understanding of class rooted in the process of production. They began searching for a new revolutionary "counter-power" to capitalism. This new movement, dubbed *Autonomia Operaia* (Workers' Autonomy) privileged local autonomous organising, alternative lifestyles and subculture, and in some cases armed struggle against the state. Their attempt to find a shortcut to challenging capitalism led to the marginalisation of the revolutionary left in the workers' movement, and ultimately to a series of brutal defeats.

This article will chart the experience of Europe's most active revolutionary left from the highs of leading workers in militant struggle to the lows of lifestylism and terrorism. The issues described below are not

---

2. Foot 2003, p.8.
3. Harman 1998, p.198.

simply of historical interest. Autonomist politics still linger as a dead weight in many parts of the left today. By understanding these politics as a product of the failure of the revolutionary left, we can better build organisations and struggles that avoid repeating the mistakes of the past.

The Communist Party and the long boom

Italy's Hot Autumn emerged after a long period of capitalist stability. Italy was dubbed Europe's *economic miracle* due to its rapid post-war reconstruction. By the late 1950s GDP was increasing at an unheard of rate of more than six percent per annum.[4] The boom transformed the economy, as dominant exports shifted from food production and textiles to modern consumer goods – fridges, televisions, washing machines and cars – still out of reach for most Italian workers. The automotive industry was at the centre of this expansion. It's estimated that in 1963, 20 percent of the total investments in Italy derived from production choices made by FIAT. The behemoth car manufacturer drove demand for mechanical parts, steel, petrol and rubber, as well as road infrastructure.[5]

The Italian Communist Party (PCI) loomed large over the left throughout this period. After years of repression under Mussolini's fascist regime, it had rebuilt itself rapidly through participation in the resistance to Nazi occupation which erupted in 1943. Many PCI militants had operated for years or decades underground, separated from their exiled leadership and relatively unaffected by the huge changes the official communist movement had undergone. While party activists tended to see the *Resistenza* as the opening stage of a social revolution that could place workers' power on the agenda, the party leadership had other plans. When PCI leader Palmiro Togliatti returned victoriously from exile in 1944, he announced a sharp change of tack.

Togliatti had spent years in exile as a key functionary of Stalin's Comintern, imposing the exigencies of Soviet foreign policy on the Communist Parties. To assist the Stalin-Churchill-Roosevelt alliance

4. Ginsborg 1990, p.214.
5. Ginsborg 1990, p.215.

in their joint effort to carve up Europe, the PCI was ordered to collaborate with the Italian state. And so in April 1944, Togliatti dutifully announced the "Salerno turn". The PCI now officially recognised the government headed by King Victor Emmanuel and the former fascist Pietro Badoglio, in exchange for cabinet positions. The party's entire program, from socialisation to opposition to the monarchy, was sacrificed at the altar of "national unity" and collaboration with the dominant bourgeois Christian Democratic Party. Having given this promise of loyalty, the Communist Party was able to continue building its influence in the resistance without fear of alienating Italy's capitalist class.

Crucially, Togliatti viewed this new orientation as a permanent strategic perspective:

> If we want the government and its action to be in conformity with the democratic will of the majority, the mass parties of the left and the Christian Democratic party must collaborate, and collaborate not in a temporary way, reserving the right to attack and destroy each other at the first opportunity, but in a permanent way, with a long prospect of common reconstructive activity.[6]

While many PCI activists treated the Salerno turn with suspicion, they were willing to give Togliatti the benefit of the doubt. The leadership fostered the illusion that they were just playing a tactical game, the strategy of *doppiezza*, or duplicity – encouraging the bourgeoisie to lower its defences. Overall the PCI was successful in building its prestige through participation in the resistance while isolating the radical elements which wanted to use the struggle to advance workers toward power.

By 1946 the party could claim two million members and its leaders looked forward to a bright future where they would be taken seriously as collaborators in building the post-war capitalist order. These plans were rudely interrupted. With the onset of the Cold War the Italian ruling class received a stern message from their American allies to end

---

6. Quoted in Blackmer 1977, p.29.

collaboration with the PCI, and the Communists were ejected from office in May 1947. The party would spend the next two decades in the political wilderness, at least at a national level, yearning for a return to governmental power.

Despite being shunned, the Communist Party doubled down on its reformist practice and theory, though it maintained a degree of revolutionary rhetoric.

While its membership declined in the decade between 1956 and 1966 to a little over one-and-a-half million members, the PCI remained a powerful force in civil society. It dominated the CGIL, the largest union federation, and accrued masses of moderate trade union officials. It organised 200,000 through women's unions, sponsored a cooperative league with two million members, and published the country's second-best-selling daily newspaper.[7] In Bologna from 1945, the PCI had a chance to demonstrate its governing prowess under the leadership of a communist mayor who was able to reassure local business that communist policy wouldn't be directed against them. The party boasted of being able to provide subsidised school meals, build municipal facilities and increase public transport, all without ever running a deficit.[8] For isolated groupings of revolutionaries, challenging the PCI for the loyalty of organised workers would have seemed like a distant dream.

Ending the industrial peace

As with any period of capitalist expansion, there were subterranean contradictions accumulating which pointed toward the possibility of a new radical rupture. The economic boom had the effect of drawing millions of southern migrants to the factories of the north. Between 1955 and 1971, some nine million Italians moved between regions, from a total population of around fifty million.[9] From the standpoint of the mainstream left, this new labour force was initially seen as diluting militancy, because many of these workers brought with them no political or union traditions. But conditions of near

---

7. Ginsborg 1990, pp.290–91.
8. Ginsborg 1990, p.203.
9. Ginsborg 1990, p.219.

full employment gave workers a confidence that hadn't existed since the war. And the concentration of industrial workers at the centre of large-scale, mass-production industries, subject to constant speed-ups and intensification, created a febrile industrial atmosphere. Though they were largely unorganised, workers from the south could be highly volatile. As one foreman explained: "the most difficult to deal with are the southerners, because they are the ones who get angry the most often and protest the most; the Piedmontese hold it against me that I've become a foreman, but they are the most tranquil and conscientious workers".[10]

The first major test of the battle-readiness of these new sections of the working class came in 1962 when the national metalworkers' contract came up for renewal. There were bitter struggles at firms like Lancia and Michelin, but FIAT would be the decisive factor in the campaign. Throughout the fifties it had been transformed into a bastion of industrial peace, through a combination of high wages and benefits, and the brutal persecution of militants. In 1955 this was symbolised by the defeat of the PCI-aligned CGIL in internal union elections.[11] This time, however, a determined lead by factory militants led to 60,000 being pulled out at the company that was at the heart of the post-war boom. Then in July, when FIAT bosses attempted to bypass negotiation with the strikers by signing a separate agreement with an employer-friendly union federation, thousands of FIAT workers besieged the union's headquarters. When the police intervened to break up their demonstration, hundreds fought back. Paul Ginsborg wrote:

> For the next two and a half days, Piazza Statuto became the site of an extended urban riot. An extraordinary series of running battles took place between demonstrators and police. The demonstrators broke windows, threw stones, set up rudimentary barricades and repeatedly charged the police lines. They were armed with slings, sticks and chains. The police replied by driving their Jeeps at the crowd, filling the

---

10. Quoted in Ginsborg 1990, p.250.
11. Wright 2017, p.9.

piazza with tear gas and using the butts of their rifles on the demonstrators. The clashes went on late into the night both on Saturday 7 July and Monday 9 July. Pajetta of the PCI and Sergio Garavini of the CGIL tried to persuade the crowds to disperse, but they were ignored and manhandled. Over a thousand demonstrators were arrested by the police, though the numbers charged were far fewer.[12]

At this harbinger of a coming earthquake in post-war class struggle, the PCI leaders and union officials displayed marked uneasiness. They dismissed the Piazza Statuto riots as the work of *agents provocateurs*. Communist Party intellectual Paolo Spriano described them as "students essentially" whose perspective was "tenaciously resistant to reality",[13] but the truth was undeniable – Piazza Statuto was a revolt of mostly young workers, many of them southerners, who felt unrewarded by Italy's "economic miracle".

The workerists

These emerging cracks in the post-war settlement between capital and labour posed a challenge for the left. In October 1961, a group of intellectuals centred around the unions and major workers' parties had published the first issue of a new journal, *Quaderni Rossi*. This journal was where the "workerist" tendency took form. The workerists attempted to analyse and give clarity to the new developments in the country's large northern factories. They rightly identified both the radical potential that existed in these struggles and the inability of the Communist and Socialist Parties to lead them. The workerists argued for a "Marxist purification of Marx", which meant going back to basics, and refocusing on workers' power at the point of production as the key to socialist transformation. Their stress on "the working-class point of view" was deliberately and diametrically opposed to the Communist Party strategy of "hegemony", which meant popular front-style top-down alliances with other designated "progressive classes" through electoral intervention.

---

12. Ginsborg 1990, p.252.
13. Quoted in Wright 2017, p.54.

This was a largely healthy reaction against reformism. But the workerists went further, laying out a novel analysis of the role of the working class in capitalism. Directly inspired by the revolt at Piazza Statuto, workerist intellectual Mario Tronti flipped the traditional analysis of the Communist Party, in which the working class is passively shaped by capitalist development, on its head. In 1962, Tronti argued that the existence of the working class and its struggles were the key motor-force of capitalism:

> We have seen that the commodity labour-power is the properly active side of capital, the natural home of any capitalist dynamism. It is the protagonist not only of the expanded reproduction of the valorisation process, but also of the continual revolutionary upheavals of the labour process itself.[14]

In Tronti's account, capital has relied throughout its history on the inventiveness and demands of the working class in order to find new avenues of growth. Every new bourgeois strategy – from technological developments, to the Keynesian welfare state, to new government coalitions – has emerged as a reaction to workers' power in production, and as an attempt to incorporate workers' struggle.

The workerists drew political conclusions from this analysis. In the absence of a revolutionary struggle for power, capital would simply use workers' struggle as a spur for its own growth. Routine union bargaining would only strengthen the system by incorporating workers' demands into capitalist development. So workers needed independence from the state and official union structures, which restrained the inherently revolutionary potential of their struggles. Priority should be given instead to struggles that could not be accommodated by capitalist development.

> We might ask: what happens when the form of working class organisation takes on a wholly alternative content? When it refuses to function as an articulation of capitalist society? When

---

14. Tronti 2019, p.31.

it refuses to *shoulder* capital's needs through meeting working class demands? The answer is that, at that moment and starting from that moment, the system's whole development mechanism is blocked.[15]

This meant the workerists tended to glorify absenteeism, sabotage and deliberately unachievable wage demands, regarding them as tactics that, at a formal level, expressed and developed workers' political and economic autonomy from the dictates of capital.

Tronti referred to this as the "strategy of refusal". He even went so far as to imply that the struggle against capitalism could be resolved at the point of production alone, writing that: "The machinery of the bourgeois state must today be smashed within the capitalist factory".[16]

They developed a highly voluntarist conception of working-class struggle – arguing that workers could challenge capitalism by subjectively rejecting its prerogatives and refusing to compromise with it. This was very different from the conception of revolutionary politics developed by communists like Luxemburg and Lenin, who argued that the day-to-day struggle for reforms under radical leadership was necessary to build the organisational power and revolutionary consciousness of the working class.[17]

Having written off the unions as hopelessly incorporated, the workerists drew inspiration from the volatile struggles of unskilled and semi-skilled workers who had confronted police with rocks and bottles in the battle of Piazza Statuto. Tronti identified these layers, to whom he referred as the "mass worker", as a new revolutionary agent. The highly skilled metalworkers who had led the struggles of the *Biennio Rosso* of 1919–20 had struggled to assert their mastery and control over the jobs in which they took great pride. In contrast, the new mass workers despised their role in the labour process. The historic mission of the mass worker was to smash the factory system entirely.

---

15. Tronti 2019, p.259.
16. Quoted in Wright 2017, p.35.
17. For an elaboration of this argument, see Bloodworth 2014.

From the workerists' perspective, the inherent radicalism of the mass worker rendered the question of developing class consciousness redundant. The forms of struggle that workers adopted would be determined not by political intervention and the "battle of ideas" in the class, but by how sections of the class were compelled to act as a result of their specific role in the productive process. As founding workerist Raniero Panzieri explained:

> [T]he subversive strength of the working class, its revolutionary capacity, appears (potentially) strongest precisely at capitalism's "development points", where the crushing preponderance of constant capital over living labour, together with the rationality embodied in the former, immediately faces the working class with the question of its political enslavement.[18]

This amounted to a form of technological determinism which downplayed the importance of politics in the workers' movement.

At various times Tronti hinted that this mass worker might be a portent of something happening across the rest of capitalist society: "the whole of society exists as a function of the factory and the factory extends its exclusive domination over the whole of society".[19] But in the 1960s he never developed this analysis. The workerists kept their focus within the factory gates.

There were deep tensions within the largely academic workerist milieu about how to translate their ideas into action. Within a few years, they split between a wing which wanted to restrict their activity to research, led by Raniero Panzieri, and a wing led by Mario Tronti and Antonio Negri, inspired by the revolts emerging around them, and committed to political organisation.

Among the activists, there were further splits over the question of orientation to the Communist Party. The workerists were forged by their common agreement that the PCI's rightward drift was a result of its separation from shop-floor struggles, but they never advanced a unified, systematic critique of Stalinism, and the

---

18. Quoted in Mohandesi 2013, p.88.
19. Quoted in Wright 2017, p.34.

reformist practice it had engendered in the Italian party. Tronti held to an extremely elitist conception of the role of the party, writing in *Workers and Capital*:

> Only through a subjective conscious intervention from "on high"...which allows you to master the functioning of the system to be destroyed can you foresee and anticipate the turning points in the cycle of capital's development, can you measure, control, manage and thus organise the political growth of the working class, obliging it to go through a whole chain of different confrontations at different levels and on some of these occasions break the chain, reverse the relationship between the parties and smash the state machine.[20]

This approach to political organising fit with Tronti's loyalty to the reformist PCI. A more radical wing led by Antonio Negri defined itself through its intransigent opposition to the PCI, the dominant current in the workers' movement.

Workerists in the Hot Autumn

Revolutionaries were given an unparalleled opportunity to put their politics to the test when Italian society exploded with social ferment in 1968. The Hot Autumn in the factories was preceded by an explosion on the university campuses, which provided the first widespread ideological challenge to Italian capitalism since 1945. After the war, universities had been transformed from ruling-class playgrounds into training grounds for the masses of civil servants, technicians and white-collar workers required to run a modern industrial economy. Hundreds of thousands of children of the middle classes and workers entered tertiary education for the first time, and were confronted by a system in an advanced state of crisis. By 1968 the universities of Rome, Naples and Bari, designed for a little more than 5,000 students, now had 60,000, 50,000 and 30,000 students respectively.[21] The curriculum was traditionalist and archaic – overwhelmingly

---

20. Quoted in Fuller 1980.
21. Ginsborg 1990, p.299.

examinations were oral, occasions where "a policeman dressed up as a teacher spends five to ten minutes in liquidating the accused with a series of questions".[22] By the late 1960s the campuses were ready to explode. As Paul Ginsborg wrote: "The decision to allow open access to such a grossly inadequate university system amounted simply to planting a time bomb in it".[23]

The student movement was not just a revolt against stuffy teachers and crowded lecture theatres – it was an ideological revolt against the values and institutions of post-war capitalism. As student leader Guido Viale wrote:

> The university functions as an instrument of ideological and political manipulation. It aims to instil into the students a spirit of subordination to the powers that be (whoever they may be). It tries to cancel, in the psychological structure of every student, the collective dimension of personal needs. It intends to destroy the possibility of establishing relations with one's neighbour which are other than purely competitive in character.[24]

Students who had grown up with an image of the United States as the liberator of Europe now had images of American war crimes in Vietnam beamed to them through the television every evening. The "economic miracle" had created vast riches for industrial magnates like Gianni Agnelli, owner of FIAT, but offered little hope of a stable job for the graduates that the universities churned out. Hundreds of thousands of students turned to revolutionary politics amidst the ferment. Then, in May 1968, Parisian students helped to spark the largest general strike in history. The news electrified the Italian student movement, and the new revolutionaries turned from the campuses to the workplaces.

In the factories, the first major strikes of 1968 were unofficial and spontaneous. Tyre manufacturer Pirelli Bicocca in Milan was typical. After years of industrial quiescence, a series of small, sectional strikes

---

22. Ginsborg 1990, p.200.
23. Ginsborg 1990, p.299.
24. Ginsborg 1990, p.301.

had emerged in defiance of the union leadership. They were driven by anger at speed-ups and piece-rate payments, and were fuelled by young semi-skilled workers with little in the way of organisational traditions. Robert Lumley gives a picture of the rapidly changing working conditions that fuelled discontent:

> From 1964 increases in workloads, rather than investment in new machinery, was the chief means of raising productivity. One worker in the vulcanization section told a researcher that in 1964 he had had eight machines to tend, but as a result of rationalizations the number had increased to seventeen, and he had to produce 390 tyres instead of 15.[25]

By September there were almost daily strikes at Pirelli, routinely involving thousands.[26]

By 1970, there were disputes in 4,000 individual factories, with new methods of struggle emerging, including sit-down strikes, internal factory marches, checkerboard strikes, and violent reprisals against hated managers.[27] It was a paper associated with Milanese industrialists which first dubbed this cycle of revolt the "Hot Autumn", likely in reference to the "long hot summer" of Black urban uprisings which shook the United States in 1967.[28]

This explosive wave of struggles had largely caught the Communist Party and major union federations off guard. A correspondent wrote in the British *Socialist Worker* at the beginning of December 1968:

> The movement has been directed by the official trade union apparatus only to the extent that it has accepted and advanced the genuine demands of the rank and file. The real leaders of the struggle have been the factory base committees and local assemblies.[29]

---

25. Lumley 1990, p.184.
26. Harman 1998, p.135.
27. Harman 1998, p.194.
28. Lumley 1990, p.208.
29. Quoted in Harman 1998, p.193.

The union leaders' preferred approach of routine bargaining every few years had proved completely inadequate to a working class faced with constant speed-ups, rationalisation and reprisals on the factory floor. Luigi, a veteran FIAT worker, explained the limitations of the official union strategy:

> So every two or three years, when the contracts were about to expire, we would have the classic sort of struggle you know, two or three days of strikes, all kept within union channels, and then the boss's repression would begin all over again. And the little politicisation achieved through those two or three days would be blocked for the next three years of boss's rule.[30]

Workers previously indifferent to the largely student and intellectual radical left were now willing to give them a hearing. This opening was created by the new sense of collective power that came from the more radical actions being taken, and by the political vacuum that was created by the abdication of the Communist Party. Workerists and other revolutionaries could now have a real impact. Toni, a Calabrian migrant worker new to FIAT, described the process of making contact with the revolutionaries:

> I began to pick up on the politics that Lotta Continua were into. At first, you know, I really didn't understand too much. I used to read their leaflets, but only in a sort of informative way, so as to know what they were saying. One day one of the student comrades from Lotta Continua hunted me out and began talking to me. He really attacked me because I was still in the union. Before I worked at FIAT I'd worked for a few months at other little factories, and all that I'd heard was that the unions were there to defend the workers. Of course, down in Calabria we don't even know what a union is; people don't know that they exist! But gradually I began to understand what they really are.[31]

---

30. Georgakas 1971, p.32.
31. Georgakas 1971, p.33.

Even the potentially alienating workerist denunciation of the unions was taken seriously by militants looking for new methods of struggle. In the same interview, Luigi expanded:

> The unions are there to make sure that workers are kept inside the system, and have less possibility of beginning to challenge it. The unions are the political extensions of the sicknesses that exist inside the government; the "long arm inside the factories" of political parties. Every group, every political party has a little hand inside the factory. The Christian Democrats have CISL, the Communists have the CGIL, SIDA are the Fascists, UIL is the Social Democrats, even some Republicans...every one of them has a certain presence inside the factory to control the situation.[32]

At the Montedison petrochemical plant in Veneto, which employed 15,000 people, the patient and systematic work of a group of workerist militants who would go on to help form Potere Operaio (Workers' Power) was paying off. In 1967, after five years of organising, they were able to organise their first industrial action. By the end of the year they were leading dozens of strikes to win a flat 5,000 lire increase for all workers in the factory, regardless of skill and job categories. The struggle relied on aggressive tactics to win, greatly increased the prestige of the workerists, and affirmed their strategic perspective – it was organised through mass democratic worker assemblies, "autonomous" from the official union and party structures.[33]

At FIAT Mirafiori in Turin, struggle was also picking up in late 1968. A student activist grouping had turned from the campuses to the workplaces, inspired by the analysis of the workerists. By June of 1969 hundreds of workers were making their way at the end of their shifts to worker-student assemblies to discuss the almost daily work stoppages occurring in the factory.

The workerists were given the opportunity that all revolutionaries dream of: the chance to test their politics in a period of industrial upsurge and social ferment. When the unions called a routine one-day

---

32. Georgakas 1971, p.37.
33. Wright 2017, p.104.

strike over rent in July 1969, the worker-student assembly at FIAT managed to escalate things by calling a demonstration outside of the factory's main gates in Corso Traiano. Soon things spilled over into streetfighting in the surrounding suburbs. The clashes were to continue into the early hours of the morning, as workers with rocks and molotov cocktails were pitted against police truncheons and tear gas.[34] The official slogans of the unions against rent rises were completely ignored in favour of the now infamous workerist catchcry: *Che cosa vogliamo? Tutto!* (What do we want? Everything!)

By the end of the 1960s two new revolutionary groups had emerged from the workerist tendency: Lotta Continua (Continuous Struggle), built from the worker-student assemblies in Turin, and Potere Operaio (Workers' Power), based in Veneto. Both were committed to ruthless opposition to the Communist Party's reformism, but they had different conceptions of what sort of party the working class needed. Potere Operaio, shaped by the thought of Antonio Negri, opted for a caricatured version of "Leninism", a centralised and disciplined vanguard party, which owed more to the Stalinist tradition than the real record of the Bolsheviks. Adriano Sofri founded Lotta Continua as a network of "internal vanguards", spurning formal leadership and structures in favour of decision-making through mass assemblies. Both took the essentials of the workerist analysis into the upsurge of the Hot Autumn, and both won the loyalty of thousands, while influencing countless more.[35]

Workerism in crisis

Despite these early successes, problems with the approach of the workerists soon emerged. The most radical struggles of 1968–69 had largely bypassed the official union structures, but by 1970 many of the union leaders recognised the need to accommodate the new mood. Starting with the more militant metal and chemical unions and then

---

34. Quoted in Wright 2017, p.114.
35. It was not just the question of organisation that separated Potere Operaio and Lotta Continua. While PO was a "pure" workerist party focused almost exclusively on struggle at the point of production, Lotta Continua intervened into social movements, and combined workerist analysis with Maoist tendencies.

spreading outwards, the official unions began to "ride the tiger" of workplace militancy in order to bring it under their control. They began to recognise new grassroots workplace "delegate" structures which were emerging relatively spontaneously, and ratified them as a new system of workplace democracy, based on factory councils.

The councils, which spread rapidly across industry, were composed of delegates from every shop or department in the workplace. Delegates were elected in a secret ballot by all the workforce, whether trade union members or not, and were subject to recall at any time. The meetings of the factory council were open to all workers. By 1975 there were more than 32,000 councils with more than 250,000 delegates, an incredible flourishing of workplace democracy.[36]

Sticking to their guns, both Lotta Continua and Potere Operaio boycotted the councils, arguing that they were nothing more than a conspiracy to reincorporate the working class back into capitalist planning. While there was some truth to this, their stance meant refusing to relate to the hundreds of thousands of workers who were moving into struggle for the first time through this process. Ironically, it also made it much easier for the union leaders to reassert their control.

The workerists could win some support in a period of offensive struggle. But they fundamentally mistook the ideas of a vanguard section of the class for those of the working class at large. The unions and PCI, far from losing support, were in fact growing alongside the new council movement. Despite building impressive organisations of thousands, the workerist parties only exerted decisive influence in relatively isolated strongholds – like FIAT Turin for LC, and Montedison in Veneto for PO. By abstaining from the council movement, they undermined the strides they had made during the working-class offensive. In particular, their approach made it impossible to challenge the hegemony of the PCI over the broader working class.

By the early 1970s the struggle had become more difficult for revolutionaries for a number of reasons.

The Italian state responded to the upsurge of the late 1960s with a "strategy of tension". A section of the ruling class hostile to any

---

36. Harman 1998, p.194.

initiatives for reform instead colluded with fascists who planted bombs to create a climate of fear and repression. The most famous of these actions, the bombing of a bank in the Piazza Fontana in Milan, was pinned on the left, and led to the murder of one anarchist activist. Rumours of coup plots abounded, culminating in an actual abortive attempt in 1970, when the fascist ex-commander Junio Borghese made a brief attempt to occupy the ministry of the interior. While the Italian ruling class quickly retreated from this high-risk strategy, this threat began pushing many radicals toward a mistaken insurrectionary perspective. That same year the Red Brigades were formed, a clandestine armed organisation which would help popularise the analysis that the situation was tending not just toward heightened class struggle, but toward civil war. This would become a recurrent theme on the far left throughout the 1970s.

Then, from 1973, an economic crisis resulted in a bosses' offensive which changed the industrial situation fundamentally. The capitalist class used the crisis as an excuse to restructure industry and victimise factory militants. The deliberately extreme demands valorised by the workerists got less of a hearing as workers' struggle became primarily defensive. The mass assemblies began to decline. Reformists had regained ground through the unions, asserted their control over the factory committees, and in 1976, far from being swept away by the struggle, the PCI received its highest ever vote.

These were all potentially surmountable problems. Class struggle always involves ebbs and flows, advances and setbacks. There has never been and never will be a continual and linear escalation of struggle to the point of power. These setbacks and downturns can be endured by revolutionaries, but they are a test of the solidity of your politics. The situation demanded a flexible but principled approach which allowed them to organise the militants who had already broken with reformism, while relating to the millions of workers who still expected the unions to defend their interests. It demanded a united front approach to the Communist Party, meaning joint struggles to strengthen the fighting capacity of the class while exposing the limitations of the PCI's reformist parliamentarism. Most importantly, it required an understanding that revolution wasn't right around the corner, and there were years of struggle ahead that activists would have to prepare themselves for.

These are all questions which the revolutionary Marxist tradition had been forced to confront before. The Third International prior to Stalinist degeneration had grappled with all of them through the experience of a wave of workers' revolutions and the construction of mass communist parties. But both PO and LC rejected these traditions, in favour of developing a new revolutionary strategy from scratch. They were quickly thrown into chaos and confusion.

Lotta Continua had largely ignored the question of relating to members of the Communist Party or proposing joint struggles in 1969–70. They preferred instead an intransigent maximalism: "We are not interested in bringing down the Christian Democrat junta, we want to destroy the capitalist system".[37] By 1971 they had performed an about-turn, claiming that fascism posed an existential threat and that unity with the Communist Party was necessary. But this unity was not proposed on the basis of ruthless critique of the PCI's betrayals. Instead Lotta Continua tended to adapt to the larger party's politics, glorifying its radical past and anti-fascist credentials. This was no aberration, but a product of their political approach. As Chris Harman wrote:

> The spontaneism of the leaders of Lotta Continua, their belief that revolutionary politics arises immediately out of the struggle, meant in 1969 articulating a hatred of strike activists against the reformist parties and union apparatuses. In 1971 and 1972 it meant articulating the feelings of those who found the Communist Party members and union activists were as worried as they were by the growth of the far right.[38]

Their lack of a systematic and principled approach to winning workers away from the influence of reformism led to a flip-flopping from sectarian abstention to ideological capitulation. By 1976 Lotta Continua were throwing themselves into the struggle to propel the Communist Party into governmental office.

---

37. Harman 1998, pp.199–200.
38. Harman 1998, p.205.

While successfully avoiding this right-wing error, Potere Operaio drew inspiration from failed ultra-left outfits like the German KAPD of the 1920s. They resurrected the disastrous "theory of the offensive" – a strategy of forcing the pace of class struggle through the brave minority actions of a revolutionary party. Their central strategy had been to leapfrog over reformist consciousness by bypassing the official structures of the labour movement, based on an extremely optimistic prediction of imminent revolution. When experience proved the continued resilience of reformist ideas in the workers' movement, they lapsed into an increasingly elitist and pessimistic view of working-class agency and consciousness. A grouping of PO militants now argued that without their intervention, working class autonomy "lives for and in the capitalist relations of production".[39] Alarmed by the seeming passivity of large sections of the working class, and the apparent threat of a right-wing coup, they believed that only a military organisation capable of destroying the capitalist state could end this cycle and shake workers from their lethargy. Unsurprisingly, calls by PO activists to militarise the struggle fell on deaf ears.

Still, Potere Operaio continued the search for signs of an imminent revolutionary upsurge. In 1973, workers at FIAT Mirafiori blockaded their workplace with mass pickets. PO theorists developed an analysis of this struggle which bore little resemblance to reality. They wrote: "Taking power at FIAT, and in all of Turin, contains an explicit allusion to the seizure of political power and to the revolutionary programme of the abolition of wage labour".[40] This analysis, deliberately ignorant of the realities of the class struggle, seemed to herald an imminent revolutionary situation based on one isolated factory struggle.

It soon became clear that the 1973 FIAT occupation was a final defiant stand by the leading protagonists of the Hot Autumn, rather than the beginning of a revolutionary challenge for power. The capitalist counter-offensive and the continued vitality of reformist workers' institutions created a new terrain in the factories, one in which radicals were increasingly marginalised.

---
39. Quoted in Wright 2017, p.135.
40. Quoted in Wright 2017, p.137.

The experience at the Innocenti plant outside Milan was typical. There, a group of militants launched a supportable campaign against management attempts to reduce the workforce while increasing working hours. They faced hostility not just from the employers, but the CGIL-dominated factory council. The conflict came to a head in October 1975, when PCI and CGIL stewards clashed physically with members of the Workers' Coordinating committee. The following day six leading radicals were sacked.[41] The right-wing newspaper *Corriere Della Sera* noted the re-establishment of CGIL control in the factories: "Rigidly marshalled by the unions…Fiat workers are ever less receptive to extreme suggestions".[42] Sergio Bologna, one of Negri's collaborators, provided a sober assessment of the period in contrast to the euphoric analyses of Potere Operaio:

> [A] deeper division has occurred: not between factory and society, but within the factory itself, between the working-class right and left. In sum there has been a reassertion of reformist hegemony over the factories, one that is brutal and relentless in its efforts to dismember the class left and expel it from the factory.[43]

As the movement in the factories was being rapidly crushed under the weight of repression, the revolutionaries gradually shifted their focus from the workplaces to the streets. Amidst the inflationary crisis of the mid-1970s, campaigns for housing rights, the reduction of transport fares and electricity fees, and various social movements like the women's liberation movement exploded. In 1977 Bologna wrote of this period: "the extra-parliamentary groups began their suicidal retreat from the factory, and in general ceased to give much attention to problems of the composition of the class. This has led to a situation where, today, the factory and the working class are almost unknown entities".[44]

---

41. Wright 2017, p.156.
42. Quoted in Edwards 2009, p.72.
43. Wright 2017, p.157.
44. Bologna 1980, p.40.

Workerism had foundered in the face of the realities of class struggle, sending leading PO figures like Antonio Negri in search of a new strategy. It was in this context of demoralisation and confusion that autonomism emerged from the crisis of workerism.

The birth of autonomism

"Autonomia Operaia", as the new movement was known, is difficult to define because of its vague organisational and political parameters. It was in reality a label adopted by a network of organisations, collectives, social spaces and struggles, informed and inspired by the analysis of intellectuals like Negri, Franco Berardi and Oreste Scalzone. It began life as a network of workplace militants, often led by activists from the dissolved revolutionary organisations. By 1975 the centre of autonomist organising had shifted away from the workplace. An autonomist "proletarian youth movement" emerged which organised around squats and social centres, and focused on demands for greater consumption and the "right to luxury". This helped spur a closely related student movement which reached its climax in 1977 before rapidly deflating. Increasingly after that point, the movement was defined by different strategies which reflected the further fragmentation and demoralisation of the movement. One wing was concerned with subverting capitalist culture, while the other degenerated into myriad tiny clandestine armed groups which swore to wage war on the employers, the fascists and the state.

A series of political perspectives united the autonomists struggling in these different fields. The autonomists were united by a rejection of the need for leadership exercised by centralised political parties. They tended also to deny the centrality of the industrial working class, focusing instead on the equal value of every struggle against the system. Their strategy for revolution was based on building forms of "counter-power" by progressively liberating space from the rule of capital and the state. They believed in the possibility and necessity of a strategy of permanent offensive against the system.

Autonomism took the emphasis on subjectivity at the heart of workerism to its extreme – progressively severing the tie between their "revolutionary" objectives and a concrete analysis of capitalism or an orientation to working-class struggle. While autonomism tended to preserve workerism's key theoretical categories, particularly the focus on "autonomy" from all political processes and state institutions, it was also its ideological opposite – a thoroughgoing trashing of the fundamental Marxist dictum that "the emancipation of the working classes must be conquered by the working classes themselves".

In many ways autonomism only really existed as a negative critique of Marxism, as a way of escaping the strategic dilemmas which had entrapped the left during the Hot Autumn, by simply choosing to ignore them. Sylvère Lotringer reflected this in her glowing 1980 appraisal of autonomist politics:

> A body of workers, it breaks away from labor discipline; a body of militants, it ignores party organization; a body of doctrine, it refuses ready-made classifications... Autonomy has no frontiers. It is a way of eluding the imperatives of production, the verticality of institutions, the traps of political representation, the virus of power.[45]

Failing to overcome the impasse of the early 1970s, autonomists chose to re-conceptualise social change in a way that erased class struggle as the central category for understanding capitalism, as Lotringer explained:

> The nature of social confrontations has changed drastically. Politics up to now was tied to the relationships of production: the conflict between exploiters and exploited. This conferred on the working class an indubitable centrality. In post-industrial societies...the opposition between factory and society is slowly disappearing. Factories are no longer the focus for struggles. Consequently, political antagonisms can be defined as a properly social, even micro-social, conflict. Class struggle has yielded to more subtle confrontations.[46]

---

45. Lotringer and Marazzi 1980, p.8.
46. Lotringer and Marazzi 1980, p.10.

This rejection of class antagonisms and conscious political intervention in favour of vagueness, fluidity and sophistry dressed up as novel theory would lead the movements of the 1970s to disaster.

Antonio Negri and the "social worker"

In response to the impasse that radicals faced in the mid-1970s, Antonio Negri and his collaborators established the defining feature of autonomist politics – the rejection of an analysis of class rooted in the process of production, and the identification of a new revolutionary subject: the "social worker". They would develop from this a political practice which focused on social layers that played a marginal role in production, and whose "proletarian status" would be defined by a denial of access to commodities, rather than a denial of control over labour.

In his 1975 essay *Proletari e Stato*, Negri argued that in the context of capitalist crisis, the whole of society has now become involved in the process of production, far outside the boundaries of the factory. The role of the state had imposed factory-like discipline on all of society. One consequence of this is that the distinction between productive and unproductive labour disappears. All labour produces value at all times.[47]

Since the process of capitalist exploitation now took place on a society-wide scale, socially and economically marginalised groups such as students, the unemployed and casual labourers must be counted as core sections of the proletariat. The new role of the capitalist state had dramatic implications for social struggle:

> It transforms exploitation into a global social relation. Jail equals factory… In reality, the operation of real subsumption does not eliminate the [class] antagonism, but rather displaces it to the social level. Class struggle does not disappear; it is rather transformed into all the moments of everyday life. The daily life of a proletarian is posited as a whole against the domination of capital.[48]

---

47. Fuller 1980.
48. Negri 1984, p.xvi.

Negri here enacted a theoretical sleight of hand, inventing a new revolutionary subject – the "social worker" – to avoid confronting the relative decline of the factory struggle, and workerists' marginalisation. He thus liquidated the Marxist conception of class in order to avoid facing up to the practical problems that the movement faced.

This argument had some precedents in the debates on the far left, particularly in feminist circles. The blindness of workerist politics to questions of women's oppression had prompted some militants to set up women-only organisations, like Lotta Feminista. They were responding to a crudeness on the part of the workerists which mirrored some of the worst elements of their syndicalist predecessors. One Potere Operaio article about women entering the workforce summed up their basic attitude:

> It is about time to stop shedding tears about women's "equality", [which] like every lecture about civil rights is fucked up. Capital has already "equalised" women at Mirafiori, assigning them to the assembly lines.[49]

Essentially, they argued that women simply had to be organised as workers, which meant conveniently that all specific political demands centred around challenging oppression could be ignored.

Mariarosa Dalla Costa's small pamphlet, *The Power of Women and the Subversion of the Community*, pioneered a critique of this framework. In it Dalla Costa set out to demonstrate that in performing domestic labour, women themselves produced surplus value. In doing so, she would be the first of the workerists to advance a case for the claim that the extraction of surplus value could occur outside the process of production. Dalla Costa's revision of Marx was an attempt to remedy the blindness of workerist politics to social relations outside the workplace, but it meant obscuring the central role of the workplace altogether.

This breakthrough laid the basis for Negri to theorise the "social worker", entirely disconnected from the labour process. In Marx's

---

49. Quoted in Wright 2017, p.122.

terms, productive labour is that which produces the surplus value that allows capitalists to accumulate. It is not a moral claim about the social usefulness of any particular form of work, but a crucial economic one: "This distinction between productive and unproductive labour", Marx wrote, "has nothing to do with either the particular speciality of the labour or with the particular use value in which...[it]...is incorporated".[50] Unpaid labour in the home produces use values which enable the reproduction of capital's most important commodity, labour power. This understanding does not downplay domestic labour's importance, as some feminists assume. It clarifies its specific role and importance while demonstrating why those who perform it (mostly women) do not have the potential social power they have in paid work. Profits do not cease flowing if women refuse to perform their domestic duties, even if this might lift a burden from their shoulders.

It is their role at the centre of productive labour which gives the working class its specific social power, its ability to stop the flow of profits on which capitalists rely. While other oppressed and exploited groups are capable of political contestation and disruptive struggle, no other social layer in history has possessed this capacity.

The understandable but flawed feminist criticism of the workerists should have been taken as a challenge to deepen their understanding of the relationship between the industrial working class, other social layers and the role of social oppression – a series of questions they had so far neglected. In the end, they simply adopted the feminist critique of workerism wholesale, before taking it even further, collapsing all distinction between productive and unproductive labour and abandoning one of the essentials of Marxist analysis.

This argument was mirrored by Lotta Continua. One of its leaders spoke of the proletariat as "all those sectors who, having been invested by the strength and content of the workers' struggles over the past few years, have now found, or are beginning to find, their own autonomous growth as a movement as a mass organisation: the unemployed, the state and local government employees, the young people, the soldiers, the social struggle etc".[51]

---

50. Quoted in Harman 2010, p.122.
51. Quoted in Harman 1998, p.344.

So by 1975, workerism, a form of Marxism originally obsessed with a narrow conception of class struggle at the point of production, flipped over into its opposite, a celebration of plurality and the equal strategic validity of all forms of resistance. At a time when struggles were becoming more fragmented, Negri delusionally posited that capitalism itself had brought about a greater level of unity in the working class and massively extended its scope and power. The trajectory of the autonomist-led struggles of the mid-1970s would bluntly refute this hypothesis. While the radical students of 1968 made a priority of connecting their struggles to the workplaces, the generation of the "proletarian youth revolt" of the mid-1970s revelled in politics that were overtly "anti-work", and often anti-worker. By focusing consciously on the liberation *from* labour in contrast to the liberation *of* labour, the political and theoretical emphasis of the workerists provided a bridge between the factory struggles of the late 1960s and these new forms of practice.

The autonomists' most provocative and significant actions centred around demands for more leisure and consumption, liberated from the necessity of labour. *Autoriduzione* became a common practice – using collective pressure and threats to force a reduction in the price of concert and movie tickets. In supermarkets the same process was labelled "proletarian shopping".

The movement proclaimed the "right to luxury" as a contradictory response to the increasingly austerian politics of the mainstream left. Amidst the economic crisis, in October 1976, Communist Party leader Enrico Berlinguer announced a "war on waste...and laxity in work and study", signalling that the PCI would expect workers to bear the brunt of rescuing economic growth. But it also reflected a disturbing drift in the conception of the sort of liberated society the autonomists were fighting for. Steve Wright has written illuminatingly:

> Potere Operaio...explicitly rejected the normative value that Marxists had traditionally assigned to the goal of labour freed from the domination of capital, replacing it with an ethic of consumption unfettered by the dictates of accumulation. Yet if such an approach stemmed from a refusal of that asceticism

which many on the left hoped to impose upon working people, it also drastically simplified the problems involved in reappropriating the wealth produced under the logic of capital. At its worst, the conception of communism and revolutionary struggle which some workerists were to develop during the 1970s can be characterised as a sort of "capitalism without labour".[52]

This perspective was rejected by militants who still maintained that the vision of a communist society was inseparable from a vision of the liberated potential of human labour. The Alfa Romeo Autonomous Assemblies, whose members would quit Autonomia, would write:

> By guaranteed wage we understand the right to life conquered with the guarantee of a job. Because in a communist society, each must contribute according to their abilities and receive from society according to their needs… The comrades of Marghera [Negri's group] say: when all men [sic] are freed from the necessity of labour, because they no longer need to work in order to eat or clothe themselves or satisfy their desires, then we will have true freedom! To this we reply that we are not against labour, but against the capitalist organisation of labour whose end is not social progress but profit… [In the South] the proletarian masses seek to resolve their problems with jobs.[53]

At the extreme end, Negri's theory presented organised workers as a privileged layer holding back a confrontation with capital:

> Some groups of workers, some sections of the working class, remain tied to the dimension of the wage, to its mystified terms. In other words, they are living off income as revenue. Inasmuch, they are stealing and expropriating proletarian surplus-value – they are participating in the social labour racket – on the same terms as their management. These positions – and the trade union practice that fosters them – are to be fought, with violence

---

52. Wright 2017, p.128.
53. Quoted in Wright 2017, p.147.

if necessary. It will not be the first time that a march of the unemployed has entered a large factory so that they can destroy the arrogance of salaried income.[54]

Given this assessment, it is unsurprising that autonomism gradually ceased to be a movement based on workers in the large factories, and became instead a movement of youth and social movement activists.

Goodbye to the revolutionary party
The rejection of a party organisation in favour of "networked" social movements and struggles was a defining feature of autonomism. This too was a direct product of the failure of the workerist groups. During their internal crisis in the early 1970s, Potere Operaio initially moved further towards a tightly centralist model of organisation. This was rejected by many of its militants. Disoriented and torn apart by internal debates about armed struggle, the contradictions of the organisation blew it apart. In late 1973, following the occupation at Mirafiori, Potere Operaio decided to dissolve itself: "We have rejected the logic of the political group in order to be within the real movement, in order to be within organised class autonomy".[55] Potere Operaio's leaders, in liquidating their group, hailed the creation of the "party of Mirafiori". They had seen in the FIAT occupation a model of resistance – an immanent process of creating communism which sidestepped the problems of generalising class consciousness and confronting the state.

Their blindness to these strategic challenges allowed them to insist that the revolutionary party was obsolete. Autonomist Franco Berardi's account of this development is typical, in that it takes for granted an authoritarian model of organisation before rejecting party organisation outright:

> [W]ithin the takeover itself was contained the possibility of transcending those vanguard organizations that had come near to assuming the role traditionally played by the workers'

---
54. Quoted in Fuller 1980.
55. Quoted in Thoburn 2003, p.163.

movement: a role of authoritarian leadership, of bureaucratic intransigence in the face of the passions and the new types of needs expressed.[56]

Within the space of a few short years Lotta Continua would follow suit, dissolving into the social movements in 1976. In practice, the "structurelessness" of the party meant that it inevitably came under the control of a chosen group of political leaders, who were all the more unaccountable for the fact that their positions were not recognised.

Lotta Continua's tensions would come to a head at the Rimini Congress, in the aftermath of the general election of June 1976. The leadership had developed a perspective that the election would be a massive breakthrough for the radical left, allowing them to aid the Communist Party in forming a government which would open up the space for a struggle for workers' power. While the PCI increased its vote, it did so by cannibalising votes from the radical left groups, rather than expanding the left vote as a whole. LC leader Adriano Sofri admitted that by investing hopes in the Communist Party, the leadership had made "the most disastrous error in our history".[57]

The mood of despair generated by the dashing of false hopes created a climate where all sorts of grievances could be raised, fusing together disparate hostility to the party's leadership and organisational methods. This began when women members took the platform after Sofri's opening address, insisting that women meet separately before the congress could resume. Women had been caucusing separately since the previous December, when a contingent of male LC stewards had physically interjected into a women-only demonstration for abortion rights to argue against their exclusion. For the women involved, this had summed up the party's undemocratic, militarist, male culture. The proceedings of the conference then became entirely insular, focused on every group and individual expressing their feelings about their party experience. References to the external political situation, the state of the class struggle, disappeared completely. At the end of the proceedings, Sofri declared

---

56. Berardi 1980, p.51.
57. Harman 1998, p.208.

that it was up to the congress's participants to decide whether Lotta Continua was a project worth salvaging. Within months the organisation had disbanded.

Having failed in their task of providing clarity and a line of march for the movement, it was convenient for the former leaders of the workerist organisations to argue that the entire notion of a party was obsolete. Through the traumatic experience of their crisis and then collapse, thousands of militants from Potere Operaio and Lotta Continua left, and moved into hundreds of smaller activist collectives and autonomist assemblies.

Activists disillusioned with the revolutionary organisations now began to see a "movement of the movements" as an alternative to the stale and repressive structures of the party. The attitude that social struggles needed to be autonomously led on their own terms was recorded in the official notes of LC's Rimini Congress:

> There has developed a just demand that one's own existence and condition in society should be recognised as the basis for one's own participation... This was a demand that arose not only from the women but also from the workers and the young people.[58]

The social movements now increasingly demanded independence not just from the reformist party system and union bureaucracies, but from the revolutionary organisations themselves. This would make it difficult for revolutionaries to find ways to link diffuse struggles, win the movements to strategic positions, or relate them to the central power of the organised working class. The collapse of the revolutionary groups reinforced the fragmentary tendencies within the movement.

Revolutionary counter-power

With the discovery of the "social worker", the "strategy of refusal" described by the workerists was taken to a radically voluntarist conclusion. Instead of focusing on workers at the point of production,

---

58. Red Notes 1978, p.83.

revolutionary change was identified in the process of ordinary people across society rejecting capitalism in their everyday lives. Autonomists described this as the process of developing "counter-power". In the 1960s workerists had spoken of "workers' autonomy" as a process of self-organisation of struggle, separate from unions and political parties. Now "autonomy" was taken to mean that people could organise a new society independently from capitalism.

The "proletarian youth revolt" spread through autonomist spaces that emerged all over the country, from the social centres established through squatting, to the entire networks of "free radio stations". Squatting had begun in the mid-'70s as a method of securing housing for working-class families. By early 1977 it's estimated that the youth of Milan alone had occupied more than 50 buildings, with about 2,000 consistent squatters involved.[59] *Radio Alice* and *Radio Popolare* became Brechtian experiments in socialist mass communication, giving people a voice to share their experiences.

The main goal of these experiments was to carve out small spaces to have experiences "outside" of capitalist exploitation, not to mount an offensive against it. The occupations thus became an end in themselves. As a publication of one of the Milan circles put it:

> We hold festivals because we want to have fun, to be together, to affirm our right to life, to happiness, to a new way of being together. We occupy buildings because we want to have places to meet, to debate, to play music, put on plays, make things up, to have somewhere that's a definite alternative to family life.[60]

Particular importance was attached to "being together", and to the exploration of interpersonal dynamics through consciousness raising. There was a proliferation of photography and music workshops, yoga classes. One particularly low point was the "Proletarian Youth Festival" organised by Lotta Continua and others in June 1976. Rather than a moment of liberation, it more closely resembled the infamous

---

59. Lumley 1990, p.300.
60. Quoted in Edwards 2009, p.76.

Fyre Festival of 2017.⁶¹ Water and sanitation were not provided, power was cut, and food stalls were raided by attendees against the urgings of festival organisers.⁶²

This form of "resistance" could easily find legitimation in Negri's new conception of revolutionary strategy. He wrote:

> The struggle against the capitalist organisation of production, of the job market, of the working day, of the restructuring of energy, of family life, etc., etc., all this involves the people, the community, the choice of lifestyle. To be communist today means *to live as* a communist.⁶³

The autonomist Lucio Castellano argued similarly: "The 'socialist' question…of the proletariat taking political power, is not even posed, because the new power which is emerging has no statist representative, cannot be delegated, cannot be separated from that which it performs".⁶⁴

The notion that a small minority of revolutionaries could begin to build communism in the margins of the capitalist system is at best wishful thinking, at worst deliberate obfuscation. Though autonomists such as Negri and Holloway have time and time again defended these projects as an incipient form of "territorial counter-power", they represented a retreat from serious revolutionary objectives. Even a million occupied apartment buildings and pirate radio stations would still leave capitalist control of the production process and the state intact. Only a powerful movement based at the point of production, and mobilised on the streets to smash the state institutions, can challenge capitalist power.

The high point of autonomist influence coincided with the high point of its internal tensions, in the student revolt of 1977. The movement was spurred in February by a series of proposed education

---

61. The Fyre Festival was supposed to be a glamorous music festival in the Bahamas in April 2017, with luxury accommodation and top-tier talent. However guests arrived to find a shambolic setup, and it was eventually cancelled.
62. Edwards 2009, p.78.
63. Quoted in Callinicos 2001.
64. Castellano 2021, p.463.

reforms which broke with the principle of mass education established in the post-war period. Student occupations and protests swept the country, including a 50,000-strong march in Rome.[65] The movement took a bitter turn on 17 March, when a student demonstrator was shot dead by a policeman in Bologna. That a protester could be killed in the city that was the jewel in the crown of PCI local government left an indelible impression on the students.

What distinguished it from the wave of struggle that began nine years earlier was the gulf that separated the struggling student elements from the mass of workers and the rest of society. While the student movement of 1968 in Italy was popular enough that it had managed to drag a reluctant Communist Party into voicing support, the tide had now turned.

In February 1977, PCI members forced entry into a student occupation at the University of Rome, having concluded that "the resumption of didactic and scientific activity" in the university was "politically essential and essential for democracy".[66] Luciano Lama, head of the CGIL, heavily protected by trade union and PCI stewards, came to address the occupation. Lama was shouted down, and violent clashes broke out between autonomists and the stewards of the PCI. Eventually, riot police cleared out student occupiers to the cheering of PCI members. The Communist Party had retained its hegemony over the left wing of civil society during the upsurge, and was more than willing to use this influence to isolate and marginalise the autonomists, as Bologna noted:

> Now it is to be the factory mass meeting that expels the extremist: the mass tenants' meeting that decides to expel the young hooligan; and the college assembly to expel the "undesirable" student with his pistol and iron bar.[67]

Predictions that the "social worker" would bring about unity in the working class sadly turned out to be wishful thinking, as the movements

---

65. Lumley 1990, p.295.
66. Quoted in Edwards 2009, p.89.
67. Bologna 1980, p.58.

fragmented. As collective social struggle declined, the "liberated areas" fell into crisis. The youth centres, unable to win demands for public funding, either closed down or ended up as the "self-management of misery".[68] Many of the free radio stations confronted the reality of the continued existence of the state, and were cleared out by the police. This downturn hit the left hard across the world. Where revolutionary organisations existed and were able to carry out an orderly retreat, a minority of militants could be sustained through the downturn. But in Italy, most activists saw only two options ahead of them – retreat into their personal lives or to join the growing ranks of the clandestine armed organisations.

"The only path possible is that of attack"

Negri's analysis of the nature of capitalism led to an extremely optimistic assessment of the power of spontaneous struggle. If capitalism itself is bringing on higher forms of unity within the working class and resistance exists everywhere, then there is no need to intervene with tactics and a program. There's no need to weigh the balance of forces, detect weak links in the movement or wage ideological arguments. As Negri put it, delusionally, in the midst of the capitalist counter-offensive:

> [T]he working class, its sabotage, are the stronger power – above all, the only source of rationality and value. From now on it becomes impossible, even in theory, to forget this paradox produced by the struggles: the more the form of domination perfects itself, the more empty it becomes; the more the working class refusal grows, the more it is full of rationality and value... We are here; we are uncrushable; and we are in the majority.[69]

With the ground cut out from under the mass movement, the notion that Potere Operaio had toyed with in the early 1970s – that the militarisation of the struggle was the only path forward – became widespread in Autonomia. The years of hope which characterised the

---
68. Lumley 1990, p.307.
69. Quoted in Wright 2017, pp.159–60.

late 1960s and early '70s ticked over into the *anni di piombo*, the years of lead.

Political violence, or at least its invocation, had featured as an element of the struggles since the Piazza Statuto in 1962. Violent reprisals against hated managers, foremen and even conservative white-collar workers had featured in the euphoria of the industrial upturn. A favourite chant of the striking and occupying FIAT workers was "Agnelli, Indochina is in your factory", referencing the guerrilla struggle in Vietnam.

Even the Red Brigades, who would become the most notorious of the clandestine terrorist organisations, had begun in 1970 as an auxiliary support for the struggles in the factories. Its founding members were participants of the Hot Autumn, and their early actions consisted of monitoring suspected "bosses' agents" among the workforce, distributing advice on sabotaging production, beating up foremen and burning their cars.

Their principle aim, however, was spelled out in the bulletin *Sinistra Proletaria*:

> It is time to move ahead to a general confrontation in order to establish the principle among the proletarian masses in struggle that "no one has political power unless they have military power"; to educate the proletarian and revolutionary Left to the need for resistance and partisan actions; to unmask the oppressive and repressive power structures that divide the class.[70]

This perspective contained a logic of escalation which led directly from small-scale kidnappings and interrogations of factory managers in 1972, all the way to the infamous capture and execution of former prime minister Aldo Moro in 1978. These methods, which in the early 1970s were often denounced, or at best tolerated on the margins of the movement, came to exert a serious influence by the latter half of the decade. There are a few related reasons for this development.

---

70. Quoted in Lumley 1990, p.282.

Firstly, while fears of a reactionary coup had receded into the background by the mid-'70s, the state resorted to heavy repression in response to the movement of 1977. On 11 March Pier Francesco Lorusso, a militant associated with Lotta Continua, was shot dead by police in Bologna.[71] Two days later the student occupation at Bologna University was cleared with the use of armoured cars.[72] That this could take place in Bologna, where the PCI now governed as the party of "law and order", impressed upon many radicals the need to confront the state openly. Tragically, a series of futile reprisals against the police only encouraged further state repression, which led to the murder of several more radicals in the following months.

Secondly, political violence took on an increasingly substitutionist character, and was seen as a necessity amidst the despair and confusion that followed the defeat of the movement of 1977. As one interview with a Red Brigade member recounted: "We came out of '77 in good shape... At the same time, we could see that those people who had made different choices didn't know what the hell to do any more; from the first of January 1978, they didn't know what to do".[73]

Armed activity peaked alongside the suppression of the mass movements – the great bulk of it took place between 1977 and 1980. Just a fortnight after the occupation of the University of Rome, a demonstration of some 60,000 young people in the capital degenerated into a four-hour guerrilla battle with police. Shots were fired on both sides, and some of the demonstrators chanted a slogan in praise of the P38 pistol, the chosen weapon of the *Autonomi*. Thousands of autonomist activists were initially willing to throw themselves behind clandestine activity, joining the myriad armed splinter groups which emerged. Their methods rapidly led to marginalisation and fed a cycle of state repression further isolating them from the working class. Increasingly, a high proportion of their activity was indistinguishable from conventional criminal activity with little or no connection to broader social objectives: bank robberies, kidnapping, extortion and gunfights with the police.

---

71. Lumley 1990, p.295.
72. Edwards 2009, p.139.
73. Edwards 2009, p.175.

Lastly, the autonomists tended to endorse the Red Brigades' conception of violence as *the* key weapon in the class struggle, and joined them in urging an immediate confrontation with the state. This was the logical conclusion of their political perspective of a constantly escalating revolutionary struggle. While Negri disagreed with the Red Brigades' conception of a single centralised proletarian army ("The BR don't believe in the 'hundred flowers' of armed struggle. One flower is plenty"[74]), he hailed spontaneous violence as inherently constructive. As always, plying the trade of the theorist, Negri was able to dress this reactionary nonsense in pseudo-Marxist language, claiming that violence was the only way to generate the class unity necessary to overthrow capitalism:

> [T]he armed struggle represents the only fundamental strategic moment – ie, the only possibility of achieving a recomposition of the proletariat and a consolidation of the struggles, and destroying, along the way, capital's weapons of provocation, of repression and containment that are designed to isolate and newly compartmentalise the various class sectors.[75]

Autonomists thus tended to fetishise illegality as the yardstick for any movement's revolutionary character, rather than the political consciousness of the masses who participated in it.

The state adopted an increasingly intransigent approach toward these methods, with the support of the PCI. In 1979 a Communist Party-aligned judge issued warrants for the arrest of a dozen leading autonomists, including Negri, on false accusations of collusion with the Red Brigades.[76] In the wave of recriminations and mass arrests that followed more than 3,000 radicals were imprisoned, leading some to claim that Italy contained the largest population of political prisoners outside the USSR.

Assisted by a state more than willing to deal out brutal repression and a weakened and divided left, the capitalist class was able to stabilise

---

74. Edwards 2009, p.62.
75. Wright 2017, p.159.
76. Edwards 2009, p.185.

Italian society in the 1980s. Using the ostensible threat posed to Italy's republic by the "extremist" movement as an excuse, the PCI moved to explicit collaboration with the Christian Democrats. In what PCI leader Berlinguer referred to as the "historic compromise", the party gave support to a series of Christian Democrat governments even as they implemented brutal austerity, and provided cover for the repression of the remnants of the radical left.

The last decisive showdown of the Hot Autumn was at Fiat Mirafiori in Turin, the heart of the Hot Autumn. In 1979, Fiat succeeded in sacking 61 militants in the plant, accusing them of having participated in violence during the struggles of the preceding decade. By the early 1980s FIAT had managed to sack 23,000 workers there, including the leading radicals, in the worst working-class defeat since the Second World War,[77] which opened up space for a new economic boom based on a huge decline in working-class living standards. Increasingly detached from any connection to the factory, and isolated by their own clandestine methods, the autonomists had little to offer these struggling workers.

The autonomists' emphasis on hyper-militant tactics organised by an elite minority had led the workers' movement on the path to the worst industrial defeat of the post-war period. By this time, autonomism mainly exerted influence to the extent that it encouraged mindless militancy, an approach which mitigated against a serious reckoning with the disaster of the late 1970s.

Autonomism and revolutionary politics today

Autonomism has repeatedly re-emerged as an influential set of politics in radical movements – from the struggles in Latin America in the 1990s, the anti-capitalist movement of the early 2000s and movements like the Indignados in Spain in 2011. It has tended to gain popularity in places where the "traditional left" has been discredited by the experiences of reformism and Stalinism. Autonomist politics have thrived where the working class has failed to assert its leadership over movements for social change.

---

77. Callinicos 2001.

Autonomism jettisoned what was undoubtedly the best feature of workerism – its focus on the working class as the only force capable of exercising the social power necessary to challenge capitalism. The politics of autonomism can be best understood as a substitutionist response to the crisis of the radical left in mid-1970s Italy. Instead of realising that the struggle had reached an impasse and that deeper strategic debates were necessary for revolutionaries to survive, they searched for a new shortcut to revolutionary advance. They were willing to abandon working-class agency and revolutionary organisation, to chase all sorts of fads, in order to avoid confronting tough realities about the situation they faced. The actions championed by the autonomists, whether the squatting and fare evasion of the "marginali" or armed terror, were doomed attempts to compensate for a working class that was seen as no longer revolutionary.

Since the 1970s, Negri has been championed by the postmodernist academic milieu. His own intellectual contribution has assisted in giving a left-wing gloss to anti-Marxist and fundamentally conservative theory. His work encourages people to contemplate the existence of "figures" of resistance unmoored from an analysis of the structures of capitalist production. Negri's own search for a new immanently revolutionary social subject who can sidestep the project of winning masses of people to a conscious socialist project continues to this day. In his 2019 essay "Empire, Twenty Years On", Negri writes: "migration constitutes a major force of internationalism and an ongoing insurrection against the border regimes of nation-states and the spatial hierarchies of the global system".[78] Refugees are assigned the role of the new proletariat, whether they are conscious of this or not.

Turning away from the working class made it impossible for the autonomists of the 1970s to develop a coherent and viable revolutionary strategy. Autonomists then vacillated between ignoring state power or attempting to confront it head on. The baleful legacy of these politics continues to shape the left to this day. Lifestylist solutions to capitalism – like squatting, dumpster-diving and veganism on the one

---

78. Negri and Hardt 2019.

hand, and the individualised violence of "black blocs" on the other – both belong to the heritage of autonomism.

One influential expression of this heritage is John Holloway's *Change the World Without Taking Power*, a book which cut with the grain of the anti-capitalist movement at the turn of the twenty-first century. Holloway's autonomist-inspired world view rejects the traditional revolutionary objective of capturing state power, in favour of creating new ways of living in the "cracks" of capitalism. For Holloway, this could mean anything from gardening, to composing music, to spending time with your kids. Virtually the only practice which he considers incapable of pointing toward an alternative to capitalism is collective working-class struggle for better wages and conditions, insisting that: "to take wage labour (or simply labour) as the basis of the anti-capitalist movement is quite simply to entrap that movement within capital".[79]

In focusing on the politics of separate organising, of lifestyle, difference and marginality, many of the themes developed by autonomists would prefigure contemporary liberal identity politics. The Italian autonomist Lucio Castellano wrote in 1980:

> Blacks, women, young people, the elderly, gays: national, professional, linguistic and religious minorities: what dominated the "movement" over these years was the search for a "non-political" identity that centred on a difference to be recognised and respected, on the basis of which to negotiate spaces for the management of resource.[80]

To combat these politics and develop movements capable of winning power for the working class, we need to learn from the failures of the workerists. The workerists took a decisive step, challenging the bureaucratic reformism of the Italian Communist Party and rediscovering the centrality of struggle to the socialist movement. But importantly, they never developed an understanding of reformist consciousness, and they abdicated their responsibility to challenge

---
79. Quoted in Blackledge 2012.
80. Castellano 2021, pp.465–66.

reformists for leadership of the class's struggles. This led them on a path to abandoning the working class, their own revolutionary organisations, and the objective of a socialist society in its entirety. To win socialism, revolutionaries need to be able to prove the superiority of their political approach in every arena, from the workplaces to the streets, by connecting day-to-day struggles against exploitation and oppression to the ultimate goal of overturning the capitalist system.

References

Berardi, Franco 1980, "Anatomy of Autonomy", in *Autonomia: Post-political Politics*, Sylvère Lotringer and Christian Marazzi (eds), Semiotext(e).

Blackledge, Paul 2012, "Holloway in Perspective", *International Socialism*, 136, Autumn. http://isj.org.uk/in-perspective-john-holloway/

Blackmer, Donald LM 1977, "Continuity and Change in Post-war Italian Communism", in *Communism in Italy and France*, Donald LM Blackmer and Sidney Tarrow (eds), Princeton University Press.

Bloodworth, Sandra 2014, "Lenin and a theory of revolution for the West", *Marxist Left Review*, 8, Winter. https://marxistleftreview.org/articles/lenin-and-a-theory-of-revolution-for-the-west/

Bologna, Sergio 1980, "The Tribe of Moles", in *Autonomia: Post-political Politics*, Sylvère Lotringer and Christian Marazzi (eds), Semiotext(e).

Castellano, Lucio 2021, "Autonoma, Autonomies", in *The Golden Horde: Revolutionary Italy 1960–1977*, Nanni Balestrini and Primo Moroni (eds), Seagull Books.

Callinicos, Alex 2001, "Toni Negri in Perspective", *International Socialism*, 92, Autumn. https://www.marxists.org/history/etol/writers/callinicos/2001/xx/toninegri.htm

Edwards, Phil 2009, *More Work! Less Pay! Rebellion and Repression in Italy 1972–7*, Manchester University Press.

Foot, John 2003, *Modern Italy*, Palgrave Macmillan.

Fuller, Jack 1980, "The New Workerism", *International Socialism*, 8, Spring. https://www.marxists.org/history/etol/newspape/isj2/1980/no2-008/fuller.htm

Georgakas, Dan (ed.) 1971, "Italy: New Tactics and Organization", in *Radical America*, 5 (5), September/October. https://files.libcom.org/files/ItalyNewTactics&Organization.pdf

Ginsborg, Paul 1990, *A History of Contemporary Italy*, Penguin Books.

Harman, Chris 1998, *The Fire Last Time*, Bookmarks Publications.

Harman, Chris 2010, *Zombie Capitalism: Global Crisis and the Relevance of Marx*, Haymarket Books.

Lotringer, Sylvère and Christian Marazzi 1980, "The Return of Politics", in *Autonomia: Post-political Politics*, Sylvère Lotringer and Christian Marazzi (eds), Semiotext(e).

Lumley, Robert 1990, *States of Emergency: Cultures of Revolt in Italy from 1968 to 1978*, Verso.

Mohandesi, Salar 2013, "Class Consciousness or Class Composition?", in *Science & Society*, 77 (1), January. https://www.scienceandsociety.com/contents_jan13.pdf

Negri, Antonio 1984, *Marx beyond Marx: Lessons on the Grundrisse*, Bergin & Garvey.

Negri, Antonio and Michael Hardt 2019, "Empire, Twenty Years On", *New Left Review*, 120, November/December. https://newleftreview.org/issues/ii120/articles/empire-twenty-years-on

Red Notes 1978, *Italy 1977–8: Living With An Earthquake*, December. https://files.libcom.org/files/IMG-Italy1977-8-Red%20Notes.pdf

Thoburn, Nicholas 2003, *Deleuze, Marx and Politics*, Routledge.

Tronti, Mario 2019, *Workers and Capital*, Verso.

Wright, Steven 2017, *Storming Heaven: Class Composition and Struggle in Autonomist Marxism*, Pluto Press.

MICK ARMSTRONG

The sixties radicalisation and the emergence of Trotskyism on the Australian left

Mick Armstrong is the author of numerous pamphlets and articles on revolutionary organisation and the Australian labour movement, including *The Industrial Workers of the World in Australia*, *The Labor Party: A Marxist analysis* and (with Tom Bramble) *The Fight for Workers' Power: Revolution and Counter-Revolution in the 20th Century*.

From the Great Depression right up until the 1970s, the organised revolutionary left in Australia was tiny. The remnants of the once powerful revolutionary syndicalist Industrial Workers of the World (IWW) had withered away by the late 1920s, as had the various pre-Communist socialist groups, and it was not until May 1933 that the first very small Trotskyist organisation was formed in Sydney. Even then, the Trotskyists found it very difficult to make headway in the face of the much larger Stalinist forces of the Communist Party of Australia (CPA).

The CPA was never a mass party on the scale of the French or Italian Communist Parties. However in proportion to population it was for much of its history the largest in the English-speaking world. The CPA built a sizeable implantation in the unions and entrenched itself among sections of the trade union bureaucracy. Its Stalinist ideas also had a strong influence on the outlook of the Labor left. From the mid-1930s onwards the CPA's world view also had a significant impact on middle-class liberal and cultural circles. Broadly speaking, most people who saw themselves as left-wing viewed Russia positively as a genuine socialist society, and had top-down conceptions of social change. All of this meant, when combined with their own political mistakes, that Trotskyist groups throughout this period consisted of tiny isolated circles with a national membership of never more than 40–50 and by the mid-to-late 1960s considerably less than that.

So the new revolutionary currents that emerged out of the radicalisation of the late sixties and early seventies were to a large extent starting from scratch. The overwhelmingly young and inexperienced revolutionaries had next to no living Marxist tradition to build on. The connections with the genuinely revolutionary politics of Lenin's Bolsheviks and the early Communist International had been decisively broken. To the extent that faint echoes of that revolutionary tradition still survived, they were distorted by Stalinist muck that negatively impacted even many of those who saw themselves as rejecting Stalinism. There were of course a few revolutionary books available, such as Trotsky's *History of the Russian Revolution* and Lenin's *State and Revolution*. But there was not much else other than the hard to access publications of various small overseas Trotskyist groups. Even these were unreliable: in a number of cases these organisations had degenerated in a sectarian direction due to long years of isolation from the working-class movement and under the weight of Stalinist hegemony on the left.

So the young revolutionaries were faced with the major challenges of laying the basic foundations of new socialist groups at the same time as they were rapidly attempting to clarify their ideas on all the fundamentals of Marxism, and on a series of immediate political questions such as the Vietnam War, party structure and innumerable tactical and strategic issues. All of this in the context of a mass radicalisation that produced a hothouse atmosphere of bitter debates in the student and anti-war movements with rival Stalinist, reformist, pacifist, anarchist and liberal forces.

No wonder then that there were all sorts of mistakes, false starts and dead ends. New revolutionary groups quickly arose and then seemed to disappear overnight. There was no shortage of splits, over-polarised faction fights, sectarianism and bad behaviour. Cynics on the left would even at the time dismiss the various attempts to build small revolutionary organisations as a futile or even counterproductive exercise. I strongly differ.

There are no guarantees in politics, but a start had to be made somewhere to begin to build a clear-cut revolutionary alternative to the ALP, the CPA and the union bureaucracy. Given the minuscule size of the revolutionary left going into the radicalisation, that was never going to be an easy task. But the effort needed to be made. Many of the young revolutionaries undoubtedly were overly impatient, and had grand expectations about their ability to build a mass party virtually overnight. But expectations could only be tempered by actually trying to build. Political ideas and strategies and methods of organisation had to be developed and tested out in practice on the political battlefield. Lessons had to be learnt and experience gained. Debates had to be had out and organisational conclusions drawn. We in Socialist Alternative would like to modestly claim that we have learned much that is positive from those experiences which will help us play a part in laying the basis for a much more serious revolutionary organisation in the future.

Some on the left who disparage the "sectarian debates" of small revolutionary groups would argue that instead of attempting to build straightforward revolutionary organisations, a better alternative would have been to build a broader and looser socialist organisation open to both revolutionaries and reformists. I have made the case elsewhere that broad left parties are not a substitute for a clearly defined revolutionary organisation, as they are simply incapable of offering a fundamental challenge to capitalism.[1] I won't rehash that argument here except to point out that in Australia in the 1960s and 1970s there were numerous attempts made to build broad left formations of various descriptions, both inside and outside the ALP. Their track record was one of disaster piled upon disaster. They have all collapsed and left no positive legacy. They were wracked, but even more so and with a few added ones thrown in, with all the vices that supposedly only afflict small Trotskyist groups – sectarian wrangling, highly charged walkouts and bitter splits, a serious lack of democracy, grandstanding, authoritarian guru-style leaders, the stacking of meetings, gross political opportunism, get-rich-quick schemes and more than the occasional punch-up between factional opponents.

---

1. See Armstrong 2018 and 2014 and also Percy 2013.

The sixties radicalisation

As I will focus on the emergence of the new Trotskyist currents out of the sixties/seventies radicalisation I need to briefly say something about the period itself. Though not as intense a radicalisation, this was the most prolonged period of mass radicalisation internationally since the immediate aftermath of the 1917 Russian Revolution.[2] In Australia the radicalisation began on the campuses in roughly 1964/65. It quickly became focused around opposition to conscription and the Vietnam War, with the anti-war movement peaking in about 1970 with the inspiring and hugely controversial Moratorium marches. In the intervening years the movement had moved sharply to the left and been polarised politically. The defeat of Labor in the November 1966 elections and its subsequent retreat from its anti-war stance under the new right-wing leadership of Gough Whitlam was an important turning point. Young activists moved to the left, seeing parliamentarism as useless and began, as one account puts it, "to grope for revolutionary alternatives to the time-honoured institutions of the bourgeoisie".[3]

Anti-war sentiment was not, however, simply confined to the campuses. As early as May 1965, a Gallup opinion poll revealed that 37 percent of the population opposed sending Australian troops to Vietnam, and over the next five years a majority of the population (and an even larger majority of the working class) came to oppose the war.[4] Students played a pivotal role in the vibrant anti-war street protests. But this intersected with and reinforced a working-class industrial rebellion which got seriously underway in 1968 and continued into the mid-1970s.[5] It was not until the late seventies that the political radicalisation had been fully contained – the last throw of the dice being the mass civil liberties campaign in Queensland against the Bjelke Petersen government's ban on street marches.[6]

Students, both university and high school, played a much greater role in this period of revolt than in previous eras. In part this reflected

---

2. For an overview of the international revolt see Harman 1988.
3. Melbourne Revolutionary Marxists 1975, p.5.
4. Hastings 2002, pp.22 and 40.
5. For the student revolt see Armstrong 2001, Hastings 2002, Russell 1998 and Percy 2005. For the working-class upsurge see Bramble 2008, Parts 1 and 2.
6. For the Queensland civil liberties campaign see Ferrier and Grassie 1978/79.

the massive increase worldwide in student numbers. The students were the shock troops of the anti-war movement, shouldering the bulk of the mass building work. For example in the lead-up to the first Moratorium march in Adelaide, 400 mostly student campaigners leafleted "almost all of the Adelaide metropolitan area and ten country towns. In all, 90% of the state was leafleted and 500,000 leaflets were produced".[7]

The students brought with them all the virtues and vices of youth and of their specific social location as students – idealism, moral outrage and the capacity to rapidly grab hold of new ideas and move seemingly spontaneously into action. On the other hand they did not have anything like the social power of workers to fundamentally challenge the capitalist system, or even the capacity to maintain stable organisations. Their idealism could at times turn into a rampant moralism and voluntarism that had a destructive political impact.

The Origlass group

I will use a broad definition of Trotskyism to include all the currents that saw themselves as revolutionary Marxists in the tradition of Lenin and Trotsky; that defended the 1917 Bolshevik Revolution and the early revolutionary years of the Communist International; that opposed the Stalinist counter-revolution in Russia and opposed the parliamentary road to socialism and popular fronts. This definition encompasses both the so-called orthodox Trotskyists who viewed Stalinist Russia as a degenerated workers' state and those currents that saw Stalinist Russia as dominated by a new bureaucratic ruling class, whether that be state capitalist or bureaucratic collectivist.

The first Australian organisation that called itself Trotskyist – the Workers Party (Left Opposition) of Australia – was formed in May 1933 as a revolutionary rival to the thoroughly Stalinised Communist Party. It was a tiny Sydney-based organisation made up largely of activists from the unemployed movement of the Depression years who had been in or around the CPA. The initial leading figure was former CPA Central Committee member Jack Sylvester, a leader of the Unemployed

---

7. Hastings 2002, p.42.

Workers Movement and the CPA's small Workers Defence Corps, who had been expelled from the CPA in 1932.

The Workers Party was far from being politically clear, let alone fully Trotskyist, at its formation, having not entirely broken with the CPA's wildly sectarian Third Period Stalinism. Australian revolutionaries had been largely isolated from developments in the world Communist movement and the emergence of the Left Opposition to Stalinism. The only connection those rebelling against the Stalinist control of the CPA had with the international Trotskyist movement in the early 1930s was the arrival of copies of the US Trotskyist paper the *Militant*. The lack of political clarity fostered splits and divisions that were sharply accentuated by the failure of the Workers Party (renamed the Communist League of Australia in 1938) to break out and win the mass working-class influence which Sylvester and the other militants who formed it had hoped for. A series of political mistakes – both by the international Trotskyist movement and the Australian comrades – further compounded their isolation.

From the late 1930s through to the mid-1960s the dominant figure in the tiny Trotskyist circles in Australia was Nick Origlass.[8] Origlass was a serious blue-collar working-class militant. Alongside other Trotskyist militants, including Laurie Short, he led an important strike in the ship repair yards of Balmain during World War II in defiance of the pro-war class-collaborationist Stalinist leadership of the Ironworkers Union and established a significant profile in Sydney's then heavily working-class Balmain.[9] However the Trotskyists were not able to recruit and caderise a significant membership out of the industrial struggles in which they were involved during the war and the immediate post-war industrial upsurge.

At the end of World War II the Trotskyists organised internationally in the Fourth International (FI), founded in 1938, believed that a worldwide revolutionary wave would enable them to sweep aside both the Stalinist Communist Parties and the reformist social democratic parties and win the leadership of the working-class movement. But this overblown perspective failed to eventuate, both in Australia and

---

8. For a biography of Origlass see Greenland 1998.
9. Gollan 1972.

internationally. In the more right-wing climate that developed as the Cold War between the US and Russia intensified, some of Origlass's close collaborators, most notably Laurie Short, moved sharply to the right. Short eventually defeated the Communists to become the right-wing leader of the Ironworkers Union in 1952.[10]

By the mid-1950s the Trotskyists were reduced to essentially a loose friendship circle of older blue-collar militants and an occasional lawyer or middle-class intellectual around Nick Origlass. According to Denis Freney, who after leaving the Communist Party joined the Origlass group in 1957, it had a grand total of just 12 members nationwide, with virtually no activity outside Balmain. Its only publication in the mid-1950s was irregularly produced and hard to read, being produced on an ancient roneo machine. It contained a few pieces on Australian politics but mainly consisted of articles written by the Greek leader of the Fourth International, Michel Pablo, that had been badly translated from French by Origlass. They also occasionally produced a small roneoed newsletter for the group's activities inside the ALP.[11]

All of this severely limited the group's ability to make any serious gains out of the turmoil in the CPA provoked by the crushing of the 1956 Hungarian workers' revolution by Russian tanks and new Russian leader Nikita Khrushchev's secret speech denouncing Stalin.[12] Dissident CPers were not enchanted by meetings consisting of hours-long monologues from Origlass and an organisation whose activity was at best sporadic, with no regular readable paper or magazine. Bob Gould and subsequently Freney were two of the very few ex-CPers who joined the Origlass group in the immediate aftermath of Hungary. A bit later one or two others joined.

In the late 1950s probably more ex-CPers were won to Trotskyism, or at least to the Healyite version of it, by a lone individual, Gavin Kennedy, who was briefly in Australia, than by the Origlass group. Kennedy, a precocious 16-year-old with considerable flair and

---

10. The political biography of Short by his daughter Susanna is well worth reading. Short 1992.
11. Freney 1991, p.92.
12. See Birchall 1974 and Harman 1974.

energy, had been a member of the British Trotskyist group headed by Gerry Healy, which from 1959 was known as the Socialist Labour League (SLL). However according to John Percy this group, which included the future NSW Labor MP George Petersen, "disintegrated, partly as a result of the bureaucratic and authoritarian practices of Healy's SLL becoming more apparent, and also because Kennedy had returned to Britain".[13] In 1960 the tiny remnants of the Healyite group united with the Origlass group.

Compounding the various political problems and the lack of growth of the Origlass group (by the 1960s known as the International group) was the impact of long-term entry work in the ALP from 1941. By May 1958 Origlass had become a Labor councillor in Balmain and he was soon joined by his close comrade Issy Wyner. There was a gradual adaption to these reformist circles. Indeed by the 1960s for many Australian Trotskyists (and not just those aligned with Origlass) membership of the ALP had become something of an article of faith. A number of them simply engaged in what was derisively called "resolutionary socialism" – passing worthy left-wing resolutions in ALP branch meetings which were then filed in the appropriate rubbish bin at head office – a practice which masked their failure to actively build a genuinely revolutionary opposition to Laborism.

Origlass proved to be one of the most dedicated supporters of the international Trotskyist current associated with Michel Pablo, loyally following him through all the splits and divisions in the Trotskyist movement. In the early 1950s Pablo, then the Secretary of the Fourth International, had moved sharply to the right, greatly softening his opposition to Stalinism. He argued that Trotskyists had to accept that there would be centuries of Stalinist "worker states". He called for a liquidationist perspective of burying the Trotskyist forces in long-term entry work, be it in the Stalinist CPs or the social democratic parties or the petty-bourgeois nationalist parties in the global south, whichever was the largest force. This project of entrism *sui generis* (entrism of a special kind) was not aimed at establishing revolutionary parties in opposition to the Stalinist Communist Parties, but was merely an

---

13. Percy 2005, p.41. See also Greenland 1998, pp.222–26.

attempt to influence them in a supposedly progressive direction. Pablo argued that under the growing threat of imperialist war the Stalinists would be forced to turn left.[14]

Despite initially going along with much of Pablo's program, not all of the orthodox Trotskyists (the current that saw Russia as a degenerated workers' state) were prepared to go all the way down this thoroughly liquidationist pro-Stalinist road. The supporters of the US Socialist Workers Party (SWP) headed by James P Cannon split away from the International Secretariat of the FI, forming the International Committee of the FI. Cannon was backed by smaller groupings around Gerry Healy in Britain (which previously had buried itself deep inside the Labour Party), Pierre Lambert in France and Nahuel Moreno in Latin America.

However by the early 1960s a number of Pablo's previous supporters, including the Belgian Trotskyist Ernest Mandel, Pierre Frank in France and Livio Maitan in Italy were moving towards a reunification with the US SWP, then the largest Trotskyist group other than the Sri Lankan Lanka Sama Samaja Party (LSSP) which by then had politically collapsed into reformism. Various political differences had opened up among the formerly united Pabloite bloc, including over what attitude to take to the growing dispute in the international communist movement between Khrushchev's Russia and Mao's China. Mandel and Maitan were for a period enthusiastic supporters of Mao, while Pablo adopted an increasingly pro-Russian standpoint, even supporting Russian nuclear testing. In Australia Origlass called for critical support for Khrushchev and was increasingly sympathetic to the CPA.[15] By 1965 Pablo was supporting a market economy in a supposedly "self-managed socialist society".[16] Pablo bitterly opposed the reunification and was eventually expelled from the FI in December 1965. Origlass's tiny group was one of the very few that stuck with Pablo.

In the early 1960s in Australia a few younger people were attracted to Trotskyism. These new forces, along with some of the former members of the Healyite group, proved to be a problem for Origlass as

---

14. Hallas 2003.
15. Greenland 1998, p.234.
16. Freney 1991, p.397.

they threatened his support for Pablo and ongoing control of the group. In 1964 the International group, which then had roughly 30 members, divided pretty much down the middle between Origlass supporters and a disparate opposition bloc. The oppositionists, including Bob Gould and Roger Barnes, were critical of Origlass's highly personalised style of operation and of some elements of Pablo's liquidationist politics. However they were neither able nor seriously willing to build a coherent revolutionary organisation with clear political lines of demarcation when it came to membership. Their continuing commitment to fairly conservative long-term entry work in the ALP was but one reflection of their rather swampy centrist politics.

The CPA fractures and opportunities open up

By the late 1960s the Stalinist monolith was fracturing. Rivalry between Russia and China for control of the world Communist movement led to a smallish, largely Melbourne-based Maoist split from the CPA forming in 1964 the Communist Party of Australia (Marxist Leninist) – CPA (ML). The 1968 Russian invasion of Czechoslovakia was to provoke a further split by pro-Moscow loyalists hostile to the CPA's criticism of the invasion.

Accentuating the CPA's crisis was the fact that the party was initially sidelined by the youth rebellion sweeping the campuses and high schools and impacting young workers. The dull grey authoritarianism of Stalinist Russia had little appeal to this new radicalising generation. Moreover the CPA and the mainstream peace groups it influenced initially took a conservative stance in the anti-war movement, opposing calls for the unilateral withdrawal of US and Australian troops. The CPA's slogan was the pathetic "Stop the bombing, negotiate". This was to the right of the position of the ALP in the November 1966 elections, which under the leadership of Arthur Calwell called for the withdrawal of Australian troops. When, in the wake of its electoral defeat, Labor dumped Calwell for the more right-wing Gough Whitlam, the CPA endorsed their decision to abandon support for the withdrawal of Australian troops. The CPA increasingly came across as fuddy-duddy conservatives to many student radicals. These new activists were influenced by countercultural ideas and the

May '68 revolt in France. Their approach combined militant street protests and campus occupations with often strident moralism and wild ultra-left rhetoric.

This opened up space for a diverse assortment of leftish currents – initially Labor-aligned groups like the Youth Campaign Against Conscription and the Vietnam Day Committee, then a bit later, groups more independent from Labor with liberal libertarian politics – on a number of campuses: Students for a Democratic Society (SDS) inspired by SDS in the United States, in Brisbane the Society for Democratic Action and in Adelaide Students for Democratic Action. As well there emerged young Maoists inspired by the Chinese Cultural Revolution, New Leftists, anarchists and currents influenced by Trotskyism. The traditional Labor Clubs (which were independent from the ALP and had commonly been strongly influenced by the CPA) had an explosion of membership on a few campuses, with new forces emerging from them, the most prominent example being the Maoists at Monash. By the late sixties and early seventies there was a multitude of collectives, organising centres and radical discussion groups with diverse politics.

In Sydney in 1965 Bob Gould, Mairi Gould, Ian Macdougall and a few of the others who had split from Origlass formed the Vietnam Action Committee (VAC). The VAC outflanked the CPA and the peace establishment by organising more radical demonstrations against the war, including against the 1966 tour of US President Lyndon Baines Johnson. It attracted a leftish milieu including Sydney University student John Percy and his younger brother Jim, who were evolving towards Trotskyism.[17] In 1967 Gould and the Percys launched Resistance – a broad socialist youth group to the left of the CPA. Resistance, though influenced by Trotskyism, was also impacted by anarchist, Third Worldist, countercultural and Maoist ideas. The controversial Third World bookshop in Goulburn St became a key organising centre for radical youth activism in Sydney.

The Percys argued for a more organised and explicitly Trotskyist group. In what was to become a common pattern, they had come

---

17. Percy 2005, pp.64–66.

under the influence of the US Socialist Workers Party. The lack of a serious local Trotskyist tradition and the relative intellectual poverty of the broader Australian left understandably meant that young proto-Trotskyists tended to look for inspiration, a political program and a practical orientation to more established overseas Trotskyist groups, especially those in Britain and the US, and to a lesser extent France. This proved to be something of a mixed blessing. It distorted the development of a number of groups by importing international factional battles that they were ill-prepared to deal with. As well there was a tendency to ape the approach of the larger overseas group on even quite narrow tactical and organisational questions which were not of local relevance or easily generalised.

Despite his formal adherence to Trotskyism, Gould for three years fought the Percys' push to establish an explicitly Trotskyist organisation. Gould formed an unprincipled alliance with semi-anarchist and countercultural types in an attempt to maintain Resistance as a fairly loose swampy outfit. But by 1970 when Resistance split, the time for broad, politically ill-defined socialist youth groups was passing. The radicalisation had significantly deepened and a layer of young would-be revolutionaries were looking for more coherent politics and organisations. There had been years of increasingly militant struggles on the campuses and on the streets against the Vietnam War and a range of other issues. By the late sixties the working class was beginning to move into action in Australia and internationally – highlighted by the May '68 revolt in France and the general strikes in Australia in 1969 to free jailed union official Clarrie O'Shea.[18] The US was losing the war in Vietnam and riots were engulfing the Black ghettos of US cities. Politics had become a lot more serious. There was a sense of urgency. For the young radicals, revolution seemed to be on the immediate agenda.

At the same time, the counterculture that initially had helped fuel the youth rebellion against the social and sexual conservatism of the Cold War years was now being co-opted by capitalist commercialism. As the class struggle picked up and politics became more contested

---

18. Wood 2013.

and polarised, the counterculture increasingly became an obstacle – organising "down to earth" festivals, getting back to nature on a hippy commune and spending half of your time stoned was directly counterposed to serious political action to challenge capitalism.

In August 1970 the Percy-led majority in Resistance founded the Trotskyist Socialist Youth Alliance (SYA) at a conference attended by 45 comrades predominantly from Sydney. Subsequently in 1972 the "adult" organisation, the Socialist Workers League (SWL), was established, laying the basis for what was to become the Socialist Workers Party, later the Democratic Socialist Party and then Socialist Alliance (though the latter abandoned revolutionary politics and disavowed Trotskyism) and also for the Revolutionary Socialist Party that was later to fuse with Socialist Alternative.

The delay until 1970 in forming an explicitly Trotskyist organisation (other than the remnants of Origlass's International group) meant that major opportunities to build a serious revolutionary socialist organisation out of the initial years of the radical upsurge had been missed. A personal example: in 1968 I was a 17-year-old from a blue-collar working-class family starting at Melbourne University. I had identified as an anti-Stalinist socialist for some years; had read Trotsky's *History of the Russian Revolution* at school and was further inspired by the May '68 revolt in France. But there was no Trotskyist organisation in Melbourne I could join. There was no revolutionary socialist newspaper that I could have bought even as late as May 1970 at the massive Moratorium march against the Vietnam War. It was not until September 1970 that the first edition of the Socialist Youth Alliance's paper *Direct Action* came out, just in time for the second round of Moratorium marches when it sold extremely well in Melbourne, Sydney and Adelaide.

The delay in establishing a revolutionary Marxist organisation allowed space for other currents to grow out of the radicalisation. In Melbourne and a bit later Adelaide the main force to the left of the CPA in the late sixties and early seventies was the Maoists. Inspired by the Chinese Cultural Revolution – mistakenly seen as a radical anti-bureaucratic revolt – and Mao Zedong's proclamation that "It is right to rebel", young student Maoists waving their Little Red Books built a strong presence on a number of campuses, in particular Monash and La Trobe in Melbourne and Flinders in Adelaide. At its height the Maoist-controlled Worker Student Alliance (WSA) had possibly 800 to 1,000 members nationwide.

However all this changed in the wake of China's rapprochement with the US in the early 1970s. Chinese foreign policy moved openly in a reactionary direction after US President Richard Nixon's visit to China in 1972, and the subsequent purge of the "Gang of Four" and other supporters of the Cultural Revolution. Ever loyal to Beijing, the Maoists of the CPA (ML) in turn moved sharply to the right, searching for an alliance with the "patriotic bourgeoisie", glorifying Australian nationalism, and losing much of their appeal to student radicals. The Worker Student Alliance became Students for Australian Independence, abandoned carrying the red flag and became increasingly violent towards their Trotskyist opponents on the left. By the late 1970s the CPA (ML) was supporting US imperialism as a counterweight to Russian imperialism, which they argued was the main threat to Australian "independence". They effectively backed the right-wing Fraser Liberal government against the ALP which they saw as being soft on "Soviet social-imperialism".[19]

In Brisbane the libertarian/semi-anarchist Self-Management Group (SMG) headed by the former University of Queensland student radical Brian Laver evolved out of the Society for Democratic Action (SDA). As SDA radicalised it gave birth to the Revolutionary Socialist Student Alliance/Revolutionary Socialist Alliance and then the short-lived Revolutionary Socialist Party (RSP) which also contained currents sympathetic to Marxism and was moving in a Trotskyist direction. The SMG, however, was strongly influenced by the semi-anarchist ideas of the British group Solidarity and the French group Socialisme Ou Barbarie. On some issues the SMG initially had relatively better positions than much of the left of this era, being much more critical of the Stalinism and Third Worldism then rampant in left-wing circles, as well as what later became known as identity politics.

For a few years the SMG was the largest, most coherent and active far-left force in Brisbane. At its peak it had two to three hundred

---

19. For the rise and decline of the Maoists see Herouvim 1982 and 1983.

activists organised in an array of student and workplace cells, and its own small, armed Defence Committee. It built significantly among university and high school students but also recruited a number of blue-collar workers in the meatworks and metal trades, including some prominent former CPA industrial militants, and had a presence at the Evans Deakin shipyards, the most militant workplace in Brisbane.[20]

However the group evolved in a sectarian and abstentionist direction which made it increasingly incapable of intervening effectively in union struggles and the protests against the sacking of the Whitlam government in 1975. It eventually abandoned its support for the Vietnamese struggle against US imperialism, spent an enormous amount of effort attempting to disrupt the activities of the "Marxist left", and degenerated into a personality cult around Brian Laver. It split in 1977 in three directions. One section around Drew Hutton and Greg George eventually meandered off towards Greens-style politics while another moved in a more fully fledged anarchist direction. More positively, a significant Marxist Tendency also developed. Many of the members of the Marxist Tendency, which included John Minns and Ian Rintoul, went on to join the Brisbane branch of the International Socialists.

The delay in forming a sizeable Trotskyist organisation also allowed space for the CPA to make something of a comeback. Sidelined by the radical youth revolt, a section of the CPA leadership around Laurie Aarons recognised that the party had to shift leftwards and appeal to a rebellious young audience if it was to have any hope of a future. It jettisoned some of its conservative baggage and Aarons pushed through a split with politically conservative Moscow loyalists, who formed the Socialist Party of Australia (SPA) in 1971.

The split with the SPA and the modernising of the party gave the CPA a more radical image, making it more attractive to some New Leftists who were beginning to see the need for party organisation. The CPA's re-imaging and distancing itself from Stalinism helped enable the party to play a major wrecking role on the left over the next five years. In the process it disoriented and demoralised a layer of impressive

---

20. Briedis 2010.

working-class militants and numerous young activists. The CPA was a key obstacle that needed to be confronted and overcome if a healthy revolutionary left was to be established.

The CPA initiated the Left Action Conference in April 1969, putting on a leftish face with grandiose talk about workers' control in an attempt to seduce student and ex-student radicals and undermine opponents to its left.[21] As one of the CPA's left critics put it:

> The Conference was all that the CPA desired. It was one that masqueraded as an attempt to unite the left – it had the very opposite effect. It resulted in the most serious fragmentation that had so far occurred. The CPA staved off a threat to replace it as the main radical force and reasserted its claim to be the party with whom all radicals had first to come to terms. Previously they had been prepared to unite against it; now there were conflicting attitudes.[22]

The Left Action Conference helped kill off the loose Revolutionary Socialist Alliance (RSA), uniting a broad cross-section of the far left, from Maoists to proto-Trotskyists to semi-anarchists, which briefly had seemed to pose a real threat to the CPA. For a short period this constellation of radical forces could work together, united by the glue of hostility to the conservative stance of the CPA in the anti-war and student movements. However this was a fragile and false unity, bound to be torn apart as the immense political differences between these various currents were clarified. The CPA's feint to the left peeled off sections of the RSA influenced by left reformism and centrism. But the conference also helped clarify that there was no ongoing basis for unity in one organisation between the increasingly hardened Stalin-loving Maoists and revolutionary socialists actually interested in fighting for working-class liberation. There have been many totally unnecessary and irresponsible splits on the left, but this one was vital if there was to be any road forward for the emerging revolutionary forces.

---

21. Mansell 1980. For the reformist degeneration of the CPA see O'Lincoln 1985.
22. Melbourne Revolutionary Marxists 1975, p.7.

In April the following year the CPA gained its own tame "Trotskyist" in the form of Denis Freney, the chief spokesperson for the RSA. Freney, one of the few remaining active and relatively younger members of Origlass's International group, joined the party arguing that it had broken with Stalinism in a revolutionary direction. He quickly evolved into a CPA hack and bitter red-baiter of the revolutionary left. Then in 1972 the majority of the Adelaide Revolutionary Marxists, which had evolved out of Students for Democratic Action at Adelaide University, joined the CPA. They took over a CPA state branch severely depleted by the split with the pro-Moscow loyalists and formed the core of the CPA's Left Tendency. In Melbourne a few New Left former students around one of the better Marxist journals of the period, *Intervention*, joined the CPA. The Left Tendency also grew in Sydney, where there was also a small coterie of people in the CPA who sold the British International Socialists' paper *Socialist Worker*.

Some Left Tendency members were influenced by variants of Trotskyism, in particular the writings of Ernest Mandel, though support for the authoritarian and obscurantist ideas of Louis Althusser was particularly strong at Sydney University. The Left Tendency argued there was no need to build a small revolutionary organisation in opposition to the CPA. Winton Higgins, one of the Left Tendency's prominent spokespeople, claimed in an article, "Reconstructing Australian Communism", that the CPA had already broken with Stalinism and was well on the road to being transformed into a genuinely revolutionary party.[23] This was delusional. The CPA may have junked much of its traditional Stalinist baggage, but it was essentially moving in a liberal reformist direction, albeit reflecting the more radical times with a left-wing sounding face. Moreover, the hardened CPA apparatchiks were never going to allow a bunch of radical young upstarts to take over their party. Within a few short years the CPA's faux leftism had completely vanished. It went back to tailing the ALP and the trade union bureaucracy, playing a key role in pioneering the wage cutting Prices and Incomes Accord of the Hawke/Keating government. The CPA may have turned away from Stalinism, but the

---

23. Higgins 1974.

liberal politics it embraced in the 1970s proved thoroughly reactionary. The CPA celebrated virtually every passing fad of the liberal middle class and academic left. It abandoned any vestige of Marxist or even class politics in favour of post-modernism, and played a key role in promoting identity politics on the left. The Left Tendency members either dropped out or were co-opted and swallowed up.

The anti-war movement peaks

The student and anti-war movements peaked with the mass Moratorium marches in 1970 and by the end of 1971 had begun to decline. A number of radicals and individual revolutionaries in search of a political home drifted into the ALP in the lead-up to the December 1972 election of the Whitlam government. This was especially the case in Victoria, where the Whitlam-orchestrated federal ALP intervention in November 1970 to purge the left-leaning state executive had provoked a furious reaction. A new left-wing faction emerged, the Socialist Left, which for a short period got out of control of the old left semi-Stalinist trade union officials who had previously bureaucratically run the Victorian party.[24] This briefly opened up a space for intervention by revolutionary forces. However within a year or two the left union officials had largely regained control and moved to bureaucratise and moderate the Socialist Left. They subsequently reached a grudging accommodation with Whitlam. By 1975 the space for fruitful intervention into the ALP Socialist Left was well and truly over.[25]

Another section of those radicalised by the movement were looking for something more clearly revolutionary to continue their activity and overcome their isolation as the movements sharply subsided. They began to join a variety of revolutionary groups or to form totally new ones. Further impelling them in this direction was the political impact of increased working-class industrial militancy, which made class politics more central to the outlook of a section of the student and ex-student radicals. There were attempts to organise various forms of worker-student alliances, some socialist former students became

---

24. For the ALP left in this period see Oakley 2012 and Armstrong 2011.
25. This was very much confirmed from my own experience of ALP entry work as a member of the Socialist Workers Action Group.

active in the teachers' and other white-collar unions and a few even "industrialised" in blue-collar jobs.

As well, a considerable array of socialist discussion groups, campus clubs, radical bookshops, activist collectives, live-in organising centres and reading groups studying Marxist classics like Lenin's *State and Revolution* and *What Is To Be Done?* had developed. Some of these started to link up in broader socialist alliances. These alliances were often quite short-lived, as the clarification of political differences led to splits. It was out of this rather chaotic process that more politically formed Trotskyist groups began to cohere.

One reflection of the trend towards a more serious outlook among sections of the radical milieu was the rapid change in orientation of a number of the semi-anarchist/counterculture types that had blocked with Bob Gould in 1970 to oppose turning Resistance into an explicitly Trotskyist organisation. They flipped over to an ultra-hard but spurious version of "Leninism", and along with other small grouplets helped establish the local offshoot of the British SLL in late 1971. Ironically, they initially banned Gould from joining until the mid-1970s, when he became a member of their Central Committee.[26]

The SLL, or Healyites, was one of the most sectarian, authoritarian and hysterical Trotskyist currents. The SLL denounced the Socialist Youth Alliance and every other Trotskyist group that ever emerged as reactionary middle-class betrayers of the working class. It spent its time publishing tub-thumping calls to build the revolutionary leadership as the final crisis of capitalism was upon us. Along with its crude workerism, this could appeal to some former student radicals such as Nick Beames, who had been involved with SDS in Hobart precisely because it seemed so, so hard – the real Bolsheviks.[27] In some ways the SLL's appeal was quite similar to that of the early Maoists.

The SLL may possibly have become the largest Trotskyist group, with a couple of hundred members in the mid-1970s, but it had an extremely rapid membership turnover. It drove its members incredibly hard, demanding a massive commitment of time and money to fund a

---

26. Percy 2005, pp.204–7.
27. For a critique of the politics of the British SLL see Hallas 1969. For an insight into the orientation of the SLL in Australia see *Workers News* 1976.

projected daily paper. Various members who resigned were physically assaulted and had their books stolen. The SLL in Britain and Australia and its other international offshoots inevitably blew themselves apart in a series of crises and purges. Its Australian remnants formed the Socialist Equality Party.

The other main Trotskyist group that briefly emerged in this period was the Communist League (CL). The CL was influenced by the Mandelite wing of the Fourth International and the International Marxist Group (IMG) in Britain, which two of its founding members, John and Sue McCarthy, had been members of while staying there. The Australian Mandelites initially cohered in the Labour Action group in Brisbane and it was only after some hesitation that they joined the Socialist Workers League (SWL) at its founding conference in January 1972. Their reservations about joining the SWL in part reflected the tensions between the Mandelite wing of the FI and the wing of the FI associated with the US SWP, with which the Percy-led SYA/SWL was then aligned. The unity did not last long, with the Mandelites quickly splitting away to the left in August 1972 to form the CL. The CL included not just former Labour Action group members but also various other SYA/SWL members from outside Brisbane who were critical of the SYA/SWL's political orientation. The CL became for a short period the main Trotskyist group in Brisbane and had a presence in Sydney and a dissident branch in Melbourne.

In their paper *Militant* the CL furiously denounced the SYA/SWL as centrists, soft on the ALP and focused on "middle class" single-issue protest campaigns rather than orienting to the new working-class vanguard which they claimed had developed in Australia and other Western countries. However in a rather contradictory fashion the CL supported the Mandelite current's international perspective of promoting guerrilla warfare in Latin America and other countries. To give you a feel for their stance, one of the CL's favourite chants went:

> *What's the word? Johannesburg.*
> *How's it done? With a gun.*
> *One solution. Revolution.*

The CL was an unserious organisation, prone to crisis and politically unstable. It lost the bulk of its Melbourne branch to form the Melbourne Revolutionary Marxists and included in its ranks some members with sectarian, Spartacist-style politics. By the late 1970s its members had become increasingly demoralised. Under pressure from the leadership of the FI the majority of CL members rejoined the SWL in two stages, albeit in the case of a number of members quite reluctantly. The remaining more leftish elements fragmented.

By the mid-1970s there was a plethora of Trotskyist or semi-Trotskyist groups. In the second half of 1975 the Socialist Workers Action Group (SWAG), the precursor organisation to Socialist Alternative, was involved in regroupment discussions initially involving a series of small independent revolutionary groups – the Workers' League in Hobart, the Labor Power group in Brisbane, a group of students in Canberra and, and in Melbourne – the Melbourne Revolutionary Marxists (a split from the Communist League), *The Link* (a semi-syndicalist group), plus elements of the CPA Left Tendency. And there were at least four or five other nominally Trotskyist groups, including some ultra-sectarian variants such as the Spartacist League. This fragmentation to a considerable extent reflected the fact that no serious revolutionary organisation had been built in the preceding decade and a half. If by the early sixties an organisation of a few hundred members with an experienced and tactically astute leadership had already existed, many of the rough edges of the newly radicalising forces could have been smoothed over and innumerable needless splits avoided.

SWAG had its origins in the short-lived *Tocsin* group in Melbourne influenced by Ted Tripp, an old 1930s Trotskyist, who ran Marxism classes at the Victorian Labor College at Trades Hall.[28] In 1971 the Tocsin group split, with one section linking up with the Healyites. Another section went on to form a loose discussion group, the Marxist Workers Group, in which Dave Nadel, a leading student radical at Monash in the sixties was prominent. Nadel, a key organiser of the 4 July 1968 protest and riot against the Vietnam War at the US

---

28. For the history of SWAG see Lee Ack 2019 and Ilton 1984. For the subsequent development of the International Socialist current in Australia see Armstrong 2010.

Consulate in Melbourne, had been around the Maoists in the Monash Labor Club but had evolved from Labor left-style politics towards orthodox Trotskyist views.

Under the influence from 1972 onwards of Tom O'Lincoln and Janey Stone, who had been members of the International Socialists in the US, the Marxist Workers Group gradually clarified its politics, breaking with people influenced by anarchism. It evolved towards explicitly International Socialists-style politics, seeing Stalinist Russia as an exploitative class society that needed to be overthrown by a working-class revolution.[29] The group put a heavy emphasis on the need to build a militant rank-and-file movement in the unions to challenge the reformist stranglehold of the union bureaucracy. It stridently opposed the Australian nationalism then dominant on most of the left and competed with the Maoists in terms of street militancy.

In late 1972 the Marxist Workers Group reorganised as the Socialist Workers Action Group on a more developed political basis and with a formal membership. It put out an initial issue of a paper, *The Battler*, in the lead-up to the December 1972 elections. But when I joined SWAG in October 1974 it was still a tiny Melbourne-based group with only about 18 members and two small campus clubs at Monash and La Trobe universities – the RevComs. It managed to recruit out of leading a major student occupation at Monash in late 1974 and subsequently from the mass struggle against the 1975 Kerr coup that overthrew the Whitlam Labor government. SWAG changed its name to the International Socialists (IS) at a regroupment conference in December 1975, where it was joined by comrades from the Workers League in Hobart and subsequently some comrades in Canberra. However it still had only a little over 30 members.

By 1975 the economic and political climate had shifted substantially and this posed major new challenges for the working-class movement and the left. The long post-war economic boom that had underpinned rising living standards and industrial militancy around wages had come to an end with the recession of 1974 and

---

29. For the political development of the International Socialist current see Birchall 2011.

a sharp rise in unemployment. The November 1975 Kerr coup that overthrew the Whitlam government had sharply polarised politics along class lines. The IS believed that this deepening social crisis would open up substantial prospects for growth of the revolutionary left and for building a base in the working class. However we seriously over-estimated the ability of our tiny group to take advantage of the changed situation. As well, while we did correctly predict that this sharp change in the political situation would provoke a crisis on the left, we could not and did not foresee the full scale of the abandonment of anything approaching class politics by the bulk of the left over the following decade and a half.

We had to adjust substantially and that inevitably led to tensions and debates. We could not financially sustain for long the fortnightly paper that we had decided to launch at our December 1975 conference. Nor could we sustain our project of "industrialisation" – sending student members into factory jobs, in our case, the metal trades. We subsequently concluded – under the influence of the British IS – that industrialisation was not a politically sensible way of attempting to build a working-class base. Despite these serious mistakes, the IS managed to grow in the course of the 1970s. The group put concerted effort into breaking out of Melbourne and became a national organisation with new branches in Sydney, Brisbane, Adelaide and Canberra. We gradually rebuilt our student work that had been substantially downgraded because of the industrialisation perspective. By 1980 the IS had about 100 members. In early 1990, having overcome a split in our ranks in the mid-1980s and being renamed the International Socialist Organisation (ISO), it was the second largest far-left organisation after the DSP, though with fewer than 200 members it was still far too small.

To sum up

The sixties and early seventies radicalisation in Australia saw many thousands of students and young workers and more than a few older ones turn to various forms of revolutionary politics. Many more could have been won to an ongoing commitment to socialist politics if there had been a serious anti-Stalinist revolutionary organisation active in the early years of these struggles. But the tragedy was that there was no Marxist organisation with even a couple of hundred members already in existence in 1965. An organisation with clearly defined politics grounded in a solid Marxist theoretical tradition combined with a democratic and level-headed organisational approach could have made a substantial impact during the mass struggles of the following decade and grown substantially. A strong, ideologically coherent organisation could have fast-tracked the clarification of ideas among the new radicals, lessening to some extent the wastefulness of years of disputes and splits. It could have begun the vital task of breaking out of the radical student and ex-student milieu and establishing some initial roots in the working-class movement.

In the absence of such an organisation, the young proto-revolutionaries of the late sixties and early seventies had to thrash out their politics and methods of organisation on the fly in the heat of battle against the entrenched reformist and Stalinist forces active in the anti-war movement. In the prevailing superheated atmosphere it was inevitable that we made a huge number of mistakes and failed to fully seize the opportunities that had opened up. These were incredibly vibrant and exciting times as the radicalisation deepened, shaking up the whole of Australian society. However it was far from plain sailing politically. A huge array of new political currents arose and often complex political questions were posed. Everything seemed up for grabs and it was all too easy to get carried away.

Young student radicals turning to Marxist politics had to break politically with the hyped-up moralism and faux radicalism and penchant for middle-class fads that so deeply infected student politics. While the nature of these fads has changed, the general tendency remains, precisely because of the isolation of students from the political discipline of the working class – the only class that actually had the power to overthrow capitalism and usher in a genuine socialist society. Some of the young radicals were badly impacted by the youth culture of the time, with its swampy semi-anarchist, spontaneist prejudices. Others embraced Third Worldism, the Chinese Cultural Revolution and Maoism – all utter disasters. Some were seduced by the Communist Party's seeming turn to the left in the late 1960s.

Others, repelled by Stalinism and looking for a genuinely revolutionary working-class alternative were attracted to one or other of the international Trotskyist currents. Unfortunately some of those currents had highly defective politics. The long decades of isolation of the Trotskyist organisations from the working-class movement had bred both sectarian and opportunist tendencies and a penchant to look for get-rich-quick schemes to break out. As well, the long-term corrupting influence of the predominance of Stalinism on the left had impacted even a number of the political currents that saw themselves as hostile to Stalinism, resulting in a tendency towards a top-down approach to politics and undemocratic methods of party organisation. And precisely because no Trotskyist organisation had been built with any serious credibility or influence in the working class and a leadership with a track record of success, there was also a pronounced tendency to fragmentation. No organisation had established the political authority or social weight to prevent splintering – often on highly sectarian lines. So the opportunity for revolutionaries posed by this tremendous period of radicalisation was nowhere near to being fully seized.

There was however one major accomplishment. The mass radicalisation had helped remove a great obstacle to the future advancement of the socialist movement. It had effectively broken the Stalinist CPA that had for decades poisoned the left and undermined working-class struggle, and whose support for the horrors of authoritarian rule in Russia and its bloc had served to discredit the very idea of socialism among the bulk of the Australian working class. But no even moderately sized revolutionary socialist party had been built to replace the CPA: a party that could then go on to continue to draw in more forces even after the high points of struggle had passed.

That remains the ongoing challenge for Socialist Alternative – to play whatever role we can in helping lay the basis for such a revolutionary party.[30] We can't know when the next great radicalisation will break out and we don't know the exact form it will take. It definitely

---

30. For a discussion about strategies for building revolutionary socialist organisations see Armstrong 2018.

will not simply be a repeat of the sixties. But seriously building Socialist Alternative today, both numerically and in terms of experience in intervening in debates, controversies and struggles and of broader Marxist political education, is vital preparation for giving us the best chance of making the most out of future upheavals. We don't want to miss the moment again.

References

Armstrong, Mick 2001, *1,2,3, What Are We Fighting For? The Australian student movement from its origins to the 1970s*, Socialist Alternative.

Armstrong, Mick 2010, "The origins of Socialist Alternative: summing up the debate", *Marxist Left Review*, 1, Spring. https://marxistleftreview.org/articles/the-origins-of-socialist-alternative-summing-up-the-debate/

Armstrong, Mick 2011, "Jim Cairns: the tragedy of relying on parliament for fundamental change", *Marxist Left Review*, 3, Spring. https://marxistleftreview.org/articles/jim-cairns-the-tragedy-of-looking-to-parliament-for-fundamental-change/

Armstrong, Mick 2014, "A critique of the writings of Murray Smith on broad left parties", *Marxist Left Review*, 7, Summer. https://marxistleftreview.org/articles/a-critique-of-the-writings-of-murray-smith-on-broad-left-parties/

Armstrong, Mick 2018, *From Little Things Big Things Grow*, 2nd edition, Socialist Alternative. https://www.sa.org.au/node/4002

Birchall, Ian 1974, *Workers Against the Monolith. The Communist Parties Since 1943*, Pluto Press.

Birchall, Ian 2011, *Tony Cliff. A Marxist for His Time*, Bookmarks.

Bramble, Tom 2008, *Trade Unionism in Australia. A history from flood to ebb tide*, Cambridge University Press.

Briedis, Tim 2010, "*A map of the world that includes Utopia*": *the Self Management Group and the Brisbane libertarians*, BA Honours thesis, Sydney University. https://www.academia.edu/16074437/A_map_of_the_world_that_includes_Utopia_the_Self_Management_Group_and_the_Brisbane_libertarians

Ferrier, Carole and Graeme Grassie, 1978/1979, "The struggle for democratic rights in Australia", *International Socialism* (2nd series), 3, Winter. https://www.marxists.org/history/etol/newspape/isj2/1978/no2-003/ferrier-grassie.html

Freney, Dennis 1991, *A Map of Days. Life on the Left*, William Heinemann Australia.

Gollan, Daphne 1972, "The Balmain Ironworkers' Strike of 1945", *Labor History*, 22 and 23.

Greenland, Hall 1988, *Red Hot. The Life and Times of Nick Origlass*, Wellington Lane Press.

Hallas, Duncan 1969, "Building the leadership", *International Socialism* (1st series), 40, October/November, pp.25–32. https://www.marxists.org/archive/hallas/works/1969/xx/building.htm

Hallas, Duncan 2003, "Fourth International in decline: From Trotskyism to Pabloism, 1944–1953" in *Trotsky's Marxism and other essays*, Haymarket. https://www.marxists.org/archive/hallas/works/1973/xx/fidecline.htm

Harman, Chris 1974, *Bureaucracy and Revolution in Eastern Europe*, Pluto Press.

Harman, Chris 1988, *The Fire Last Time: 1968 and After*, Bookmarks.

Hastings, Graham 2002, *It Can't Happen Here. A political history of Australian student activism*, The Students Association of Flinders University.

Herouvim, John 1982, *"An Alien Association". Australian Maoism and the Communist Party of China, 1971–1977*, MA thesis, La Trobe University. https://www.marxists.org/history/erol/australia/alien-association.pdf

Herouvim, John 1983, "Politics of the Revolving Door: The Communist Party of Australia (Marxist-Leninist)", *Melbourne Journal of Politics*, 15, January.

Higgins, Winton 1974, "Reconstructing Australian Communism", *Socialist Register*, Merlin.

Ilton, Phil 1984, *A history of the Socialist Workers' Action Group*, International Socialists (Australia).

Lee Ack, Tess 2019, "The SWAG years: Revolutionary organising in 1970s Australia", *Marxist Left Review*, 17, Summer. https://marxistleftreview.org/articles/the-swag-years-revolutionary-organising-in-1970s-australia/

Mansell, Ken 1980, *The Marxism and Strategic Concepts of the Communist Party of Australia, 1963–1972*, Honours thesis, La Trobe University, https://labourhistorymelbourne.org/wp-content/uploads/2019/03/cpa-thesis-ken-mansell.pdf

Melbourne Revolutionary Marxists, 1975, *A Call For The Revolutionary Regroupment Of The Australian Left*. https://www.reasoninrevolt.net.au/objects/pdf/d2194.pdf

Oakley, Corey 2012, "The rise and fall of the ALP left in Victoria and NSW", *Marxist Left Review*, 4, Winter. https://marxistleftreview.org/articles/the-rise-and-fall-of-the-alp-left-in-victoria-and-nsw/

O'Lincoln, Tom 1985, *Into the Mainstream. The decline of Australian Communism*, Stained Wattle Press.

Percy, John 2005, *A History of the Democratic Socialist Party and Resistance, Vol. 1: 1965–72 Resistance*, Resistance Books.

Percy, John 2013, "An international balance sheet of the 'broad party' strategy", *Marxist Left Review*, 5, Summer. https://marxistleftreview.org/articles/an-international-balance-sheet-of-the-broad-party-strategy/

Russell, Lani 1998, *Today the Students, Tomorrow the Workers! Radical Student Politics and the Australian Labour Movement 1960–1972*, PhD thesis, University of Technology Sydney. https://www.marxists.org/history/erol/australia/students.pdf

Short, Susanna 1992, *Laurie Short: A Political Life*, Allen and Unwin.

Wood, Katie 2013, "Fighting anti-union laws: the Clarrie O'Shea strikes", *Marxist Left Review*, 5, Summer. https://marxistleftreview.org/articles/fighting-anti-union-laws-the-clarrie-oshea-strikes/

Workers News 1976, *The Canberra Coup! A documentary on the sacking of the Labor Government, November 11, 1975*.

TESS LEE ACK

East Germany 1953: Workers' forgotten rebellion against Stalinism

Tess Lee Ack is a long-term socialist living in Melbourne.

I N JUNE 1953, workers across East Germany rose in the first major rebellion in the Eastern Bloc. For a brief period, the iron grip of Stalinism was loosened, and only the intervention of Russian tanks saved the regime from ignominious collapse.

The opening of state archives following the fall of the Berlin Wall and the collapse of the Soviet Union cast considerable new light on the events of 1953. It has now been established that the uprising was more widespread and prolonged than previously thought, and that "contrary to the traditional assumption that the disorders quickly subsided after Soviet military intervention...the events of June 16–17 marked only the peak of a rebellion which continued...throughout the summer of 1953".[1]

It is no coincidence that the uprising erupted shortly after Stalin's death in March 1953, when a fierce power struggle was taking place within the Russian leadership. The uprising "opened up divisions both within and between elites in Moscow and East Berlin [where it] plunged the apparatuses of power into uncertainty and confusion"[2] and had lasting repercussions for the regime in the German Democratic Republic (GDR).

---

1. Ostermann 1996, p.2.
2. Dale 2005, p.10.

Seventy years later, the 1953 uprising remains an inspiring example of workers resisting tyranny against all the odds, and fighting for a world free of exploitation and oppression. Their slogan "We want to be free human beings, not slaves!" still resonates today.

The Cold War and the division of Germany

Despite its depiction as a war for democracy, World War II "ended in an ignoble maze of obvious intrigue and jockeying for advantage",[3] with the Allies carving up the world between them. The US and the Soviet Union came out on top, with the USSR gaining control over Eastern Europe and creating states in its own image: bureaucratic state capitalist dictatorships in which workers were an oppressed and exploited class.

Germany was divided into four zones of occupation, administered by the US, Britain and France in the west, and by the USSR in the east. The capital, Berlin, was likewise divided into four sectors, leaving West Berlin as an isolated enclave within the Russian zone.

The hostility between the Western powers and the USSR erupted into the open in 1946–47. In March 1946 Churchill made his famous "iron curtain" speech.[4] A week later the US president enunciated the "Truman Doctrine", which hoped to "contain" communism by "stemming the tide of Soviet expansionism".[5] The Cold War was decisive in shaping approaches to post-war Germany.

Both Russia and the US were apprehensive about the possibility of social unrest or even revolution, as had occurred after World War I, and viewed with alarm the revival of the workers' movement. Under the Nazi dictatorship, the possibilities for working-class resistance were extremely limited. Nonetheless there had been instances of small-scale strike activity, sabotage, absenteeism, petitions.[6]

As the war came to an end, Anti-Fascist Committees ("Antifas") sprang up, more than 500 in all, and overwhelmingly working-class in composition. In Leipzig alone, there were 38 local committees claiming 4,500 activists and 15,000 adherents.

---

3. Kolko 1990, p.388.
4. Churchill 1946.
5. Fulbrook 2002, pp.132–33.
6. Gluckstein 1999, p.217.

The Antifas were determined to rip out Nazism... In some places workers took over their factories and management fled. Antifas set up their own factory militias and replaced police chiefs and mayors with their own nominees. The situation in Stuttgart and Hanover was one of "dual power", the Antifas having set up their own police forces, taken over a raft of powerful local positions and begun to run vital services like food provisioning.[7]

The Antifas lasted for only a few weeks before being suppressed – in both the Western and Soviet zones. But many of the participants would again be actors in 1953.

On 20 June 1948 the US, Britain and France merged their zones. Russia reacted days later with a blockade of the movement of goods and food to Berlin. The US and Britain countered by airlifting supplies to the Western sectors until the blockade was lifted in May 1949. The division of Germany was now inevitable. The Federal Republic of Germany (FRG, West Germany) was officially established on 23 May 1949; the establishment of the German Democratic Republic (GDR, East Germany) followed on 7 October.

Creating a Stalinist state

Walter Ulbricht had been a leading German Communist Party (KPD) functionary since 1923. Favoured by Stalin, he was charged with the "operational leadership" of the party during the war, which he spent in Russia.[8] In April 1945, he was sent with a small group of KPD veterans to direct party activity in the Soviet Occupation Zone (SBZ).

The KPD's "Action Program" of June 1945, dictated by Moscow, contained no reference to socialism. It upheld private industry and property and called for the "establishment of an anti-fascist, democratic regime, a parliamentary democratic republic with all democratic rights and freedoms for the people" – but key posts went to trusted veteran communists. Ulbricht is reported as saying: "It's got to look democratic, but we must have everything in our control".[9]

---

7. Gluckstein 1999, p.220.
8. Epstein 2003, p.103.
9. Quoted in Epstein 2003, p.103.

As the Cold War intensified, however, this program was abandoned. Moscow decided to expedite the integration of the GDR into the Soviet Bloc. Stalin and Ulbricht pushed for a merger of the KPD and the Social Democratic Party (SPD). Given the bitter sectarian feuding between these parties during the Weimar years,[10] this was opposed by many rank-and-file members of both parties. SPD leader Otto Grotewohl initially resisted, but capitulated under pressure from Ulbricht and the Soviet Military Administration. In April 1946, the KPD and the SPD merged as the Socialist Unity Party (Sozialistische Einheitspartei Deutschlands, SED).

The SED subsequently became the ruling party of the GDR, with Wilhelm Pieck as state president and Grotewohl rewarded with the position of prime minister. But as First Secretary of the SED Central Committee, Ulbricht was the real leader. He

> brought a hard-edged Stalinism to the GDR. During the late 1940s and 1950s he deployed a regime of terror against the East German population – as well as against veteran communists. He zealously transformed the GDR into a Soviet satellite state.[11]

The establishment of the SED was accompanied by a series of purges which began in July 1948 and continued until 1953. Carried out in close cooperation with Soviet officials, the aim was to create a "disciplined and ideologically pure party" – ie, one that would unquestioningly obey the dictates of Moscow. Prominent among the targets were former SPD members and "non-conformist Communists": members of organisations such as the Communist Party Opposition (KPO) and the Socialist Workers' Party (SAP), both of which had a presence in the region before 1933. Nor was the party leadership exempt: by 1950 ten of the fourteen members of the 1946 Central Secretariat had been demoted, expelled or had fled the country.[12]

---

10. The ultra-left Stalinist madness of the "Third Period" and the condemnation of Social Democrats as "social fascists" was largely responsible for this. See Gluckstein 1999, chapter 5.
11. Epstein 2003, p.261.
12. Dale 2005, p.15.

Party membership fell from 2 million to 1.2 million between 1948 and 1952. The proportion of working-class members fell to 38 percent, reflecting "the shift from the party's roots in the working-class movement to its position as the hegemonic state party".[13]

> From being a party of the industrial proletariat, it was increasingly becoming a party of managers, bureaucrats and officials, who enjoyed all kinds of perks and privileges which were unavailable to the people they were supposed to represent.[14]

Many KPD veterans, while not expelled, were sidelined. They had been loyal to the party during the Weimar years but were uneasy with aspects of the new state.

> They detested the more lenient approach to former Nazis that accompanied the introduction of Stalinist economic practices in the later 1940s. [They] deeply resented being elbowed aside…by the ambitious young apparatchiks who were being systematically fostered by the regime, [viewing them] as "conformists, subservient grovellers, crawlers, obsequious yes-men".[15]

However, there was no organised opposition among long-time KPD cadres. This was partly due to habits of party discipline and fear that criticism would be viewed as the abandonment of their socialist principles. But another factor was "political terror, in the form of public and secret investigations…[that] left many longtime communists reluctant to express political doubts".[16]

The broader population was also subjected to severe repression. In 1950, for instance, 78,000 people were sentenced for "crimes" broadly

---

13. Dennis 2000, p.32.
14. Pritchard 2000, p.156.
15. Pritchard 2000, p.179. Lutz Niethammer notes that "approximately four fifths of the [SED] had no leftist background at all. They were apolitical people who had been mobilised by the party in the late 1940s and 1950". Niethammer 1993, p.15.
16. Epstein 2003, p.123.

defined as political. One 19-year-old was sentenced to death for distributing leaflets criticising the electoral system.[17]

Exploitation and resistance

In an economy devastated by the war,[18] recovery was hindered from the outset by inadequate supplies of raw materials and the GDR's low industrial potential. Reparations were a further burden: by the spring of 1948 over 1,900 factories had been dismantled and shipped to Russia, reducing the productive capacity of the SBZ by about 26 percent.[19] Up to 1953 about one quarter of East Germany's national product was spent on occupation costs and reparations payments.[20] When war damage was taken into account, the total loss of productive capacity was about 50 percent compared to 1939.

Boosting productivity – which in the late 1940s remained at less than half its 1936 level[21] – was a priority for the authorities. In October 1947, Order 234 reintroduced piecework and other forms of productivity-based wages. Echoing Stakhanovism in the USSR in the 1930s, workers who "contributed most to raising productive norms were to be designated 'activists' and receive financial and political rewards".[22] In 1949 the USSR took over management and ownership of key German companies, setting up Soviet Joint-Stock companies (SAGs). Working conditions in SAGs were often poorer than in similar enterprises: hours were longer, accidents more common and rest periods less frequent.[23]

Workers resisted these attacks. Reviling piecework as a method

---

17. Dale 2005, p.14.
18. Some key indicators: industrial output in 1947 was down by a third compared to 1938; food production was half the pre-war level; 20 percent of housing stock was destroyed; and a large percentage of Germany's working-age men were dead or crippled. Henderson n.d.
19. The production capacity of the steel industry was reduced by 85 percent in 1946 owing to the dismantling of factories. Baring 1972, p.6.
20. Fulbrook 2002, pp.126–27.
21. Kopstein 1996, p.399.
22. Kopstein 1996, p.400.
23. Geerling et al 2020, pp.4, 10. Workers in SAGs such as the Buna and Leuna chemical plants, the Agfa film factory in Wolfen, the Sachsenwerk electrical machinery manufacturers in Dresden and several engineering firms in Magdeburg were at the forefront of events in June 1953.

of increased exploitation, they revived the traditional slogan "Akkord ist Mord" (piecework is murder).[24] Six months after the push began, the proportion of the labour force receiving piecework and productivity wages had only risen by 3 percent. Bosses lamented that "many foremen could not be stopped from putting all the piecework tickets into a common urn in order to ensure equality of reward".[25] There was a state of "permanent guerrilla war against the activists", who were despised by their fellow workers. Many had their tools stolen and were physically abused.[26] Kopstein notes that widespread resistance meant that "the attempt to create a Stalinist East German labour aristocracy failed in the face of a strong egalitarian working-class solidarity".[27] He concludes that the working class retained "an amorphous, disorganised power that, even with a good dose of Stalinist terror, could not easily be diminished".[28]

During the three years immediately after the war, there was a marked revival of trade-union consciousness and shopfloor militancy in the SBZ. According to one historian, workers in this period exerted "considerably more leverage over their...workplaces than had ever been the case during the Wilhelmine or Weimar periods". He quotes a visitor to the SBZ in 1947 who was "told quite bluntly" by the shop stewards' committees in several factories that "nothing happens here without our consent".[29]

Part of the explanation for this was that East Germany contained a relatively high concentration of organised socialists. In the pre-war years it was home to at least a third of KPD members (100–120,000) and 60 percent of SPD members (581,000).[30] Many had held onto their political traditions and beliefs under the Nazi dictatorship; a sizeable minority had taken part in illegal resistance.[31]

24. Kopstein 1996, p.402.
25. Kopstein 1996, p.403.
26. Dale 2003, p.35.
27. Kopstein 1996, pp.407–8.
28. Kopstein 1999, p.421.
29. Pritchard 2000, p.43.
30. Dale 2003, p.30.
31. Merson 1985, p.89.

Wismut: an early warning sign

The uranium mines in Thuringia and Saxony were crucial to Stalin's goal of producing nuclear weapons. The Wismut SAG employed a volatile mix of forced labour, returning prisoners of war and refugees from Germany's former eastern territories. They endured harsh discipline, heavy-handed policing and appalling conditions: forced to live in overcrowded barracks with poor sanitary conditions and a shortage of fresh water. All this combined to make the area ripe for revolt.

In Saalfeld on 16 August 1951, a drunken fight and the arrest of several miners led to a strike and violent protests demanding their release. A crowd of about 3,000 stormed the local prison and police precinct, where "panic-stricken officials climbed out windows, onto rooftops and down trees in order to avoid the swinging picks of rampaging miners who refused to return to the pits until their…mates were set free".[32] Several police were injured, about a thousand windows smashed, weapons stolen and criminal files burned. Desperate to get production resumed, the authorities ordered the immediate release of the miners and forbade the use of firearms.[33] Protest subsided following this victory. Security was subsequently stepped up, but the treatment and material position of the Wismut miners improved. This combination of "carrots and sticks" succeeded in "maintaining peace in the region so that mining could proceed on schedule".[34]

Some of the features of the Wismut rebellion would be repeated in 1953 – including the SED leadership's attempt to blame "Western agents" for stirring up discontent.

The "construction of socialism"

In March 1952 Stalin offered to allow the unification of Germany, on condition that it remained unarmed and politically neutral. But in May the General and European Defence Community treaties were signed, cementing the FRG's integration into the Western alliance. In response, Stalin ordered the full transformation of the GDR into a Soviet satellite.

---

32. Port 1997, p.145.
33. Bruce 2003, p.27.
34. Port 1997, p.168.

At its Second Party Conference in July 1952 the SED adopted a Five-Year Plan for the accelerated "construction of socialism". The plan centred on rearmament and the rapid expansion of heavy industry. It also included attacks on private enterprise, the collectivisation of agriculture and repressive measures against the middle class and the churches. This was sold as the "intensification of the 'class struggle' against landowners, capitalists, priests and other 'enemies of the people'".[35] But the Plan had nothing to do with socialism: its main aim was to increase accumulation in order to compete militarily with the West. It would be paid for by reducing spending on consumption, that is, by lowering workers' living standards.

Under pressure from the USSR, the GDR leadership allocated 2 billion marks – 10 percent of its 1952–53 budget – to the rapid build-up of its military. This was to be financed by the raising of taxes and prices, cuts to social welfare and reduced consumption[36] – "guns over butter". The paramilitary *Kasernierte Volkspolizei* (KVP, "garrisoned people's police", later to become the East German army) was formed in July 1952. Aggressive recruiting saw its numbers swell from 90,250 in December 1952 to 113,000 by mid-1953.[37] The build-up of armed forces, weaponry and police diverted resources from production and exacerbated labour shortages.

The response of many thousands of East Germans was to simply leave the GDR. Emigration to West Germany rose steadily, reaching 166,000 in 1951, 182,000 the following year, then climbing sharply to 226,000 in the first half of 1953,[38] despite the construction of a fortified border in 1952. So many farmers emigrated that roughly 13 percent of the country's productive land remained fallow.[39] Given a poor harvest in 1952, a food crisis was inevitable.

Shortages of basic foodstuffs and consumer goods meant that workers faced rationing and higher prices. Coal was in short supply, leading to prolonged interruptions of heating and electricity. At the

---

35. Stibbe 2006, p.40.
36. Grabas 2015, p.186; Kopstein 1996, p.411; Dale 2005, p.17.
37. Diedrich 1992, pp.363–64.
38. Dale 2005, p.17.
39. Baring 1972, p.17.

same time, factories were cutting overtime. So while the cost of living was rising, take-home pay was shrinking. Living standards in 1952 fell below those experienced in the disastrous "hunger crisis" of 1947.[40] Most workers saw their real wages drop by roughly 33 percent.[41]

But not all suffered equally. Emigration had made it difficult to find qualified personnel to manage industries and public services. So the "technical intelligentsia" (engineers, technicians, scientists and managers – including former Nazis) received higher wages, bonuses and privileges including access to higher quality and scarce commodities in special shops (*Handelsorganisation* or HO).[42]

This was not what workers expected of a supposedly socialist state: "it was regarded as axiomatic among most workers…that the construction of socialism should mean…a system of greater equality… As one older comrade…put it: 'If Karl Marx knew how his teachings are being interpreted…he'd roll over in his grave'".[43] Soviet intelligence agents were soon reporting back to Moscow about growing unrest.

> By November 1952, sporadic food riots had broken out in a number of the major industrial centres…and throughout the following spring the internal reports show an unmistakeable increase in…shopfloor discontent from all across the GDR, ranging from "rabble-rousing" to anti-SED graffiti to alleged sabotage.[44]

To facilitate the intensified exploitation of the working class, the SED needed to muzzle workers' organisations. The FDGB (Free German Trade Union Association) was cowed into submission by a government campaign attacking it for "concentrating on promoting its members' interests instead of adopting a 'correct attitude toward work quotas and piece rates'".[45] Workers increasingly "lost faith in the labour movement… which was now becoming the primary instrument of their oppression"

---

40. Grieder 2012, p.37.
41. Ross 2000, p.55; Kopstein 1996, p.412.
42. Pritchard 2000, pp.195–96.
43. Ross 2000, p.53.
44. Ross 2000, p.54.
45. Baring 1972, p.13.

and "just another branch of management".⁴⁶ As a result, large numbers of workers left the FDGB: 3,714 in January 1951 and another 10,500 by April.⁴⁷

Works councils were harder to subdue. Created on the initiative of experienced union activists and firmly rooted in the workplaces, these "classrooms in the arts of industrial action" were key to the revival of labour movement traditions.⁴⁸ Their powers were progressively whittled away or handed over to the FDGB.

Economic conditions deteriorated further in 1953. In April the Kremlin refused the SED's requests for aid, and recommended the adoption of a "softer line".⁴⁹ But instead, the SED decided to squeeze industrial workers even harder. On 9 April, the Council of Ministers announced a series of price rises and the withdrawal of food subsidies for two million "non-essential" workers.⁵⁰ In a drive to raise the intensity of labour, the regime had tried to persuade workers to accept higher work quotas "voluntarily", but without success. So in May the government announced a compulsory 10 percent increase in work norms.

The "construction of socialism" produced a toxic combination of excessive demands on production capacity, economic crisis and growing opposition. With party activists finding it increasingly difficult to sell government policy, the regime stepped up repression. There was a ferocious crackdown on "economic criminals", with the passage in 1952 of a draconian law which mandated at least a year in prison for the most trivial thefts.⁵¹ The number of prison inmates "mushroomed from 30,092 in July 1952 to 61,377 in May 1953".⁵² Even before the June uprising, there were demonstrations outside prisons demanding the release of prisoners.⁵³

---

46. Pritchard 2000, pp.194, 205.
47. Collins 2017, p.65.
48. Dale 2003, p.33.
49. Baring 1972, p.20.
50. Stibbe 2006, p.42.
51. Dale 2005, p.16.
52. Dennis 2000, p.63.
53. Sperber 2004, p.625.

The death of Stalin and its impact

Following Stalin's death on 5 March 1953, Malenkov, Beria and Khrushchev jointly led the Soviet government. The ensuing succession struggle generated significant changes in Soviet policy.

For some months, Moscow had received numerous disconcerting reports of growing instability in Eastern Europe in response to the imposition of Stalinist policies. By May 1953, the Soviet leadership had concluded that the Eastern Bloc regimes should moderate these policies, if not abandon them altogether. This conclusion was further reinforced by an outbreak of strikes and riots among tobacco workers in Bulgaria, serious trouble in Czechoslovakia[54] and the growing unrest in the GDR.

A meeting of the Presidium of the USSR Council of Ministers on 27 May discussed the "severe weaknesses" of the East German state, acknowledging that "the presence of Soviet troops is the only thing enabling the current regime…to survive". The GDR was in danger of collapse unless the SED took steps to rectify its "unacceptably simplistic and rash policies". Ulbricht in particular was subjected to harsh criticism for pursuing a hard-line agenda and ignoring advice from the Kremlin.[55] Molotov, Beria and Malenkov were tasked with preparing a program of political and economic reform for East Germany.[56]

The "New Course"

In early June, Ulbricht and Grotewohl were summoned to Moscow and instructed to abandon the "construction of socialism" in favour of a "New Course". The collectivisation of agriculture and expropriations were to be halted, living standards improved by shifting emphasis from heavy industry to consumer production, price rises revoked, the withdrawal of food subsidies reversed, even some political prisoners released. Many of the measures against the middle classes, small businesses, farmers and Christians were to be wound back.[57]

---

54. Kramer 1999a, pp.15–20. See also Ostermann 2001, p.16.
55. Sperber 2004, p.627 speculates that Ulbricht's zeal may have gone "beyond what Stalin himself wanted, or at least at a faster pace than [he] intended".
56. Kramer 1999a, p.28.
57. Some ten days later, the Czechoslovakian and Hungarian party leaders were summoned to Moscow and received similar instructions. Sperber 2004, p.625.

After the SED leaders returned to Berlin, the Politbüro met almost continuously for five days under the watchful eye of Soviet High Commissioner Vladimir Semyonov. He had been instructed to "take an active part in the [Politbüro's] meetings"[58] – ie, to ensure they toed the line. Tensions within the upper echelons of the SED had increased following Stalin's death, and the intervention by Moscow further unsettled the regime. Serious divisions within the SED leadership opened up, posing a threat to Ulbricht's authority. "Reformers" such as Herrnstadt and Zaisser[59] now felt confident to openly articulate alternative views.

On 11 June the party paper *Neues Deutschland* published a communiqué from the Politbüro, pledging that the government would rectify the "grave mistakes" of recent years and announcing the New Course. However, on one crucial point Ulbricht dug in, insisting that the 10 percent increase in work norms would under no circumstances be rescinded.[60]

The abrupt change of policy caused widespread confusion and revealed deep divisions between reformers and hard-liners within the party. The latter were shocked and disoriented, seeing the New Course as a retreat. One die-hard Stalinist bitterly commented that: "If Comrade Stalin were still alive, there would be no New Course".[61] Some were so dispirited that they renounced their party membership, and many others called for the resignation of the party leaders.

Within the working class, the announcement did nothing to assuage discontent; on the contrary, workers' anger was fuelled by the retention of the higher work norms. They alone, it seemed, would not benefit from the New Course. But workers were emboldened as well as angry. There was a widespread belief that "the U-turn had resulted from the pressure of mass discontent, that it represented a victory of the masses over the functionaries".[62] A secret report prepared by

---

58. Kramer 1999a, p.32.
59. Rudolf Herrnstadt was editor of the party newspaper *Neues Deutschland*; Wilhelm Zaisser was the Minister of State Security. Both were supporters of the New Course.
60. Pritchard 2000, p.206.
61. Pritchard 2000, p.218.
62. Dale 2005, p.19.

the Central Committee later conceded that "when the communiqué was published, a large proportion of workers regarded it as a sign of weakness and even impotence on the part of the SED".[63] In a now familiar pattern, the inadequate concessions of a beleaguered dictatorship transformed resentful discontent into open defiance. The combination of extreme economic hardship, the abruptness of the turn, the disagreements within the SED leadership, the confusion this created among the rank and file of the SED and uncertainty about what was going to happen about the new quotas produced an explosive situation.

Between 12 and 16 June a series of strikes broke out at East Berlin building sites, at least one of which raised the demand for a general strike. On 15 June workers at the Friedrichshain Hospital construction site sent a message to Grotewohl complaining that "the only people to benefit from the new line were the capitalists" and demanding the immediate withdrawal of the higher quotas.[64]

16–17 June

The next day, 16 June, the FDGB paper *Tribüne* published an article defending the norm increase. The FDGB executive expected workers to believe that: "The work quotas are not being raised in order to force down wages but in order to produce more, better and cheaper goods for the same amount of work but with more economical working methods".[65]

This raised the workers' fury to a new pitch; determined to take action against the new quotas, workers on sites across Berlin's Stalinallee went on strike. A propaganda banner reading "Block 40 raises its norms ten percent" was ripped down and replaced with one reading: "We demand a lowering of the norms!"[66] Construction workers had a history of militancy, having successfully fought off previous attempts to slash wages. Moreover, they were in a strong position: the

---

63. Kramer 1999a, p.40.
64. Baring 1972, p.42.
65. Otto Lehmann (FDGB executive member) in *Die Tribüne*, 16 June 1953. Quoted in Baring 1972, pp.146–47.
66. Richie 1998, p.683.

Stalinallee was a prestige project, and there was a shortage of some 40,000 building workers. Early that morning the Stalinallee and Friedrichshain workers gathered and decided to demonstrate at the FDGB headquarters. But first, they marched to nearby sites, persuading other workers to join them. Finding the FDGB building closed, they headed to the House of Ministries.

Along the way thousands of other workers joined them, transforming the march into a mass demonstration that moved "with unwavering will and elemental power".[67] A crowd of about 10,000 gathered at the House of Ministries, demanding that Ulbricht and Grotewohl come out from the now barricaded building to address them.[68] Instead they were fobbed off with lesser officials.

The Politbüro had met that morning and reluctantly decided to withdraw the higher norms. But the officials' assurances to this effect were howled down. The wording of the Politbüro resolution was somewhat equivocal: the higher norms would be "voluntary" and their implementation reconsidered "in conjunction with the trades unions".[69] Most workers suspected, not unreasonably, that the authorities would restore the higher norms at the first opportunity, and they didn't trust the unions to represent their interests. At the same time, the possibility that they had won a major concession reinforced their sense of the regime's vulnerability.

Heated arguments continued back and forth between the workers and the officials. At one point an elderly worker climbed onto a table to address the crowd. A *Pravda* correspondent reported:

> He said that he had been sent to a concentration camp by Hitler as a fighter for the rights of workers, and now he saw his duty to defend these rights once again. The people applauded him. From this man we heard the demands of the strikers...annulment of the increased work norms; decrease in prices in the state-owned

---

67. As described by SED official Heinz Brandt, quoted in Harman 1998, p.66.
68. One account has it that Ulbricht and Grotewohl were hiding in the cellar and were spirited out of a side door some hours later. Richie 1998, p.683.
69. "Politbüro statement on the quota question", 16 June 1953, quoted in Baring 1972, p.152.

> retail stores (HO); general increase in living standards for workers; abandonment of the formation of the People's Army; holding of free elections...[70]

Following this a younger worker climbed onto the podium and called on the crowd to march through the city and spread the call for a general strike. This was greeted with a "hurricane of approval" and the march set off. Demonstrators threw rocks and bottles at the giant monument to Stalin in central Berlin and called on the government to resign.[71]

On the way, the workers encountered several loudspeaker vans sent out by the government to broadcast that the work norms had been rescinded and calling on the demonstrators to return to work. Instead, they hijacked one of the vehicles and used it to broadcast the call for general strike and a mass demonstration at 7am the next day. One of the hijackers later recalled "a wonderful feeling of strength, because we had dared to act like this in the face of that regime".

> [F]eelings of uncertainty gave way to a sense of strength, limited goals gave way to more adventurous ones, and petitioning the government turned into confrontation with the regime. From out of a strike a rebellion had begun to grow.[72]

A host of "self-appointed couriers" carried the call for a general strike to workplaces in the suburbs. Railway construction gangs, their wages and conditions already savagely cut, had been ordered to increase work norms by 20 percent, and when they complained, 200 of them were sacked. Hardly surprising then that "the arrival of cyclists from the Stalinallee [was] the signal for an immediate stoppage of work".[73] By the afternoon protest marches were taking place all over East Berlin.

---

70. P Naumov, "Report on the Events in Berlin on 16 and 17 June 1953", in Ostermann 2001, pp.202-3.
71. Dale 2003, p.8; Kramer 1999a, p.44.
72. Dale 2005, p.22.
73. Brant 1957, p.67.

Despite all the warning signs, the events of 16 June took the government by surprise, and a degree of panic set in. With the Politbüro split, the party and state apparatus were paralysed by indecision. The SED was in such a state of disarray that on 17 June,

> functionaries on the ground were left to face a difficult situation with nobody to tell them what to do. Many simply ran away... Others lamely surrendered to the demands of the protesters...
> At the Betrieb Mifeu, the workers [demanded that] all SED functionaries leave the works immediately, whereupon the frightened young apparatchiks obediently went home and only felt able to return with a police escort. Throughout the GDR, there were thousands of instances of SED functionaries falling prey to mysterious and sudden illnesses, or failing to return from holiday, or surreptitiously taking off their party badges.[74]

The regime doubted the reliability of its own security forces, so initially only small numbers were deployed, with orders not to open fire.[75] The Soviet authorities however were in no doubt about how to proceed. Semyonov took charge, announcing that Russian troops would be sent to Berlin to quell the rebellion. He ordered the SED leaders to evacuate to the Soviet headquarters in Karlshorst, where they "remained passive spectators of events".[76] By the early hours of 17 June Soviet troops occupied strategic positions such as railway stations and post offices in the larger towns, the docks and harbours on the Baltic and the uranium mines in the Erzgebirge.

Meanwhile, word was spreading throughout East Germany with breathtaking speed. Some historians (especially of the pro-US variety) attribute this to broadcasts by RIAS (Radio in the American Sector).[77]

---

74. Pritchard 2000, p.219. See also Baring 1972, pp.94–95.
75. Kramer 1999a, p.48; Dennis 2000, p.66. The next day, with huge numbers of strikers and protesters on the streets, most police "locked their guns up so that the insurgents could not get at them, and so rendered themselves helpless". Sperber 2004, p.688.
76. Sperber 2004, p.637.
77. For example Ostermann 2001, pp.172–74. RIAS was a German-language radio station set up by US military authorities in 1946 in the American sector of Berlin to broadcast propaganda to the SBZ.

A recent study of the range and signal strength of RIAS debunked this myth. Some of the towns that witnessed the greatest upheaval, such as Görlitz, could not even receive RIAS. Moreover, RIAS was ordered not to broadcast the call for a general strike, due to US fears that this might cause a military confrontation with the Soviet Union.[78]

Workers used every available means of communication and transport to get the word out. Truck drivers and rail workers played an important role. In less than 24 hours, wildcat strikes in Berlin blossomed into strikes and demonstrations all over the country.

In Berlin, bicycles and cars equipped with loudspeakers provided communication between columns of marchers as they converged on the city centre. Twelve thousand workers from the steel plant in Hennigsdorf marched all the way – 27 kilometres. By 9am, despite teeming rain, the numbers at the House of Ministries had swelled to around 25,000. As protesters and KVP troops faced off, Soviet armoured cars and troops arrived, driving into the crowd. The demonstrators scattered, reconverging at Marx-Engels Platz where 50,000 packed the square. Without warning, Red Army tanks charged into the crowd at full speed, crushing a man to death. There was a stampede as people tried to get out of the way, pursued by tanks and armoured cars.

At noon Soviet authorities declared a state of emergency. The assembly of more than three people was forbidden. Many protesters ignored this announcement, despite now being shot at. But eventually the Russian troops and loyal elements of the German security forces prevailed over unarmed demonstrators.

Soviet military force was deployed throughout the GDR, with heavy fighting occurring in some places. The Russian army arrested strike leaders, blocked factory gates, dispersed crowds and occupied urban areas. Martial law was declared before many strikers had the chance to act. In Erfurt, for example, Soviet troops blocked the gates of one factory with trucks armed with machine guns to prevent workers from marching.

Between 60 and 100 protesters were shot or crushed by tanks, hundreds were injured and at least 20 were summarily executed

---

78. Crabtree et al. 2018, pp.302, 304, 311.

– including three policemen found guilty of disobeying orders.[79] Despite this appalling toll, most accounts – including by Western commentators – agree that the Soviet troops "acted with great restraint".[80]

While Russian military force ultimately prevailed, recent research refutes claims that the "revolutionary wave had already begun to ebb" before their intervention.[81]

> On the 18th, despite military rule that saw public places and workplaces occupied by Soviet troops and tanks, over 44,000 demonstrated, while all districts of the country witnessed new or continuing strikes, involving well over 100,000 workers – including many who had not struck the previous day. In defiance of the military crackdown, activists in some factories maintained their organisations and planned further activity... The 18th also saw an increased level of activity in the countryside, notably meetings, rallies, and clashes with the local authorities.[82]

How extensive was the uprising?

Estimates of the number of towns and cities where strikes and demonstrations occurred vary, as do estimates of the total numbers involved. Between 16 and 21 June, according to Gareth Dale, "between 1 and 1.5 million people, 6 to 9 percent of the total population, participated in strikes, demonstrations and rallies. Over 700 towns and villages were affected, and at least 0.5 million workers in well over 1,000 workplaces stopped work".[83] A survey by the FDGB estimated that

---

79. Dale 2005, p.10; Stibbe 2006, p.44.
80. Baring 1972, p.80. US intelligence officials praised Soviet troops for their "remarkable discipline, restraint, and cool-headedness" (Kramer 1999a, p.54), while seeing the uprising as an "excellent propaganda opportunity" (John Foster Dulles, quoted in Ostermann 2001, p.213). Churchill wrote to the British Commandant that the Soviet authorities had "the right to declare Martial Law in order to prevent anarchy" (Ostermann 1996, p.21).
81. Baring 1972, p.76.
82. Dale 2003, p.21.
83. Dale 2005, p.9. These figures are at the higher end, arrived at by evaluating numerous sources. For details, see Dale 2003, pp.1–4. For a map showing centres of unrest, see https://germanhistorydocs.ghi-dc.org/sub_document.cfm?document_id=2999.

almost three-quarters of the workforce in Berlin's metal industries took action.⁸⁴

Building workers and employees in the larger state-owned factories were among the first to go out, but strikes affected all sectors, and events across the country tended to follow a similar pattern. Early on the morning of 17 June, groups of workers gathered to discuss how to "show solidarity with Berlin". As Brant puts it, "the word 'solidarity'…assumed the force of law".⁸⁵ In many places, there was a ripple effect:

> Once one department of a factory had decided to strike, the other departments almost invariably followed suit, and once the personnel of a whole factory had marched out on to the streets, the men of other factories quickly joined them.⁸⁶

At the Sachsenwerk factory in Dresden a group of workers marched to nearby factories, singing the *Internationale* and bringing out their employees along the way. Action was not always unanimous: some workers stayed at their posts, while waverers frequently had to be persuaded with arguments about the need for unity.

On the afternoon of 17 June,

> a wide variety of insurrectionary and riotous events occurred… Town radio stations and loudspeaker systems were taken over, and used to broadcast calls to rally. Over 100 offices of state institutions…were ransacked; files were opened and in many cases seized or destroyed. In one town the Stasi headquarters was occupied and "the whole building was completely taken apart from top to bottom". Other popular targets were police stations and prisons, dozens of which were stormed. Over 1,300 prisoners were freed.⁸⁷

---

84. Dale 2003, p.2.
85. Brant 1957, p.81.
86. Baring 1972, p.68.
87. Dale 2005, p.27.

Often, buildings were not only ransacked, they were burned to the ground. In many cities, "local government and Party offices, even prisons, were surrendered without a struggle"[88] while police stood by. The scale of unrest was in any case too great for them to handle without Soviet aid. But also, the SED leaders' doubts about their reliability proved justified; some police, KVP and even Stasi personnel either joined the demonstrations or deserted their posts. Nor were they the only defectors. Scores of SED and government officials, as well as many members of the party's youth organisation (FDJ) and FDGB members and officials joined in the strikes and demonstrations.[89] Some demonstrations were actually led by union functionaries, notably veterans of the pre-1933 unions.[90]

Marches and rallies mostly started peacefully, but workers in some areas fought back when security forces were sent in. As the day wore on, clashes became more violent, particularly in major centres of unrest such as Magdeburg, Halle and Leipzig.[91]

There were numerous attacks on those seen to represent the regime. In Brandenburg a public prosecutor and a hated judge, notorious for handing out harsh sentences for petty crimes, were beaten up and taken to the market square to be "interrogated" by a crowd of 5,000 angry demonstrators. It was only the intervention of strike leaders that prevented them being lynched on the spot, though both men later died of their injuries.[92]

Who participated...and who didn't?
Other sectors of the population were drawn into the nationwide protests, among them farmers, school students and housewives. But "these elements were not typical of the social groups from which they came and were...far less numerous than the much larger working-class contingent".[93] Workers at a factory in Halberstadt demonstrated

---

88. Brant 1957, p.188.
89. Dennis 2000, p.66.
90. Ross 2000, p.55.
91. See Brant 1957, chapter 8.
92. Brant 1957, p.84. For a detailed account of strikes and protests in Brandenburg, see pp.80–87.
93. Grieder 2007, pp.152.

their advanced consciousness by voting to reserve a place on the strike committee for a woman;[94] but because most strikers were industrial workers in male-dominated sectors, women (mainly housewives) constituted a minority among the demonstrators. However, they were prominent in actions such as the storming of jails and police stations.[95]

The revolt was not confined to the cities. There were protests in some rural areas, mostly in districts south of Berlin. These were areas where the economy relied upon both industrial and agricultural production and consequently there were strong connections between peasants and workers, who "lived side by side and interacted with one another socially".[96] Things were quieter in predominantly agricultural areas.

There were other sectors of the population whose support for the uprising was minimal or non-existent: the middle classes, the intelligentsia (especially university lecturers and students, writers and artists), most white-collar employees employed in administration and church leaders.[97]

Semyonov reported to Molotov on 18 June: "Representatives of the intelligentsia took almost no part in the strikes and disturbances.... Classes in schools and in institutions of higher learning...continued in a normal fashion".[98] As he noted in his report on 24 June: "The implementation...of measures to improve the situation of the intelligentsia [ie the New Course]...determined to a significant degree its loyal conduct and favourable attitude toward the government". He also praised "the loyal behaviour of the Evangelical and Catholic churches".[99]

The partial exception to this was members of the "technical intelligentsia" located in the factories. For example, more than

---

94. Sperber 2004, p.633.
95. Grieder 2012, p.39. The SED leadership in Leipzig estimated that a quarter of the demonstrators there were housewives. Sperber 2004, p.633.
96. Witkowski 2006, p.261.
97. Stibbe 2006, p.48; Dennis 2000, p.68; Brant 1957, p.78; Fulbrook 2002, p.155.
98. "Telephonogram from Vladimir Semyonov and Vasilii Sokolovskii to Vyacheslav Molotov Reporting on the Situation in East Berlin", in Ostermann 2001, p.217.
99. "Report on the Events of 17–19 June 1953", in Ostermann 2001, pp.273, 274.

80 percent of the scientists and technicians employed at the electronics factory in Berlin-Köpenick joined the strikers,[100] while some engineers and other technicians sat on strike committees and played an active role in leading the movement.[101] Their close day-to-day connection with industrial workers was a key factor.

Spontaneity and organisation

Most historians stress the spontaneity of the uprising and the lack of coordinated leadership. Baring identifies two distinct stages on 17 June. The first involved striking workers marching into city centres, tearing down pictures of party leaders, political posters and banners, occupying public buildings and trying to release political prisoners. "In everything they did the workers displayed remarkable discipline...due to the influence of the strike committees." The second stage saw wider layers of the population joining in, but the central strike committees set up in many towns "did not have the authority of the workers' committees and so were unable to exercise effective control".[102]

As the demonstrations grew later in the day, "the actions became ever less coordinated"; assaults on party and government buildings were "largely expressions of anger and outrage rather than for strategic purposes".[103] Brant describes the focus on releasing prisoners as a "fatal error", as the government "could scarcely be threatened by... undernourished political internees".[104] There were few serious attempts to seize control of key road and railway junctions, media or transport and communications; nor were there any efforts to seize weapons from the security forces, or to use firearms against them.[105] Where protesters did try to seize post offices and telecommunications centres (Dresden, Halle, Leipzig and Görlitz), they were beaten back.

Often, "the thrust of protest was less towards an assault on centres of power and more on [acts of] symbolic liberation [which] could function to mobilise protest...without directly affecting the sinews of

---

100. Brant 1957, p.77.
101. Dennis 2000, p.68; Dale 2003, p.41.
102. Baring 1972, pp.73-74.
103. Fulbrook 1995, p.184.
104. Brant 1957, pp.188-89.
105. Fulbrook 1995, p.184; Pritchard 2000, p.209.

state power".[106] Military intervention "raise[d] the costs of protesting, multiplied the uncertainties facing participants, and contributed to a partial fragmentation of the sense of unity that had marked the rising's earlier stages".[107]

But as Kopstein notes, "the absence of [political leadership] did not prevent the initiation of collective action that threatened to bring down the regime".[108] And in fact there was a greater degree of organisation than had been previously thought, especially in areas where there were stronger left-wing traditions and a history of working-class and community solidarity.

At crucial moments, individuals and groups took the initiative. "These interventions were in one sense 'spontaneous' (ie, impromptu) reactions…but, equally, they were socially and politically determined, shaped by previous experience."[109] Many workers who initiated strikes and marches "had either done so before or had learned of such practices…from relatives, through an immersion in the culture of the labour movement".[110]

The rapid spread of the strikes was a product of both the leadership of conscious militants and the receptiveness of wide layers of the workforce to arguments for collective action.

> In the disciplined and purposeful manner in which the strikes, demonstrations and factory occupations proceeded, one could perceive the traditions of collective action of the labour and trade union movements. Also, the experience of all those old workers' movement "cadre"…who were active in the strike leaderships, contributed to imparting the spontaneously erupting strikes with a certain organised solidity.[111]

Elected strike committees often consisted of individuals with a record of standing up to management or who had spoken out against SED

---

106. Dale 2003, p.16.
107. Dale 2003, p.15.
108. Kopstein 1996, p.414.
109. Dale 2003, pp.27–28.
110. Dale 2003, p.29.
111. Klaus Ewers and Thorsten Quest, quoted in Dale 2003, p.29.

officials in workplace meetings that morning. Given the short time available to them, these committees demonstrated a remarkable level of democratic organisation and in some cases quickly exercised an astonishing degree of initiative and authority.

> To a certain extent the strike committees temporarily became "organs of power": they took on the coordination of enterprise activity...[and] led the negotiations with factory managements. They also took responsibility for maintaining peace and order in the workplaces, they protected property from damage and prevented attacks on individuals; in some cases picket lines were organised too... In countless workplaces the committees coordinated the spread of the strike to neighbouring factories, as well as the marches to town centres and sometimes, even, further activities in the local region.[112]

The main centres of struggle were the industrialised districts of Greater Berlin, Leipzig, Magdeburg, the Halle-Merseburg-Bitterfeld district and Görlitz. These were areas where workers were concentrated in very large enterprises, most prominently construction, mining,[113] machine building and the chemical and iron-ore producing industries. They were also traditional strongholds of the German left and the labour movement.[114]

Joint strike committees were established in a number of these places, and in Halle-Merseburg and Magdeburg, they temporarily seized control. Attempting to spread the strike, they took over the telephone exchange to make contact with other workplaces and commandeered vehicles to use for picketing. In Magdeburg, flying pickets broke down the doors of the Karl Marx plant in order to bring out the workers inside.

---

112. Heidi Roth, quoted in Dale 2005, p.24.
113. Mainly in iron ore, potassium and copper mines. Uranium and coal miners played a minor part in the strike, mainly because Soviet troops intervened quickly in these highly strategic industries. Baring 1972, pp.59–60.
114. In Halle-Merseburg, the KPD had been the strongest single party during the Weimar period; Magdeburg, Görlitz and Dresden had been SPD strongholds. Leipzig and Berlin had strong representation of both parties. Baring 1972, p.68; Dale 2003, p.31.

The towns of Görlitz and Bitterfeld saw the highest level of workers' organisation and control.[115] In Bitterfeld, an elected committee of representatives from the major factories plus a housewife and a student "usurped both economic and civic authority, in a matter of hours". This "perfectly structured leadership organ acted, instructed, appointed, proclaimed; all in constant…communication with the tumultuous masses in the streets, and in contact with other sites of the uprising".[116] It ensured that food and energy supplies were in rebel hands and organised units of workers who took control of the prison, the post office, town hall, SED offices, telephone exchange and Stasi headquarters. The mayor was arrested, police officers disarmed, and the police chief locked up. The strike committee sent a telegram to the government demanding its resignation, the formation of a "provisional government of progressive workers" and the dissolution of the army.

In Görlitz a "committee of popular rule" established an alternative administration, sacked the police chief, forced the mayor to approve the release of political prisoners and attempted to gain control of communications. An unarmed "workers' militia" directed the occupation of the courts, police stations, the town hall, offices of the SED, FDJ and Stasi, the regional newspaper and the railway station. The committee was even able to meet simultaneously and interact with the mass rally. "Everyone was able to put their demands", recalled one demonstrator.

But these highpoints were exceptions. Time often ran out before attempts to coordinate strike action could bear fruit. In Dresden for example a joint strike committee was stymied by the delaying tactics of local party apparatchiks. By the time an "illegal strike committee" of delegates from five factories was established, martial law had been declared and the delegates were arrested before they could meet.

---

115. The following account is based on Dale 2003, pp.19–20.
116. Manfred Hagen, quoted in Dale 2003, p.19.

Resistance continues

The overwhelming numbers of heavily armed Soviet forces suppressed the uprising relatively quickly. Mass demonstrations were violently dispersed, workers forced back to work at gunpoint, and members of strike committees arrested. But when Semyonov reported to Moscow on 24 June that the strikes in Berlin had subsided and that "a normal situation was restored",[117] he spoke too soon. The crackdown, and particularly the arrest of strike leaders, actually prompted new strikes.

Working-class defiance continued into late summer and early autumn, with sporadic strikes erupting in large industrial conglomerations.[118] Leipzig remained in a state of siege for several weeks. During July there was a mini-strike wave. On 4 July workers at the steelworks in Thale staged a sit-down strike and secured the release of a number of strike leaders. In mid-July several thousand workers at Carl-Zeiss-Jena and the Buna Chemical Works in Schkopau went out on strike, the latter demanding free elections, the release of all political prisoners, the reduction of the KVP and the transformation of the FDGB into "a combat organisation of all workers".[119] Breaking the two strikes required massive intervention by the security forces, and effectively ended the second wave of unrest.

But even after this, passive forms of resistance such as go-slows and absenteeism were common. Output in the coal mines at Zwickau, which had not struck on 17 June, fell steeply because the workers were constantly found "doing nothing, and even asleep".[120] In early September, the sick-rate in the coal-mines around Stollberg, normally 3 percent, rose to 22.5 percent.[121]

---

117. "Report on the Events of 17–19 June 1953 in Berlin and the GDR and Certain Conclusions from These Events", in Ostermann 2001, p.263.
118. Pritchard 2002, p.113. In many cases, the workers' demands included the release of arrested colleagues. Baring 1972, p.101.
119. Dennis 2000, p.69; Dale 2003, p.22.
120. Brant 1957, p.161.
121. Pritchard 2002, p.115.

The aftermath

For the SED – and their Russian masters – the pressing need now was to restore stability and forestall any further eruptions. This was achieved with a combination of political repression and economic concessions.

Repression

On 16–17 June 1,744 East Berliners were arrested, and over the following weeks the rest of the country experienced a wave of repression. The number of arrests reached a single-day peak of 6,325 on 23 June, rising to 13,000 by 1 August.[122] Of these, 1,524 people received harsh prison sentences, ranging from one to ten years or more, with three life sentences. Several hundred "anti-communists" were deported to Siberia.

The purpose of the crackdown was not just to punish the participants, but to intimidate the population. Justice Minister Max Fechner was a high-profile casualty. In interviews published in *Neues Deutschland* in early July, he had defended the right to strike as guaranteed by the GDR's constitution, and argued that neither participation in nor leadership of strikes was a crime. Denounced as an "enemy of the state" and stripped of party membership, he was arrested on 16 July and sentenced to eight years imprisonment.[123]

Not wanting to be taken unawares again, the regime overhauled the Stasi and built up its apparatus. The MfS (Ministry for State Security), founded in 1950, employed more than 10,000 people by 1952, making it larger than Hitler's Gestapo had ever been.[124] Initially the Stasi had focused on anti-Communist organisations based in West Germany. But that changed now. Not only did the Stasi experience "exponential growth" (up to 17,400 by November 1957),[125] but it also set about massively increasing its domestic surveillance program by recruiting informants to spy on the population.[126] By 1954, the Stasi had almost 145,900 agents on its books.[127]

---

122. Bruce 2003, p.27; Kramer 1999a, p.55.
123. Baras 1975, p.389; Fechner was released in 1956.
124. Sperber 2004, p.624.
125. Grieder 2012, p.44.
126. Thomson 2017, p.83.
127. Grieder 2012, p.44.

In the factories, additional surveillance was carried out by newly established *Kampfgruppen der Arbeiterklasse* (workforce combat groups) composed of workers chosen for their political reliability. All of this repressive apparatus "provided the leadership with an ever-present coercive force that contributed to the outward semblance of stability in the GDR between 1953 and 1989".[128] The flow of emigration to the West was largely stemmed with the construction of the Berlin Wall in 1961, turning East Germany into a "prison state".

The SED: purges and resignations

After the rising, Ulbricht came close to losing his position. Yet in the end he not only survived, but actually consolidated his leadership. The succession struggle in Russia remained unresolved. Malenkov and Khrushchev had been conspiring for some time to oust Beria, but the crisis in East Germany "caused a slight delay in [their] timetable".[129] Ulbricht used Beria's arrest on 26 June to discredit his opponents in the SED leadership. At a Central Committee meeting on 24 July, he implied that Zaisser and Herrnstadt had been "secretly colluding with Beria in pursuit of a 'capitulatory policy which would have ended in the restoration of capitalism'".[130]

But Ulbricht survived mainly because Moscow could not afford to take the risk of replacing him. Since Ulbricht's resignation had been a key demand of the uprising, the Kremlin feared that removing him would be seen as a capitulation, and that unrest could spill over into neighbouring Eastern Bloc states.

For a short period, the SED made a show of repentance and self-criticism. Between 20 June and early July, leading functionaries visited a number of large industrial sites, where they engaged in "long, self-critical and...extremely open discussions with the workers in an attempt to regain their confidence".[131] The response was not what they had hoped for. On 23 June Ulbricht himself tried to talk to employees at a state-owned machine tool factory, but was "greeted with shouts, boos

---

128. Ostermann 2001, p.416.
129. Kramer 1999b, p.21.
130. Stibbe 2006, p.46. See also Baring 1972, pp.108–9.
131. Baring 1972, p.103. See also Brant 1957, p.159.

and catcalls".[132] On a visit to the Leuna Works the following day, he was forced to listen to the workforce's demands for freedom of speech and the separation of party and unions.[133]

But once the situation stabilised and Ulbricht regained control, the pretence of self-criticism came to an abrupt halt. The SED was thoroughly purged: along with dissident factions in the leadership and officials deemed to have failed in their duties, many rank-and-file members were expelled. A third of these had been KPD members since before 1933.[134] But in 1953, their class solidarity won out over party loyalty.

Worker members deserted the party in droves. A report from Zschopau noted that: "it has been above all the older comrades who have…expressed the opinion that there is no longer any trust in the authorities". The widespread reports of such attitudes signalled a "rupture between the party and the class it was supposed to represent" and provides "clear evidence that, for many workers, their rejection of the SED was based not on a love of West Germany and capitalist democracy, but on a principled, Socialist rejection of Stalinism".[135]

Concessions – and working-class resilience

Repression alone was not sufficient. The SED was forced to grant significant economic concessions to placate the force it most feared – the workers. The norm increases were rescinded and most workers experienced significant improvements in pay and working conditions. By September 1954 an estimated 3.7 billion East German marks had been redistributed to the general population.[136] After 1953 "the state ensured that at least basic necessities were available…at reasonable

---

132. Stibbe 2006, p.45.
133. Dennis 2000, p.69; Dale 2003, p.21. The Leuna workers had a history of revolutionary militancy. In the disastrous March Action of 1921, for example, the factory was taken over by armed workers. Dale 2003, p.31. See also Brant 1957, pp.96–97.
134. Pritchard 2000, 216. The numbers of expelled veterans were higher in centres of revolt: 52 percent in Magdeburg, 59 percent in Leipzig, 68 percent in East Berlin.
135. Pritchard 2000, pp.213–14.
136. Stibbe 2006, p.47. The concessions are detailed in "On the present position of the party and the tasks facing it in the immediate future", SED Central Committee resolution, 21 June 1953, in Baring 1972, pp.170–72.

prices. Food, housing and utilities remained heavily subsidised and inexpensive until the very end of the regime".[137]

> Frequent unofficial work stoppages – small acts of sabotage, protest or ministrikes and walk-outs – were constant reminders of the importance of keeping the workers at least satisfied, if not happy; sops to consumerism were repeated ploys to keep levels of unrest from rising.[138]

Fear of renewed industrial conflict meant that "even the most hard-nosed factory directors learned to bargain with workers... The experiences of 1953 undermined the party leadership's ability to gain control over the shopfloor".[139]

As a result, throughout the 1950s wages rose faster than productivity in every sector of industry. Despite numerous unsuccessful efforts to rectify this problem, the regime never again dared to introduce arbitrary norm increases. Wage egalitarianism "remained a constant of East German industry [and] gradually became a social norm... Along with job security, East German workers had the power to demand...consumer prices that remained low relative to wages".[140]

From the perspective of the SED leaders, "little could be done to change economic structures or industrial relations without the risk of open rebellion".[141] To avoid this, the government was prepared to accede to economic demands – provided conflicts were kept "inside the factory and out of politics". Workers were rarely disciplined for factory rule infractions, and their criticisms were tolerated – as long as they remained "apolitical" and were not voiced in public. This strategy "was effective in keeping workers' protests well below any real level of danger".[142] But the long-term consequence was that the regime was left in a permanently

---

137. Grieder 2012, p.44.
138. Ostermann 2001, p.416.
139. Ross 2000, p.59.
140. Kopstein 1999, pp.415, 416, 421.
141. Kopstein 1999, pp.421–22.
142. Wierling 1996, pp.58, 59.

weakened state. Its inability to undertake "meaningful economic reform" – ie, suppress workers' wages – severely restricted its ability to compete with the West.

Right up until 1989, the shock of 1953 and the possibility of its recurrence was a source of acute anxiety for the SED leadership. Ernst Wollweber, the minister of state security between 1953 and 1957, later wrote that Ulbricht was "haunted" by "the fright of June 17".[143]

On the first two anniversaries of the uprising, police, the KVP and the *Kampfgruppen* were ordered to remain in a "state of heightened readiness".[144] What was a "lasting trauma" for the regime had given the working class "a certain awareness of its own strength and authority".[145]

> The spectre of 17 June assumed downright mythical dimensions in both the factories as well as in the halls of power. It became a cultural icon synonymous with workers' discontent... During the 1950s, reports around the anniversary of the 17 June uprising commonly cite various "provocations" from workers, such as moments of silence on the factory floor, drinking bouts in the canteen, high rates of absenteeism, the increased distribution of hostile leaflets and the daubing of slogans such as "Give us more to eat, have you forgotten the 17th of June?"[146]

Nature of the uprising

The SED tried to paint the uprising as an attempted fascist coup, organised by Western agents.[147] But dispatches sent by Soviet intelligence officials "provided no evidence to support...allegations of an 'imperialist conspiracy'". Their reports instead "contained many scathing comments about the SED's 'unacceptable blunders'

---

143. Epstein 2003, p.111.
144. Bessel 2002, p.71.
145. Wierling 1996, p.58.
146. Ross 2000, p.57.
147. See "On the present position of the party and the tasks facing it in the immediate future", SED Central Committee resolution, 21 June 1953, in Baring 1972, pp.160–65.

and 'extremely deficient' performance", and concluded that "the mistaken policies" and "abuses" of the SED were the "prime cause of the disturbances and unrest".[148] After months of investigation, "the state security service was forced to admit that it had found no evidence of either large-scale Western participation in or leadership of the insurrection".[149]

The mainstream Western interpretation is that it was a "people's uprising", the working class just one element in a society-wide rejection of "communism". Brant writes that the uprising could be considered a "classless revolution", driven by a "common and elementary desire for freedom", as exemplified by the West.[150] This is contradicted by the evidence, which overwhelmingly confirms that "it was above all the industrial working class...which played the leading role in the Uprising and determined its character".[151]

The most convincing argument has been made by left-wing anti-Stalinist historians, who insist that it was "first and foremost a 'workers' uprising' against Stalinism, the goal of which was not to destroy Socialism in East Germany, but to free it of its bureaucratic and authoritarian distortions".[152] One of these, Torsten Diedrich, writes that:

> the demand for the abolition of the GDR simply was not raised.
> The main reason for this is arguably that the majority of the workers in the GDR did not regard the political system in the Federal Republic...as the alternative. The thrust of the workers' rising therefore aimed at the democratic transformation of the East German state.[153]

Similarly, Martin Jänicke argues that "in 1953 the Central German working class became the bearer of the general resistance against Stalinism, 'a class whose opposition...was determined in no small

---

148. Kramer 1999b, pp.7–8.
149. Sperber 2004, p.631.
150. Brant 1957, pp.196, 197, 199.
151. Pritchard 2000, p.211.
152. Pritchard 2000, p.207.
153. Quoted in Pritchard 2002, p.113.

part by socialist traditions'".[154] Such views are given credence by numerous small incidents. For example, in the Halle market square "a large propaganda portrait of Karl Marx…was untouched, while its counterpart of Stalin was destroyed".[155]

Summarising the arguments of the anti-Stalinist historians, Pritchard writes:

> It was no accident…that the Uprising was at its most intense in precisely those towns and cities…which had long been the traditional strongholds of the German labour movement. The Uprising, they assert, bore all the hallmarks of organised working-class dissent, such as the formation of factory committees and factory councils, the shouting of traditional Socialist slogans and the singing of Socialist songs.[156]

The leading role played by the working class is indicated by their preponderance in the number of arrests. By 30 June 6,171 people had been arrested; of the 5,296 individuals whose class origin is known, 65.2 percent were workers. In Leipzig 85 percent of the 143 people arrested by 10 August were working-class.[157] Internal government documents indicate that overall at least 70 percent of those detained were workers.[158]

A revolutionary opportunity?

East German workers did not set out to make a revolution. As Brant writes: "it is doubtful whether, at the moment of downing tools, many of the building workers realised the full implications of their action".[159] But the generalisation and rapid spread of strike action inevitably

---

154. Scholmer 1964. Jänicke was a prominent advocate for a "third way", which he defined as an "attempt to synthesise positive elements of both systems [West and East], to find a middle line, to democratise socialism and to fill it with liberal content".
155. Sperber 2004, p.635.
156. Pritchard 2000, pp.211–12.
157. Pritchard 2000, p.212.
158. For examples of SED members participating in and even leading strikes, see Pritchard 2002, p.121.
159. Brant 1957, p.184.

raised the question, for both the participants and the regime. After all, any serious general strike "amounts to a gauntlet thrown not only to factory and company managements but to government itself".[160] As Rosa Luxemburg argued in "The Mass Strike", the relationship between economic and political struggles is highly reciprocal, each reinforcing the other; they "form the two interlacing sides of the proletarian class struggle".[161]

Baring observes that "the strikes were prompted...by economic considerations and it was not until the workers had massed on the streets and their ranks were swollen by passers-by that they felt sufficiently elated to call for political changes", raising demands that "gave the demonstrations a completely different character".[162]

While the higher norms were the catalyst, workers raised a range of other demands. Some were economic, such as equal pay for women, an eight-hour day and the abolition of piecework. But they also made connections between purely "material" and political issues, such as the build-up of the security forces and pay cuts for workers. So political demands were raised in most workplaces from a very early stage, and increasingly in the mass demonstrations.

In a few areas, as we have seen, events began to assume an insurrectionary character. Brant again: "the stoppage...on the Stalinallee became the prologue of a revolutionary drama and the fact that the revolution was smothered while still at the stage of insurrection does not alter its character and objectives".[163]

In 1915, Lenin argued that a revolutionary situation exists:

> (1) when it is impossible for the ruling classes to maintain their rule without any change; when there is a crisis...in the policy of the ruling class, leading to a fissure through which the discontent and indignation of the oppressed classes burst forth... (2) when the suffering and want of the oppressed classes have grown more acute than usual; (3) when, as a

---

160. Dale 2003, p.13.
161. Luxemburg 1970, p.185.
162. Baring 1972, p.73.
163. Brant 1957, p.185.

> consequence of the above causes, there is a considerable increase in the activity of the masses, who…in turbulent times, are drawn both by all the circumstances of the crisis *and by the "upper classes" themselves* into independent historical action.[164]

These conditions were all present in East Germany in 1953. But, as Lenin noted, not every revolutionary situation leads to revolution. In Russia in 1917, the revolution succeeded because of the leadership of the Bolsheviks: a mass revolutionary party built over decades of struggle, with a clear understanding of what needed to be done, and the authority and credibility to lead the working class. This most certainly did not exist in East Germany, and as has been shown time and time again (notably in Germany in 1918[165]), such an organisation cannot be built overnight in the heat of the struggle. Moreover, there was no clarity – in Germany or anywhere else – about the nature of the enemy. Most of the international left supported Russia as socialist; the Trotskyists saw Russia as a "degenerated workers' state" and its satellites as "deformed workers' states" which had "ceased to be… capitalist countries".[166] To the very limited extent that Tony Cliff's pathbreaking analysis of Russia as state capitalist was known at this time, it was rejected by the left.[167]

The balance of forces was such that the workers could not have won. The intervention of Russian troops was decisive, as it would also be in Hungary three years later.

---

164. Lenin 1974, p.213.
165. See Harman 1982, chapters 3, 4 and 5.
166. Quoted in Callinicos 1990, p.32.
167. "The Nature of Stalinist Russia" was written as an internal document in 1948. An amended version was published in 1955 as *Stalinist Russia: A Marxist Analysis*, and reprinted as *State Capitalism in Russia* in 1974.

Conclusion

The East German uprising was "the first chink in the armour of Soviet hegemony in Eastern Europe",[168] and the fallout was considerable. In Russia it influenced the CPSU leadership struggle and Soviet foreign policy, especially with regard to its satellite states. News of the rebellion triggered a wave of strikes in the forced labour camps of the gulag and was a factor in the uprising in Vorkuta (July 1953) which mainly housed political prisoners.

The reverberations were felt throughout the Eastern Bloc. In the following years, further revolts challenged the Stalinist monolith: Hungary in 1956, Czechoslovakia in 1968, Poland in 1956 and again in 1980–81.[169] The GDR, however, remained relatively stable until 1989. The long-term cohesion of the ruling party was an important factor in this, due to Ulbricht's purge of "reformers". As well, the increased level of political surveillance and repression undermined workers' confidence to engage in collective resistance beyond the individual workplace.

Despite this, however, workers were able to maintain their living standards to some extent by action (or the threat of it) at the factory floor level.

> Thanks to the spectacular intensity of the uprising, its persistence over the following days in the teeth of military occupation, and the material concessions delivered in its wake, its defeat was not experienced as total. Nor could repression rob participants of the experience of the protest itself – the euphoria and solidarity...[170]

Niethammer goes so far as to write that: "the shop floor represented a liberated milieu where people could move around, could talk, could criticise, and could even go shopping during working hours".[171]

But while the working class was not totally demoralised, no lasting organisation or leadership survived. And over time, the experienced

---

168. Stibbe 2006, p.51.
169. See Harman 1988.
170. Dale 2003, p.51.
171. Niethammer 1993, p.15.

older militants who had played a leading role in 1953 died off, their memories and traditions often dying with them. It is telling that the 1989 revolution had a very different class character. Unlike in 1953, workers as an organised force did not play a leading role.[172]

Despite its brevity and defeat, the 1953 uprising is worth remembering and celebrating as an example of the strength, courage and resilience of the working class, its capacity for solidarity, democratic organisation and collective action and its ability to lead the struggle for a better world.

References

Baras, Victor 1975, "Beria's Fall and Ulbricht's Survival, *Soviet Studies*, 27 (3), July, pp.381–95.

Baring, Arnulf M 1972 [1959], *Uprising in East Germany: June 17, 1953* (trans. Gerald Onn), Cornell University Press.

Bessel, Richard 2002, "The People's Police and the People in Ulbricht's Germany", in *The Workers' and Peasants' State. Communism and Society in East Germany under Ulbricht 1941–1971*, Patrick Major and Jonathan Osmond (eds), Manchester University Press.

Brant, Stefan 1957 [1954], *The East German Rising* (trans. Charles Wheeler), Praeger.

Bruce, Gary 2003, "The Prelude to Nationwide Surveillance in East Germany: Stasi Operations and Threat Perceptions, 1945–1953", *Journal of Cold War Studies*, 5 (2), pp.3–31.

Callinicos, Alex 1990, *Trotskyism*, Open University Press.

Churchill, Winston, 1946, "Iron curtain" speech, *The National Archives*, 5 March. https://www.nationalarchives.gov.uk/education/resources/cold-war-on-file/iron-curtain-speech/

Collins, Steven Morris 2017, *Intelligence and the Uprising in East Germany 1953: An Example of Political Intelligence*, MA thesis, University of North Texas. https://digital.library.unt.edu/ark:/67531/metadc1011823/

Crabtree, Charles, Holger Kern and Steven Pfaff 2018, "Mass Media and the Diffusion of Collective Action in Authoritarian Regimes: The June 1953 East German Uprising", *International Studies Quarterly*, 62, pp.301–14.

---

172. See Dale 2005, Part 2.

Dale, Gareth 2003, "'Like Wildfire'? The East German Rising of June 1953", *Debatte: Journal of Contemporary Central and Eastern Europe*, 11 (2). https://www.academia.edu/28659208/_Like_Wildfire_The_East_German_Uprising_of_1953

Dale, Gareth 2005, *Popular Protest in East Germany, 1945-1989*, Routledge.

Dennis, Mike 2000, *The Rise and Fall of the German Democratic Republic, 1945-1990*, Longman.

Diedrich, Torsten 1992, "Der 17. Juni 1953 in der DDR. Zu militärhistorischen Aspekten bei Ursachen und Verlauf der Unruhen", *Militärgeschichtliche Zeitschrift*, 51 (2), 8 January, pp.357-84. https://www.degruyter.com/document/doi/10.1524/mgzs.1992.51.2.357/html?lang=de

Epstein, Catherine 2003, *The Last Revolutionaries: German Communists and Their Century*, Harvard University Press.

Fulbrook, Mary 1995, *Anatomy of a Dictatorship: Inside the GDR 1949-1989*. Oxford University Press.

Fulbrook, Mary 2002, *History of Germany 1918-2000. The Divided Nation* (2nd edition), Blackwell.

Geerling, Wayne, Gary B Magee and Russell Smyth 2021, "Occupation, Reparations, and Rebellion: The Soviets and the East German Uprising of 1953", *The Journal of Interdisciplinary History*, 52 (2), pp.225-50. https://www.researchgate.net/publication/344036995_Occupation_Reparations_and_Rebellion_The_Soviets_and_the_East_German_Uprising_of_1953

Gluckstein, Donny 1999, *The Nazis, Capitalism and the Working Class*, Bookmarks.

Grabas, Margrit 2015, "17 June 1953 – The East German Workers' Uprising as a Catalyst for a Socialist Economic Order", *Vierteljahrschrift für Sozial- und Wirtschaftsgeschichte*, 102 (2), pp.182-90.

Grieder, Peter 1999, *The East German Leadership, 1946-73: Conflict and Crisis*, Manchester University Press.

Grieder, Peter 2007, "Perspectives on *Resistance with the People*", *Journal of Cold War Studies*, 9 (3), Summer, MIT Press.

Grieder, Peter 2012, *The German Democratic Republic*, Palgrave Macmillan.

Harman, Chris 1982, *The Lost Revolution. Germany 1918-1923*, Bookmarks.

Harman, Chris 1988, *Class Struggles in Eastern Europe 1945-83* (3rd edition), Bookmarks.

Henderson, David R n.d., "German Economic Miracle". https://www.econlib.org/library/Enc/GermanEconomicMiracle.html

Kopstein, Jeffrey 1996, "Chipping Away at the State: Workers' Resistance and the Demise of East Germany", *World Politics*, 48, pp.391–423. https://cpb-us-e2.wpmucdn.com/faculty.sites.uci.edu/dist/9/994/files/2021/05/chipping_away_at_the_state.pdf

Kramer, Mark 1999a, "The Early Post-Stalin Succession Struggle and Upheavals in East-Central Europe. Part 1", *Journal of Cold War Studies*, 1 (1), Winter, pp.3–55, MIT Press.

Kramer, Mark 1999b, "The Early Post-Stalin Succession Struggle and Upheavals in East-Central Europe. Part 2", *Journal of Cold War Studies*, 1 (2), Spring, pp.3–38, MIT Press.

Lenin, Vladimir Ilyich 1974 [1915], "The Collapse of the Second International", in *Collected Works*, Vol.21, Progress Publishers, pp.205–59. https://www.marxists.org/archive/lenin/works/1915/csi/ii.htm#v21pp74h-212

Luxemburg, Rosa 1970, "The Mass Strike, the Political Party and the Trade Unions" [1906], in *Rosa Luxemburg Speaks*, ed. Mary-Alice Walters, Pathfinder Press. https://www.marxists.org/archive/luxemburg/1906/mass-strike/index.htm

Merson, Allan 1985, *Communist Resistance in Nazi Germany*, Lawrence and Wishart.

Niethammer, Lutz 1993, "The Structure and Restructuring of the German Working Classes after 1945 and after 1990", *The Oral History Review*, 21 (2), Winter, pp.9–18.

Ostermann, Christian F 1996, "'Keeping the Pot Simmering': The United States and the East German Uprising of 1953", *German Studies Review*, 19 (1), February, pp.61–89, Johns Hopkins University Press.

Ostermann, Christian F (ed.) 2001, *Uprising in East Germany 1953: the Cold War, the German question, and the first major upheaval behind the Iron Curtain*, Central European University Press.

Port, Andrew 1997, "When workers rumbled: The Wismut upheaval of August 1951 in East Germany", *Social History*, 22, May, pp.145–73.

Pritchard, Gareth 2000, *The Making of the GDR, 1945–1953: from Antifascism to Stalinism*, Manchester University Press.

Pritchard, Gareth 2002, "Workers and the Socialist Unity Party of Germany in the Summer of 1953", in *The Workers' and Peasants' State. Communism and Society in East Germany under Ulbricht 1941–1971*, Patrick Major and Jonathan Osmond (eds), Manchester University Press.

Richie, Alexandra 1998, *Faust's Metropolis: A History of Berlin*, Carroll & Graf Publishers.

Ross, Corey 2000, *Constructing Socialism at the Grass-Roots: The Transformation of East Germany, 1945–65*, St. Martin's Press.

Scholmer, Joseph 1964, Review of *Der dritte Weg: Die antistalinistische Opposition gegen Ulbricht seit 1953* [The Third Way: The anti-Stalinist opposition to Ulbricht since 1953] by Martin Jänicke, Neuer Deutscher Verlag, in *Zeit*, 31, 31 July. https://www.zeit.de/1964/31/die-opposition-gegen-ulbricht/komplettansicht?utm_referrer=https%3A%2F%2Fwww.google.com%2F

Sperber, Jonathan 2004, "17 June 1953: Revisiting a German Revolution", *German History*, 22 (4), pp.619–43.

Stibbe, Matthew 2006, "The SED, German Communism and June 1953 Uprising: New Trends and New Research", in *Revolution and Resistance in Eastern Europe: Challenges to Communist Rule*, K McDermott and M Stibbe (eds), pp.37–56, Berg.

Thomson, Henry 2017, "Repression, Redistribution and the Problem of Authoritarian Control", *East European Politics and Societies*, 31 (1), pp.68–92.

Wierling, Dorothee 1996, "Work, Workers, and Politics in the German Democratic Republic", *International Labor and Working-Class History*, 50, pp.44–63, Cambridge University Press.

Witkowski, Gregory R 2006, "Peasants' Revolt? Re-evaluating the 17 June Uprising in East Germany", *German History*, 24 (2), May, pp.243–66.

SAM PIETSCH

Review: Analysing Australian imperialism

> **Sam Pietsch** is the author of a PhD about Australia's military intervention in East Timor in 1999. He has been active in socialist politics for over two decades.

Clinton Fernandes, *Sub-Imperial Power: Australia in the International Arena*, Melbourne University Press, 2022.

THE CENTRAL ISSUE in world politics today is geopolitical competition between the United States and China in the Asia-Pacific region. The Australian state is one of the US's strongest supporters in this contest, a stance publicly justified by the supposed threat posed by China to democracy and human rights.

Challenging this narrative and understanding why Australia acts in concert with its superpower ally is a priority for anyone opposed to imperialism. Clinton Fernandes' book *Sub-Imperial Power* is a welcome contribution to these efforts. Fernandes has a background in military intelligence and as an academic at the Australian Defence Force Academy. But in this book he dismantles many of the foundational myths of Australia's security establishment and opposes the imperialist logic which is making the prospect of war between the US and China ever more likely.

Short and accessibly written, this is a book aimed at influencing public discussion rather than academia. But nor is it really a work of the political left. Fernandes doesn't engage with theoretical debates about imperialism and his lack of a clear political framework reduces the book's usefulness for socialists.

Fernandes' central contention is that Australia is a "sub-imperial" power. "[I]t is subordinate to the imperial centre [that is the United States], defends the imperial order known as a rules-based international order, and projects considerable power and influence in its own region" (p.21). As a first approximation, this analysis has a lot of merit. Clearly Australia and the US are not equals. The United States is the world's sole superpower and when it comes to conflicts in the Middle East or confronting China, Australia supports the US rather than going it alone.

But Fernandes does not slide into a simplistic anti-Americanism, which sees the Australian state as betraying its own "national interest" in the service of the US. In short, "Australia is not a victim of this imperial order but a junior partner and enthusiastic – if anxious – supporter" (p.16). He argues that Australia has generally benefitted from the US-centred international order. Although not really a focus of this book, Fernandes also touches on Australia's own dominance of small regional nations such as Papua New Guinea, the Solomon Islands and East Timor. This is a step forward from left nationalist analyses which have long been prevalent on the Australian left.[1] But nor does Fernandes completely avoid the problems associated with these positions.

The strongest part of the book is its critique of the so-called "rules-based international order", which is the constantly repeated rallying cry of the US and allies like Australia in their confrontation of China. They claim to be defending a neutral set of rules which benefit all countries, in accordance with established international legal norms.

Fernandes rightly exposes how these claims serve to legitimate the US and Australia's own interests. The international order established after World War II was constructed around US economic and financial supremacy, with a banking system centred in New York and the US dollar serving as the global reserve currency. International bodies like

---

1. O'Lincoln 2021, pp.3–6; Kuhn 1997.

the World Bank and International Monetary Fund are constructed along lines dictated by the US. The rules establish the rights of private business to invest capital wherever it chooses, with free trade agreements favouring the more developed economies.

Of course, liberal economic principles can be abandoned when necessary. A prime example is the current US attempt to limit Chinese access to computer microchips. These are crucial components if China is to develop high end manufacturing capabilities, including of advanced weaponry.

The US has also established a string of military bases and alliances which surround China and threaten its vital trade routes. It's not a threat China can ignore, given the US has repeatedly toppled governments which oppose its interests, either by invasion or by fomenting internal coups. On the other hand, rhetorical commitments to democracy and human rights have never stopped the US forming alliances with friendly dictators.

Fernandes rightly argues that the status quo international order has benefitted Australia's economy, enabling the export of efficiently produced primary commodities like coal and iron ore. So having "coasted in the slipstream of US supremacy since the end of World War II" (p.41), Australian policy makers are anxious to see the existing order maintained. Nor can Australia claim any moral high ground in terms of respect for human rights or the right to self-determination, having supported, for example, the Suharto dictatorship in Indonesia and the ongoing occupation of West Papua.

Fernandes is, however, too dismissive when he describes the rules-based order as "a euphemism for imperial practice" (p.58), implying it is a rhetorical nicety which merely disguises a more brutal reality. This obscures how the legal order positively structures international affairs and does so in ways which are not exclusively to the benefit of US capital. The global economy today really does operate for the most part according to liberal norms; trade patterns are determined by nations' comparative advantages in production; capitalists from all countries are generally free to invest where they expect to reap the greatest profits; international shipping firms enjoy freedom of navigation.

Interactions between capitalist nations states will always be structured around some form of legal order, mirroring civil society inside national borders. In both cases, legal norms govern the actions of formally equal and independent juridical agents (individual citizens, nation states), providing the structure in which substantive inequalities (class position of citizens, national economic development) are given free rein. But in the absence of an international supra-state, disputes between legally equal sovereign nations always have the potential to be resolved through the use of force. As Marxist theorist of international law China Mieville argues, "[t]he chaotic and bloody world around us *is the rule of law*".[2]

So Fernandes is right to stress how the rules currently favour the US and its allies, which is why countries like China and Russia seek to restructure them. But to counterpose the "rules-based international order" with "the United Nations-centred international system…underpinned by international law" (p.57) wrongly suggests that international law could ever be an alternative to great power rivalries.

This points to a general shallowness in Fernandes' understanding of imperialism, which is focused on the overwhelming strength of the US in world affairs and how it treats poorer countries. Quoting historian Michael Doyle, he defines imperialism as "a relationship, formal or informal, in which one state controls the effective political sovereignty of others" (p.10). This is a trans-historical definition, supposedly applicable from ancient Rome through to today.

It is of limited usefulness in understanding the international system under capitalism, which consists of a political sphere of independent territorial nation states co-existing with capitalist economic development which transcends all borders. No nation is an autarchy, "independent" of international market forces. This doesn't imply a loss of sovereignty; it is the historically unique form that sovereignty takes under capitalism.[3] But equally, the need for each state to defend its particular economic and strategic interests against competitors generates imperialist rivalry.

---

2. Mieville 2005, p.319.
3. Rosenberg 1994, chapter five.

Anti-imperialist theorists have debated how to understand the evolution of the international system since the end of the Cold War. Has inter-imperial competition involving multiple great powers, of the sort which resulted in the two world wars, now been replaced by a single US empire which serves the interests of all capitalists, or which at least effectively suppresses the rivalries of the various national capitals? Or will US dominance, which was never complete, eventually be challenged by new rivals?[4]

Fernandes doesn't engage with this debate, which means he never clarifies how the interplay of sovereignty, capitalism and imperialism generate what we know as the world order. This results in two important ambiguities running through the book.

First, Fernandes does not clearly state whether or not Australia has suffered a loss of sovereignty to the US. This is a crucial issue, since he goes so far as to argue that a nation's sovereignty can be diminished due to "collaboration between both countries' elites" (p.3), an extremely broad conception. Whether Australian interests are subordinated to those of the US, and if so, why the Australian state and capitalist class would pursue such a policy, is never resolved.

At times, Fernandes stresses the benefits of the US alliance for Australian businesses. But he also implies that substantial US investment in Australia, particularly in the mining industry, has altered Australia's stance towards China in ways which are detrimental to Australian capital. He also critiques the Australian economy as being "wealthy but dependent" due to its lack of complexity (focusing on the export of raw materials with little manufacturing) with "vital sectors...integrated into the value chains of US corporations" (p.22). But if Australian capitalists have pursued economic integration with the US, this needn't imply an infringement on Australian independence. It has simply been the most profitable alternative available to them in the global economy.

Fernandes acknowledges that Australian governments have provided the US with military support because of strategic calculations, not "for sentimental reasons or because they were duped" (p.35).

---

4. Callinicos 2009, pp.15–17 summarises this debate.

Yet he also bemoans a lack of Australian strategic independence, claiming that "[t]he aim is to uphold US military dominance, hence the deliberate choice not to develop a separate Australian military strategy" (p.29). This should not be a concern for anti-imperialists. Instead, we should focus on how the US alliance serves to enhance Australia's own power. It secures the backing of the world's strongest military and offers access to advanced weapons like the latest aircraft, missiles and now submarines. Without the alliance, the Australian ruling class would probably develop its own nuclear weapons and would certainly be forced to spend far more than the current 2 percent of gross domestic product on the military.[5]

An "independent" Australia would also continue dominating smaller regional countries. Fernandes rightly denounces how Australia has meddled in the affairs of post-independence East Timor, spying on its government and seeking to deprive it of revenues from oil deposits in the Timor Sea. But he fails to mention how Australia's military intervention in East Timor in 1999 laid the basis for all of this. Fernandes has argued previously that popular pressure forced a "reluctant" Australian government to save the new nation from Indonesia.[6] In reality, Australia deliberately used its military power to control the transition from Indonesian rule, defending its own strategic and economic interests. Australian intervention was certainly an "independent" action, towards which the US was initially ambivalent. It was also a prime example of Australian imperialism.

Ultimately, Fernandes' use of the term "sub-imperial" doesn't clarify the analysis of US-Australian relations. Whatever the particular term employed, it is important to understand that the Australian state is an imperialist power in its own right, seeking to defend as best it can the Australian capitalist class's own specific interests against rival powers. In this context the US alliance has proven immensely beneficial for the past eight decades, offering a security guarantee while enabling Australia to carve out a profitable position within the circuits of international capitalism. The alliance

---

5. Stockholm International Peace Research Institute (SIPRI) 2022. The US itself spends 3.5 percent of GDP.
6. Fernandes 2004. For a critique see Pietsch 2010.

no doubt involves unwelcome trade-offs at times and it might cease to be beneficial in future if US hegemony is undermined by Chinese competition. But it has been rationally chosen by those who exercise power in Australian society.

The second ambiguity is whether Fernandes sees China as a new imperialist competitor to the US or a potential leader of anti-imperialist challenge from the Third World. At one point he refers to the "global confrontation between developed and developing countries, between North and South, between imperialism and anti-colonialism" (p.106). It isn't clear how China's economic rise and challenge to US geopolitical hegemony in the Asia-Pacific fits into this picture.

Fernandes certainly does not join the ranks of those who for whom anti-imperialism simply means opposition to the US, even to the extent of supporting the expansionism of China or Russia. But nor does he clearly oppose the authoritarian capitalism championed by the Chinese Communist Party. Although acknowledging repressive aspects of the Chinese state, particularly in Xinjiang, Fernandes presents a generally benign view of China's international role. Its economic growth has been "achieved without resorting to slavery, war or colonialism" (p.76). And although China does not seek to impose its domestic order on other countries (except Taiwan), poor nations could see its development model as an attractive alternative to failed neoliberalism.

With tensions between the US and China rising, we should unambiguously reject supporting one side or the other. Perhaps Fernandes would agree. His concluding chapter is tantalisingly titled "Neither their war nor their peace". But he can't point to any real alternatives, merely suggesting that Third World countries might be attracted to a policy of non-alignment, advanced through motions passed at the UN: "A democratic, equitable, international order would be an alternative to an imperial order whether led by the United States or a China-based alliance system" (pp.125–6). This is utopian liberalism. It fails to see that since imperialism is the necessary outgrowth of capitalism, great power rivalry is inevitable unless its economic basis is overthrown.

In relation to Australian domestic politics, Fernandes adopts a vaguely populist position, in which the interests of "the elites" are at odds with those of "the public". It's hard to disagree that for those who want to challenge Australian foreign policy "the task is to change the domestic structure of power" (p.121). But who might have the motivation and power to effect this change remains a mystery, let alone what alternatives they should be seeking.

It is to Fernandes' credit that he has written a book which challenges the anti-China consensus of mainstream commentary on international affairs. He offers a stinging critique of how the US and Australia deploy the rhetoric of the rules-based order to justify their own imperial manoeuvres. But an effective anti-imperialist politics needs to be grounded in a clearer understanding of how Australian capitalism generates distinctive imperialist interests for the Australian ruling class.

References

Callinicos, Alex 2009, *Imperialism and Global Political Economy*, Polity.

Fernandes, Clinton 2004, *Reluctant Saviour: Australia, Indonesia and the independence of East Timor*, Scribe Publications.

Kuhn, Rick 1997, "The Australian left, nationalism and the Vietnam War", *Labour History*, 72, May. https://www.jstor.org/stable/27516471

Mieville, China 2005, *Between Equal Rights: A Marxist Theory of International Law*, Brill.

O'Lincoln, Tom 2021 [2014], *The Neighbour From Hell: Two Centuries of Australian Imperialism*, Interventions.

Pietsch, Sam 2010, "Australian imperialism and East Timor", *Marxist Interventions*, 2. https://sa.org.au/mi/2/2.htm

Rosenberg, Justin 1994, *The Empire of Civil Society*, Verso.

Stockholm International Peace Research Institute (SIPRI) 2022, *SIPRI Military Expenditure Database*. https://www.sipri.org/databases/milex

DUNCAN HART

Review: An insight into inequality in Australia today

Duncan Hart is a socialist activist and unionist based in Brisbane.

Ben Schneiders, *Hard Labour: Wage theft in the age of inequality*, Scribe Publications, 2021.

AUSTRALIAN WORKERS OWE a debt of thanks to Ben Schneiders and his colleagues (Royce Millar in particular) at *The Age* for their consistent work to expose systemic exploitation and wage theft since 2015. Schneiders' book distils his journalism, exposing some of the worst, yet *extremely typical*, examples of working conditions in Australia. As an exposé of the situation for millions of Australian workers this work is worth reading for everyone concerned with the fight for workers' rights in Australia today.

Not all in this together

Schneiders' book starts by showing how the coronavirus pandemic in 2020–21 brought to light the vital necessity of "essential" workers, while showing how many of those very same workers were put more at risk of spreading the virus due to their precarious working conditions. Overwhelmingly, the areas hit hardest by the virus and lockdown measures in Sydney and Melbourne were the poorest and where most migrants lived. Workers in the west and north of Melbourne and western Sydney couldn't perform their essential work in cleaning, food services, retail or warehouses from home. These workers generally had less access to paid leave, state welfare and medical support and were employed on insecure, shoddy or illegal contracts.

The pandemic clearly exposed the lines of class, exploitation and oppression in Australia. The pandemic response also showed, as Schneiders outlines, that "the level of poverty in Australia was a political choice", as we saw practically overnight the lifting of Centrelink payments, housing the homeless and even the maintenance of wages with the Jobkeeper payment (p.29). The question is then – why is this "choice" maintained? The easing of health measures has coincided with inflation which has seen "the biggest wage cut in twenty years" (now the biggest wage cut since records began).

"A new age of slavery"

One of the most valuable aspects of *Hard Labour* is its insight into the sheer injustice of the prevailing state of affairs in workplaces across this country, and the resulting vast fortunes that are accumulated in the hands of very few. The best examples in the book are drawn from the hospitality industry, such as the Rockpool Dining Group owned by Quadrant Private Equity. As Australia's biggest "high-end restaurant conglomerate", among many other concerns, Quadrant currently manages over $2 billion in three investment funds. Schneiders describes how through perfectly *legal* accounting mechanisms, Rockpool Dining Group managed to make no profit over years, avoiding tax, while still channelling $70 million in payments to Quadrant in the three years prior to the pandemic (p.57). While the owners of Quadrant raked it in selling $310 steaks, the workers at Rockpool's various restaurants were earning as little as $12 an hour – in many cases skilled chefs employed on a 457 visa (p.31). Workers described working typically 55 hours a week, and up to 85, all while being paid for 38 hours. The workload was such that a chef reported sleeping on the pastry bench of his restaurant because he wouldn't have time to make it home before returning to work. The total underpayment for each worker was calculated to amount to up to $100,000. After the reporting in *The Age*, some millions of dollars were recouped by workers, but no doubt this was a gross underestimate of the real scale of the wage theft involved (p.52).

Despite the scandal, the owners of Quadrant have maintained their multimillion-dollar mansions.

This wage theft was carried out by implicit or explicit threats made to largely migrant workers that they needed to shut up about their pay and conditions or lose their visa. This extends across the industry. Schneiders describes a smaller hospitality group in Melbourne that literally operated two sets of books to evade legal pay rates. Then there is the example of 7-11's wage theft against international students. In the fast-food sector, employing young workers under 20 years of age is the absolute rule, enabling the bosses to get away with wages up to half those paid to adults. Regardless of the exact mechanism used, the common element across all cases was a disempowered workforce.

Much of this disempowerment has involved the establishment of an underclass of workers on temporary visas, either on various temporary work visas or as international students. Out of this large number of people – numbering 2.2 million at the end of last year, nearly back to its pre-pandemic levels – 100,000 are estimated to be here in breach of their visa conditions, placing them in an extremely tenuous situation, ripe for exploitation (p.163). Schneiders relates the story of these workers across industries and workplaces. For example, Mahani Tif arrived on a tourist visa and worked as a strawberry picker for piece rates. Once employer deductions for transport and board kicked in, she was on $3 an hour.

Farm workers that the National Union of Workers (now the United Workers' Union, UWU) had begun to organise in Victoria would speak "with great intensity about the fundamental disrespect they experienced – the bullying, the sexism, the racism – and about the extraordinary hours they worked, and of being yelled at to pick more broccoli, lettuce, or fruit" (p. 154). Workers at Rockpool described the constant surveillance and demands not to take breaks as being treated "like a slave." Thus the workers across multiple industries who spoke out asserted their humanity against the degradation that their bosses would force them into, as Schneiders documents.

Staring into the abyss

Whereas the accounts of workers striving for dignity leap from the page, the bosses are conspicuous by their absence. The only boss actually interviewed is Chris Hadley, managing director of Quadrant Private Equity. As if he speaks for the entirety of the capitalist class, Hadley simply throws up his hands regarding the disgraceful underpayment and "modern slavery" in restaurants owned by his company. He explains that "we are not operators of the business," merely "shareholders", who, hand on heart, "are very focused on…a fair, equitable and safe working environment". The underpayment and abuse at Rockpool were simple "mistakes" due to the complexity of various regulations – presumably, such complexities as what the minimum wage is and whether someone can work more than 38 hours a week without overtime pay (p.52).

While workers strive to assert *control* over their daily working lives and even their capacity to put bread on the table, the operations of the capitalist system which Schneiders discusses is more akin to a black hole – crushing *everything* that comes within its orbit, while remaining at the same time inscrutable and unknowable.

A remarkable case study outlined is the arcane internal operations of Dinner by Heston Blumenthal, an absurdly expensive restaurant that operated out of Crown Casino in Melbourne's Southbank until February 2020. As well as selling $500 meals, the restaurant underpaid its staff, by as much as $60,000 in one case.

Despite being just one restaurant, it is unclear who even owns it, as its proprietors, Tipsy Cake Pty Ltd, are based in an infamous Panama-Papers Caribbean tax-haven, Nevis, while the "directors" of Tipsy Cake, remarkably, all "live" on the Isle of Man, a tax haven located in the Irish Sea. On top of this, Crown Casino paid $7.9 million to yet another offshore, Irish-based company, Bacon and Egg Ice Cream, for the rights to use the name "Dinner by Heston" for the restaurant. Owners unknown made millions while avoiding tax, off the back of the back-breaking sweating of the restaurant's workers (pp.68–71).

Just as with the broader system of ruthless pursuit of profit regardless of any broader human cost, so too does the emergence of a large underclass of guest workers with either tenuous or no work rights appear in Schneiders' account as a qualitative development upon unplanned, sporadic and unforeseen steps. Without any politicians openly calling for it – in fact in the teeth of racist beat-ups against refugees and some migrants, and in the context of the Islamophobic "war on terror" for much of the twenty-first century – Australia has nonetheless emerged with a large strata of residents, and workers, without citizenship rights. This has developed in an ad hoc way, due to the desires of business to quickly fill "skill shortages", with the added benefit of reducing the bargaining power of workers, and also to the explosion in the higher education industry with its now hundreds of thousands of international students (pp.164–65). This guest worker underclass is a significant fact in the modern Australian working class that must be reckoned with.

Despite the purposeful opacity of the rulers of Australian (and global) capitalism, it is nonetheless readily apparent where the vast wealth generated by workers is ending up. By 2020, "Australia had a growing class of super-rich oligarchs, unprecedented in our history" (p.42). The wealth of the richest ten people in Australia rose from $60.7 billion in 2016 to a staggering $177 billion in 2021 (p.42). The richest 200 people possessed well over half a trillion dollars in 2022. In fact, as of 2022, possessing $1 billion in net wealth is no longer enough to even be in the richest 100 people in this country.[1] Australian society is a "whirring, self-perpetuating inequality machine" (p.42).

Fightback

Hard Labour is not just a story of worker disempowerment and capitalist enrichment. It also covers important recent developments in working-class organising, in particular, the Fair Work cases against Coles (which I was involved with) and other major companies, the emergence of the Retail and Fast Food Workers' Union (RAFFWU), and the efforts of the UWU in organising farm workers.

In each of these cases, while the experience of the workers and their bravery shines through, one notable weakness of these accounts is the lack of explanation from the workers themselves of the significance

---

1. Sprague and Bailey 2022.

of their own actions. Generally speaking, it is union officials who provide an overview of the various forms of workers' resistance. Yet is it the case that the union officials dominate the organisations discussed? If so, this should have been discussed as a limitation of the organising work undertaken. Or did Schneiders lean on union officials to explain the broader significance of the issues at stake, without seeking out the opinion, for instance, of worker leaders of the newly established RAFFWU?

Nonetheless, *Hard Labour* provides a useful account of the significance of the finding by Fair Work that Coles had breached the Better Off Overall Test (BOOT), which eventually led to the reintroduction of award penalty rates at most major Australian retailers and fast food outlets, such as the Woolworths empire, Domino's and McDonald's. As well as improving the pay and conditions of hundreds of thousands of workers, these cases also showed up the rank treachery of the official union for retail and fast food workers, the Shop, Distributive and Allied Employees Association (SDA).

Another chapter explains how a union could be complicit in what Schneiders and union official Josh Cullinan estimated to be around a $1 billion annual transfer in income from workers to bosses (p.116). The chapter explores the particularly idiosyncratic ideology of the SDA leadership, as the political descendants of the anti-communist Catholic activists led by Bob Santamaria of the National Civic Council, and the large factional influence wielded by the SDA in Labor as a result of their sweetheart deals with the bosses.

That influence is based on the size of the SDA's membership, giving the highly-paid bureaucrats who run the organisation a real incentive to sign agreements with huge retailers and fast food behemoths – Australia's largest non-government employers – that sacrificed workers' pay and conditions in exchange for the SDA's ability to recruit those workers.[2] The dependency of the SDA on the employers is shown up in the darkly humorous example of how McDonald's unceremoniously dropped their cooperative relationship

---

2. I have written on the period of the signing of these early "closed shop" agreements between the SDA and Australian retailers, and how employer control over payroll deductions to the union strengthened right-wing forces in the SDA. See Hart 2016.

with the association in 2019 after worker Xzavier Kelly, backed by RAFFWU, succeeded in scrapping the agreement on the basis that it failed the BOOT. The SDA agreement, which had obliterated a wide variety of penalty rates, had come at an annual cost of around $1,300 per worker, or around $100 million across all stores (pp.144–45).

In the case of the largely migrant, often undocumented farm workers that UWU has recently organised, the lesson related is crystal clear, as explained by organiser George Robertson:

> It wasn't coming up with innovative schemes to magically make outsourcing of labour-hire workers go away. It was, like, organise the workers really well through house visits and off-site organising, build relationships with community leaders at the workplace, and bring them together and take on the employer. That's what that model was. It was very simple, and that, I think, built confidence in the union that it's not impossible to organise migrant workers…(p.180)

This "old fashioned grunt-work" not only built up a membership of 5,000 in the farmworkers' division of UWU, but resulted in real wins when it came to wages and conditions at some of the biggest rural labour-hire companies in Australia. A significant landmark was reached in November 2021 when Fair Work, in response to a union case, ruled that piece rates paid on farms must amount to the minimum award hourly rate of around $25 for casual workers. This decision – if enforced – will undercut the ability of bosses to get away with the most staggering underpayments.

Final thoughts

As Schneiders notes at the outset, this is not "a work of political or economic theory. Rather, it seeks to provide some of the finer-grained detail of how inequality has increased, and how power relations have evolved between those with and those without wealth and power" (p.9). With this standpoint in mind the book is worth reading and an important account of modern labour conditions. As a revolutionary socialist and a long-time retail worker activist, I often found

Schneiders' (journalistic?) tendency to present his conclusions in an open-ended way frustrating. I would have preferred more polemical arguments based on his experiences of some of the most heinous cases of worker abuse and wage theft in Australia today.

Schneiders is right to point out that the examples of the pushback that has occurred among retail, fast food and farm workers won successes even in a situation of conservative government, indicating that working-class organisation is paramount to turning inequality around. While the author's own conclusions seem to point towards the potential for a return to a more egalitarian society such as existed prior to the neoliberal period of the 1980s, the weight of the evidence presented goes a long way towards illustrating that Australia today is characterised by a vicious class war by the bosses, which can only be answered by workers responding in kind. This is not a case of reinventing the wheel, but of rebuilding *class struggle* unionism that recognises this fact, and as a related necessity, building *class struggle* politics which can help to cohere rank-and-file worker activists who see in the grassroots struggle of workers today an indissoluble link to the final overthrow of the entirety of capitalist oppression. The mindless, ravenous thirst of the capitalists to accumulate won't be fundamentally deterred this side of the revolution.

With that said, the more people who come away from reading Schneiders' book with a renewed understanding and hatred of the oppression of workers in Australia today, the better.

References

Hart, Duncan 2016, "Challenging the Groupers: the NSW Shop Assistants' Union in the 1970s", *The Queensland Journal of Labour History*, 22, March, pp.19–29. http://brisbanelabourhistory.org/wp-content/uploads/2021/05/The-Queensland-Journal-of-Labour-History-No-22-March-2016.pdf

Sprague, Julie-anne and Michael Bailey, "Total Rich List Wealth Soars past half a trillion dollars", *The Australian Financial Review Magazine*, 26 May. https://www.afr.com/rich-list/australia-s-top-10-richest-people-revealed-20220524-p5ao7i

SAGE JUPE

Review: Socialism in the United States

Sage Jupe is an Adelaide-based socialist.

Kim Moody, *Breaking the Impasse: Electoral politics, mass action, and the new socialist movement in the United States*, Haymarket Books, 2022.

US SOCIETY IS GOING THROUGH a prolonged period of political crisis. The US ruling class is incapable of providing for the mass of ordinary people. Millions are disillusioned with the political and economic system. Yet the US left finds itself at an impasse, unable, and seemingly unwilling, to break out of the confines of the Democratic Party. As the title of his new book suggests, Kim Moody argues that this impasse needs to be broken.

Decades of neoliberalism have driven down even the most basic of living standards, and multiple systemic crises have impacted the US in recent years, including economic problems, the COVID-19 pandemic and environmental destruction.

At the same time the country has been hit with mass demonstrations: teachers' strikes in 2018, and the explosion of the Black Lives Matter movement, first in 2014 and then again in 2020.

It is within this context that the high-profile campaign of self-described socialist Bernie Sanders has taken place, and with it the growth of the Democratic Socialists of America (DSA), swelling from a few thousand members prior to 2015 to over ninety thousand in 2021.

Moody is right to describe the Sanders phenomenon as anti-climactic. Absorbed quickly within the establishment Democrat presidential campaigns of both Clinton and Biden, the Sanders campaigns doomed thousands of new anti-capitalist hopefuls to either disillusionment or accepting the botched facelift Joe Biden is attempting to give to American capitalism.

Moody, with his consistent championing of the working class, provides a refreshing perspective aimed at restoring the classic Marxist assumption that socialism cannot be won without the independent self-activity of the working class.

The impasse

The impasse Moody describes is twofold. Firstly, an impasse for the American ruling class. Moody describes a global political context of traditional right-wing parties moving further right, and social democratic parties embracing the centre. While the Democratic Party is a not a social democratic party, these shifts are reflected in American politics by the emergence of Trumpism, while the Democrats remain firmly in the centre. Neither party is capable of breaking with their own class interests to meet the needs of an increasingly disillusioned population.[1]

The second impasse is one for the working class and the socialist left, with a seemingly one-sided class war between the organised sections of finance and production, and a largely unorganised working class. While the many crises of capitalism have produced sporadic but frequent upsurges worldwide, major projects of the left, such as Syriza in Greece or Corbyn in the UK, have found themselves caught up in electoral projects tied to the centre, treading water with the status quo rather than building an alternative.[2]

1. *The Economist* 2022.
2. Armstrong 2016.

The Democratic Party

Moody describes the Democratic Party as, "by any reasonable definition a capitalist party", just like the Republicans. It is an organisation funded by major sections of US capital, including the Fortune 500 new blood such as Alphabet (Google), Amazon, hedge funds and a range of Silicon Valley capitalists. According to OpenSecrets' listing, 58 of the top hundred individual political donors in the 2020 election cycle gave to the Democrats.

The party is also run by professional politicians and bureaucrats drawn from the upper echelons of society and ideologically committed to capitalism.

Unlike the Republicans however, the Democrats have some undeserved credibility as a party the working class has more sway over and interest in. Moody provides a critical account of the trade union bureaucracy and the role their strategy of "business unionism" has played in upholding this myth.

Moody also outlines a compelling argument against "using the Democrat ballot line". Ironically the Democrats are characterised by an extreme lack of internal democracy. You can't even join the Democrats like you can the Australian Labor Party. The Democrats don't really have members – instead they have an extremely well-funded bureaucracy. So even the shift that led to the short rise of reformist Jeremy Corbyn in the British Labour Party could never happen in the Democrats.

No surprise then that the party machine itself is rigged against the left. Primaries are more a weeding-out process than an opportunity for progressives to use the ballot line. If new candidates outside of the traditional establishment want to get ahead, they quickly need to start playing by the rules. Moody shows this clearly in Alexandria Ocasio Cortez (AOC)'s 2020 run for Congress. AOC raised $10.5 million, compared to her challenger's $2 million, with some big names in her donation list: Alphabet (Google), $71,795; Amazon, $42,805; Microsoft, $30,128 and so on.

Moody's main criticism of the AOC campaign, and of Sanders' as well, is that despite the money, time and energy poured them, not just by party hacks but by genuine left-wingers, they have left no organisations behind of the kind that would be required to build the kind of mass, independent working-class struggle the US so desperately needs.

Moody also describes the trajectory of socialists in the party as "upward and rightward".

When it came to the election of House Speaker, AOC argued that there was no alternative to Pelosi. At the same time, despite easily pushing projects like the Green New Deal to the margins, Pelosi and the Democrats have not attempted to completely silence AOC or "the Squad" of liberal progressives but to integrate them. AOC was put on Biden's advisory taskforce on climate change in reward for her support of the establishment Democrats.

As Moody explores, attempts to transform the Democratic Party, or at least use it in some form to advance the interests of the oppressed have been tried and tested many times. It's also worth saying previous attempts occurred during eras of much greater class struggle than we see in the US today. Yet still, the result of attempts such as Jesse Jackson's Rainbow Coalition and the New Politics have not had any lasting effect on the party, or indeed left behind organisations fit to build an alternative to the Democrats.[3]

The alternative

Moody devotes the final chapters of his book to his perspective on where the socialist left should dedicate their energies.

His argument begins by demolishing the widely held mythology of the progressive legacy of the Democrats during the New Deal and Civil Rights era. The limited reforms that were achieved in these times were the result of working-class struggle and action, not benevolent gifts from enlightened liberals in the party. These same progressives instead played a role in winding-up and limiting the gains of these movements.

While today the working class is at a low point of struggle, and strike rates remain low, there are signs of hope. While the Sanders campaign did help popularise the word "socialism" and show an appetite for basic social provisions among young Americans, that appetite existed before he came onto the scene. In 2010, polling showed that 54 percent of

---

3. Everett 2020.

young people already approved of socialism before it rose to 58 percent in 2019 (p.76).

At multiple times during the book Moody champions actions such the 370,000-strong teachers' strikes of 2018 and the mass movement of Black Lives Matter in response to the murder of George Floyd as indications of what is possible.

He argues that the political impasse that has led to a choice between the far right and the establishment centre can only be broken by a mass social upsurge and the organisation of millions of so far unorganised members of the working class. Moody goes over debates on exactly how to go about rebuilding the unions, and lands not on convoluted strategies and small changes to bureaucracies, but the bread-and-butter organisation of the rank and file.

While involvement in elections may very well be a feature of a genuinely independent and working-class force in America, a break with the capitalist Democratic Party and the building of something independent is necessary. Moody also takes time to point out the difference between gains handed down from on-high, and genuine working-class power: "When Marx and/or Engels spoke of the working class taking political power in order to commence the transition from capitalism to socialism, they did not have in mind the president of the United States and Congress speaking and legislating from on high for a class of millions" (p.221).

For all of his insightful history and analysis of the inner workings of the Democrats, labour, industry and the US electoral system, Moody's book shines brightest in its utmost trust in the working class to struggle and build a better world.

References

Armstrong, Mick 2016, "The broad left party question after Syriza", *Marxist Left Review*, 11, Summer. https://marxistleftreview.org/articles/the-broad-left-party-question-after-syriza/

Everett, Nick 2020, "We've been down this road before: Jesse Jackson, the Democrats and the left", *Marxist Left Review*, 19, Summer. https://marxistleftreview.org/articles/weve-been-down-this-road-before-jesse-jackson-the-democrats-and-the-left/

The Economist 2022, "Donald Trump's hold on the Republican Party is unquestionable", 18 August. https://www.economist.com/briefing/2022/08/18/donald-trumps-hold-on-the-republican-party-is-unquestionable

www.ingramcontent.com/pod-product-compliance
Lightning Source LLC
Chambersburg PA
CBHW012004090526
44590CB00026B/3864